The Complete Idiot's Reference Card

Go Words Get You There Fast!

1. From anywhere online, click on the Edit menu.
2. Point at Go to, at the bottom of the menu.
3. Click Other Location.
4. Type the Go word in the text box.
5. Click OK, and you're there!

Want the Latest Go Words?

Use the Go word: GOWORD. Just follow the steps at left.

Go Words You Can Use Now!

To Go Here:	Use This Go Word:	To Go Here:	Use This Go Word:
Arts & Entertainment	ENTERTAINMENT	Games & Gaming	GAMES
		Internet Center	INTERNET
Movies	MOVIES	Internet Newsgroups	NEWSGROUPS
Music	MUSIC	World Wide Web	WWW
Business & Finance	BUSINESS	MSN Passport	PASSPORT
Career Connection	CAREERCONNECT	Member Assistance Lobby	LOBBY
Personal Finance	PERSONALFINANCE		
Chat World	CHATWORLD	Accounts & Billing	MSNACCOUNTS
Chat World Lobby	CWCHAT	News & Weather	NEWS
Games & Casino	CWCASINO	MSN News	MSNNEWS
Computers & Software	COMPUTING	The Weather Lab	THEWEATHERLAB
Safe Computing	SAFECOMPUTING	People & Communities	COMMUNITY
Software	SOFTWARE	Men	MEN
Education & Reference	EDUCATION	People to People	PEOPLE
Reference	REFERENCE	Women	WOMEN
Health & Fitness	HEALTH	Public Affairs	PUBLIC
Mental Wellness & Counseling	COUNSELING	Government Agencies & Departments	GOVERNMENT
Nutrition	NUTRITION	Science & Technology	SCIENCE
Home and Family	HOME	Astronomy & Space	ASTRONOMY
Family Interests & Recreation	FAMILYINTERESTS	Industry & Infrastructure	INDUSTRY
		Medicine	MEDICINE
For Kids	KIDS	Special Events	EVENTS
Interests, Leisure, & Hobbies	INTERESTS	Sports & Recreation	SPORTS
		Sports Media	SPORTSMEDIA
Collecting	COLLECTING		

que®

Hot Tools

Don't sweat it! If you forget which button is which, point at one with your mouse. A name pops up to remind you.

THE INTERNET EXPLORER'S TOOLBAR TOOLS
Chapters 19 and 20 have all the Internet scoop.

Open   Goes to a specific World Wide Web site.

Home   Takes you back to your start page.

Back   Takes you back one Web page.

Forward   Takes you ahead one Web page.

Stop   Cancels whatever Browser is doing.

Refresh   Reloads the current Web page.

Favorite Places   Opens Favorite Places list.

Add To Favorite Places   Adds the current Web page to Favorite Places.

Use Large Fonts   Makes fonts bigger.

Use Small Fonts   Makes fonts smaller.

BBS BUTTONS
Chapter 10 has the buzz on forums & bulletin boards (BBSs).

New Message   Starts a new conversation.

Save   Saves current message to disk.

Print   Prints the message.

Reply to BBS   Responds to current message.

Previous Message   Goes back one message.

Next Message   Moves ahead one message.

Next Unread Message   Goes to next unread message.

Previous Conversation   Goes to last conversation.

Next Conversation   Opens next conversation.

Next Unread Conversation   Goes to next unread conversation.

File Transfer Status   Opens the File Transfer Status window. See Chapter 11 for details.

Send   Posts your message.

Insert   Places a saved file in the message.

The

COMPLETE
IDIOT'S
GUIDE TO

Microsoft®
Network

by John Pivovarnick

A Division of Macmillan Publishing USA
201 W. 103rd Street, Indianapolis, IN 46290

©1995 Que Corporation

International Standard Book Number: 0-7897-0603-2

Library of Congress Catalog Card Number: 95-71745

97 96   8 7 6 5 4 3 2

Interpretation of the printing code: the rightmost number of the first series of num-bers is the year of the book's printing; the rightmost number of the second series of numbers is the number of the book's printing. For example, a printing code of 95-1 shows that the first printing of the book occurred in 1995.

Printed in the United States of America

Publisher
Roland Elgey

Vice-President and Publisher
Marie Butler-Knight

Editorial Services Drector
Elizabeth Keaffaber

Publishing Manager
Barry Pruett

Development Editor
Melanie Palaisa

Technical Editor
Martin Wyatt

Production Editor
Phil Kitchel

Copy Editor
Rebecca Mayfield

Cover Designer
Scott Cook

Designer
Kim Scott

Illustrator
Judd Winick

Indexer
Mary Jane Frisby

Production Team
*Jeanne Clark, Lisa Daugherty, Joan Evan, Bryan Flores, Trey Frank,
Amy Gornik, John Hulse, Damon Jordan, Bob LaRoche,
Stephanie Layton, Michelle Lee, Julie Quinn, Michael Thomas,
Jody York, Karen York*

Contents at a Glance

Contents

20 Browsing the WWW—World Wide Web, Not Wild, Wild West 239

Part 3 Tips, Tricks, and How-To Stuff 257

21 On the Road with MSN 259

Wilkommen, Bienvenu, C'mon In...

Hiya. Welcome aboard. My name is John, and I'll be your tour guide on this little adventure, here—and it *will* be an adventure, let me assure you. It's going to be an adventure for a couple of reasons.

MSN says "Howdy," too.

Reason 1

We're on an adventure, because this book is all about the new Microsoft Network (also known as MSN, for short).

MSN is an online service (which means you use your PC, modem, and a telephone line to hook into it) that lets you into a digital world that's just dripping with information, software, games, Internet goodies, and more. It's very new.

It's so new, in fact, that only the folks who have been testing the early versions ("beta" versions, they're called) of Windows 95 have even *seen* it. This is really *terra incognita* (Latin for "dirt in sunglasses"), so get out your pith helmet. Or pith in a helmet. Something like that.

Reason 2

This isn't a whole new reason: it grows out of the fact that MSN is such a new thing.

I've seen the beginnings of only a few online services. I joined America Online when it was relatively new, and it's gone through rapid growth and change over the last 10 years.

I got in on the ground floor of Apple Computer's eWorld—another online service (mainly Macintosh right now, but expect a Windows version soon)—as a beta tester, before it was released to the general public.

Online services at this very early stage of the game are like the pod people in *Invasion of the Body Snatchers* (the original, not those pale imitations). Like pod people, newborn online services are perfectly formed, but lack the details of a living thing.

For the pod people, that means no personality, no fingerprints, none of the scrapes and scars of living. For MSN that means no personality, too (because an online service's personality is created and amplified by its membership). And limited membership (right now) means that it doesn't have that lived-in feel: the ashtrays are still clean and the toilets are still "Sanitized for Your Protection."

Once the joint fills up, things will start to happen, and quickly. Members will make suggestions for new features. Unused areas will shrivel up and blow away. In short: Things are going to change, fast.

Reason 3

Depending on your previous online experience(s), this may be your first opportunity to explore the Internet.

The Internet can be, at once, the strangest and most ridiculously typical collection of computer users flapping their gums that you'd ever want to see.

If you don't know, "Internet" stands for INTERnational NETwork. It's a global system of computers, linked together all higgledy-piggledy, allowing fast world-wide communication.

Some of the Internet's computers are in the basements of major colleges and universities. More of them are in corporate vaults, keeping track of accounts receivable and payable while users swap recipes for Rocky Road Brownies internationally. Still other Internet computers are on military bases, and still others are in musty rooms of typical homes on typical streets.

One minute you could be corresponding with someone in your home town, the next minute a student in Prague could be asking homework advice. In that regard, the 'Net, as some call it, is like Wednesday on the old "Mickey Mouse Club," except everyday is "Anything Can Happen" day.

The Last Reason, Reason 4

A dear friend used to ask me, when we'd take an untested shortcut, travel to a new place, or try a new restaurant, "How adventurous are you feeling?"

That was our shorthand for, "We may get lost/the food may stink. How safe do you want to play it?" Because we never got lost, or had bad meals—we had adventures.

Because MSN is so new, because it will start to change and grow as it acquires more members, and because developing a real personality is never easy (just ask any 12-year-old), we're on an adventure.

How adventurous are you feeling?

How This Book Will Help

I'm going to play Davy Crocket for you (without the raccoon beanie, thanks) and blaze the trail. I'll make all the really embarrassing, first-time mistakes so you won't have to.

To that end, this book is laid out in something like chronological order. Part 1, "Getting Started," is all about, well, getting started: what you need to have, how to install the software (if it isn't already), how to nudge your modem settings, and how to sign on to MSN for the very first time.

Part 2, "Cruisin' MSN," is a general overview of the service, some tips for surviving in an electronic world, plus all about e-mail, chat rooms, file libraries, the Internet, and more.

Part 3, "Tips, Tricks, and How-To Stuff," is a mixed bag, covering stuff you may not need to know until later (using MSN while traveling, for instance), how to get help both on- and offline, and tips for saving time and money online.

There's also some information that you may not *want* to know, like what my favorite areas are online. I've been told I "share too much."

How You Can Help Yourself

If you're feeling like a complete idiot already, you might just want to sit down and read this puppy through. It may have a calming effect. ("You're feeling veeerrryy relaxed, almost *sleeeepppyyy...*")

If you already have MSN installed and running, and have already successfully signed on, you may want to skim through the set-up and install chapters (1–5) and begin right where you left off: Chapter 6, "Your First Time Online."

Everybody should read Part 2—you don't have to read it in order, but you should read it. It explains how things work, and where things are. Some useful bits of knowledge, especially in Chapter 7, "Aunt Effie's Guide to Online Etiquette."

Part 3? Well, you don't have to read it right away. Read what appeals to you, when it appeals to you. I promise to keep things light and moving right along. As a matter of fact, in the spirit of moving things along here's some...

Geeky Stuff You Can Ignore

Just for the sake of thoroughness, you'll find some information boxes and sidebars throughout this book (and all *Complete Idiot's Guides*).

These Boxes Contain Asides & Other Information

Sometimes, as I write, I think of important stuff that's related (if barely) to the subject at hand, that I think you should know. Often, these boxes contain definitions of geeky words in the text. Sometimes personal opinion, or additional information. If I can't work it unobtrusively into the main text, I usually tuck it off to one side like this.

The least you should do is read the title. If it doesn't strike your fancy, well, skip it.

Boxes Like These Contain Technical Information

Just like you don't need to know how an internal-combustion engine works to drive a car, there's some technical information you don't *really* need to know to use a computer. Boxed like this, they're easy for the technically squeamish to spot and avoid. I promise to keep them as painless as possible

If you're feeling adventurous, you may want to give them a try; if not, you won't hurt my feelings. The sun will still rise in the east and set in the west, and the Mets probably won't make the World Series again this year.

Rules of the Road

You'll find that I'm not a very pushy tour guide. I won't babble on and on about things that only interest me. (Well, not much.) The goal here is to show how things work generally on MSN. We'll do that by looking at representative areas that show how most of the areas online work.

In the instances where I want you to do something, I won't be shy. I'll put the important portion of the instructions in **boldface**, so you won't miss it.

If I want you to click on an icon, or something, I'll be horribly clever and say something like: Click the **Whatever** icon.

In cases where I need you to type something, I'll be equally witty, and say, type this in the text box: **A pickled pack of peccadilloes.** Why on earth I'd want you to type that, I don't know.

When I'm getting really pushy, and I really want you to jump through digital hoops, I'll give you step-by-step instructions like this:

1. First, do **this**.

2. Then do **that**.

3. Finally, do the **other thing**.

Otherwise, you are expected and encouraged to take all the information provided and explore on your own. Be your own trailblazer. That's the only rule. Enjoy yourself, explore, have fun. And be back on the bus by 7:30, or I'll leave without you.

Making Assumptions

I'm really good at that—that and jumping to conclusions. If not for jumping to conclusions, I'd get no exercise at all.

I'll try not to make too many assumptions about you, or your level of comfort or expertise with a computer, but I will make *some* assumptions. For example, I'll assume that your computer is assembled and works; that you know how to turn it on and off properly; and that you've got the computer basics down.

By "basics," I mean you can find stuff on your hard drive, use a mouse to point and click, double-click, format a floppy disk, and save a file. If you don't know how to do these basic things, you should get a handle on *them* before you tackle MSN. Read your computer and Windows 95 manuals and online help (in the Help menu) and get acquainted with the day-to-day skills you'll need.

Since everybody is fairly new to Windows 95, I'll give advice where I can squeeze it in, or point you to a reputable source of information.

The Ever Changing World of Online Services, MSN Included

We work very hard (us writers and the editorial staff at Que) to make sure that these books are as accurate as possible before they get shipped out. But, if you run into a situation online where things are completely different than what's described here, chalk it up to developmental changes at MSN that happened after the book went to press.

There's plenty of information in here on how to get help with new and mystifying situations, so you'll be able to handle it. Don't panic.

Trademarks, Copyrights, and Other Stuff

The Microsoft Network, also known as MSN, is wholly owned by the Microsoft Corporation—trademarked, copyrighted, and probably service marked, too.

Any other companies and products mentioned throughout this book are also copyrighted, trademarked, and otherwise owned by their respective companies. Product names are indicated by the appropriate capitalization (Apple Computer, eWorld—well, *that's* a bad example). This spares us the need of typing (and typesetting) all those annoying little symbols after the names.

If, by chance, I screw up and mis-capitalize something, it in no way reflects on the ownership of the product, just my stupidity and sad typing skills.

Part 1
Getting Started

You must think I'm such a cyber-tease, dangling all those tantalizing glimpses of things you can do on the Microsoft Network in front of you like that, while you don't actually do any of them for chapters. Well, I am, and proud of it.

It'd be nice if we could just connect to MSN, or any online service for that matter, but we can't. We have to prepare ourselves, and our computers, for the journey. It isn't difficult—there's no fasting, or wind sprints involved.

You just need to be sure that you have all the necessary accessories together before you attempt to log on for the first time. This section walks you through the process. No more teasing. Well...not much, anyhow.

EMERGENCY COMPUTER GEEKS

Chapter 1

The Top Ten Things You Need to Know

In This Chapter

This is by no means an exhaustive coverage of *everything* there is to know about using the Microsoft Network—that would mean the other 300-odd pages of this book are just padding. This is just a quick, get-your-brain-in-gear introduction to some of the more important concepts and issues involved in using the Microsoft Network.

Here's a freebie: more often than not, I call the Microsoft Network just MSN, because the Microsoft Network is an awful lot to type over and over.

1. To Use MSN, You Need Specific Hardware and Software

Chapter 2 gives you the specific details, but in a nutshell you need:

➤ An IBM-compatible computer

➤ Microsoft Windows 95

➤ MSN and Microsoft Exchange software, installed

➤ A modem

➤ A telephone line

That's it, basically—although some accessories are nice to have, too: a mouse, a printer, and an attractive love interest to peel you a grape while you navigate the service.

2. Signing In Is Simple

Once you install and configure your MSN software for your system (Chapters 3, 4, and 5 cover all this in depth), you launch MSN like any other software on your PC.

➤ You can double-click the MSN icon on your desktop.

➤ You can use the spiffy Start button to start MSN.

➤ Or, you can double-click directly on the MSN application. It's located at C:\Windows\Programs\The Microsoft Network, and its icon looks just like the one on your desktop in the first item above.

Once the software is running, signing in is as easy as typing your password and clicking Connect. Oh, make sure you connect and turn on your modem, and that your phone line is connected and working. That helps. Chapter 6 takes you step-by-step through the process.

3. While You're Online, Be Polite

Signing in with MSN is just like going to any public place (a mall, a movie theater, a party, a restaurant). All the rules of behavior and etiquette apply, plus a few extra ones that are peculiar to the online world.

Chapter 8 has some specific suggestions, but overall the Golden Rule applies: treat people the way you want people to treat you. That works all the time, both online and off.

4. All This Fun Costs Money

Your subscription to MSN isn't free. When you sign on, you've got two pricing plans from which to choose:

The Standard Plan costs $4.95 per month. You get three hours of online time, and additional hours cost $2.50 each.

The Frequent User Plan costs $19.95 per month. It includes a whopping 20 hours of online time, and additional hours cost only $2.00 each.

With either plan, you also have the additional expense of a longish (at least when I sign on, it's longish) local phone call—of course this depends on your local phone service. I have to pay; you may not. Check with your local phone company (or your last bill) for details.

Throughout this book, you'll find some helpful money saving tips and tricks piled together in Chapter 26. To check your current bill, select **Billing**, and then **Summary of Charges** from the Tools menu. (You have to be online to do this.) You can check your current bill, or even examine the bills from previous months to track your online time.

5. "Go" Words Take You Where You Want to Be—Fast

A Go word is a single magic word that immediately takes you to a specific location online. You find Go words by checking the Properties of a forum or category you enjoy (Chapter 7 explains how).

To use a Go word: Click the **Edit** menu, point to **Go To**, and click **Other Location**. Type the Go word for the service you want to open. Click **OK**. Poof! You're there.

6. You Can Use Your Favorite Places and Shortcuts to Travel Quickly, Too

Favorite Places is an empty area online where you can store a list of (*duh*) your favorite online places. To add an area to your Favorite Places, click on the place's icon to select it, and then select **Add To Favorite Places** from the File menu.

A shortcut is a desktop icon that takes you right to the designated area online when you click it. To create a shortcut, click on the place's icon to select it and select **Create Short-cut** from the File menu. A shortcut icon with the same name as the selected icon appears on your desktop.

Check out Chapter 27 to learn more about Go words, Favorite Places, and shortcuts.

7. Microsoft Exchange Handles All of Your E-Mail Online

E-mail is electronic mail. You can send and receive a lot of it online (I do). Microsoft Exchange is a separate application (it comes with Windows 95) that MSN calls upon to handle your e-mail.

When you sign in to MSN, it tells you if you have any e-mail waiting and gives you the option of firing up Microsoft Exchange (or you can do it yourself). Microsoft Exchange then copies (downloads) your messages to your computer so you can read and respond to them.

Chapter 12 covers e-mail.

8. Chat Rooms Are an Absolute Hoot

Chat rooms are areas online where MSN users meet and "chat" (type messages back and forth to each other). There are chat rooms built for groups of anywhere from two to *thousands*. You can be a *participant* and chat, or you can be a *spectator* and just follow the conversation.

Many forums feature a chat room where members discuss stuff related to the forum topic. *Chat World* is one of MSN's categories, and there are mondo-huge chat rooms for special events in the Special Events Category.

When you chat, you type what you want to say and press the **Enter** key. Your words disappear from the text box, and then appear in the main dialog display, preceded by your member ID (so everyone knows who's talking). It not only appears on *your* monitor, but also on the monitors of everyone using that chat room. They can read it and respond.

Learn more about the art of chat room conversation in Chapter 13.

9. MSN's Internet Access Makes the World Your Oyster...or Appetizer, If You're Not into Shellfish

The Internet has been getting a lot of play in the press of late, and now you can find out what all the buzz is about. You can use esoteric tools such as Gopher, WAIS, and FTP (no, not the motor oil treatment). You can strain your brain browsing through the WWW (World Wide Web) pages. You can communicate with people all over the world—and they don't have to be members of MSN. You can drop a line to anyone who has Internet access or an account with any major online service (like America Online or CompuServe).

Chapter 19 explains it all for you, just like Sister Mary Ignatius.

10. Signing Out Is a Two-Step Operation

To disconnect from MSN, you need to do two things. First, you select **Sign Out** from the **File** menu. Then you click **Yes** when MSN asks if you're really sure you want to disconnect.

You're back in your own little corner of your own little room.

Stuff That Didn't Make the Top Ten

There are some other factoids you really should know, but they didn't make the top ten. For instance:

➤ Reading text files online calls another piece of software into play: it may be your word processor, or it may be the Windows WordPad or NotePad. It depends on your software, and the kind of text file you're trying to read.

➤ Finally, the most obvious thing of all: this is fun. You're going to be exploring a strange new world, and you are one of the creatures in it. Pluck up your courage, pull on your Captain Spaulding uniform, and get ready.

Chapter 2

What You Need to Get Started with MSN

In This Chapter

➤ Basic system requirements

➤ Modem information

➤ The 411 on telephone lines

➤ Software requirements

In order to use the Microsoft Network, your computer system needs to be up to snuff. You also need to have some hardware and software installed, and you need some additional doo-dads, like a working telephone line.

You may spend most of this chapter saying, "Been there, done that," but better safe than sorry. That's my motto. Okay, that's *one* of my mottoes. You'll discover I have piles of mottoes, suitable for all occasions, many of which conflict with the others. Don't feel bad. My therapist can't figure it out either.

Minimum System Requirements

Right out of the bucket, here's a list of the *least* you need to have, computer-wise, before you can even think about running MSN.

Since the MSN software comes with (and requires) Windows 95, the system requirements are pretty much the same as those for running Windows 95.

For Windows 95 You Must Have:

➤ A PC with a 386DX processor or better (486 or Pentium).

➤ 8 megabytes (MB) of RAM. If you don't know how much RAM you've got, it's easy to find out. See the following section, "Say, How Much RAM Have I Got?"

➤ 35–40 MB of free hard disk space for Windows 95 (depending on which Windows 95 options you choose to install), and another 20 MB for MSN and the Microsoft Exchange (required for MSN). If you don't know how much free hard drive space you've got, see the section "Hard Disk Space—The Final Frontier" later in this chapter.

➤ One 3.5" high-density floppy drive, or a CD-ROM drive. One 3.5" high-density floppy drive is standard on most new PCs sold in the past two or three years.

➤ VGA or higher-resolution monitor. No clue about this one either? See the "Monitoring Your Video" section later in this chapter.

➤ A Microsoft compatible mouse or other pointing device—track ball, track pad, that sort of thing. Microsoft *says* a mouse is optional, but I wouldn't want to work without one.

➤ A modem or fax modem.

Optionally, you may want to have an audio card and speakers for sound.

Say, How Much RAM Have I Got?

You can check to see how much RAM (random access memory) is installed on your computer using the System Control Panel. Here's how:

Click the **Start** button, and select **Control Panel** from the Settings submenu. When the Control Panels window opens, double-click the **System** icon.

When the System Properties dialog box opens, it looks like the following figure. You may have to click on the **Performance** tab to see the information about your system if it's not already selected. You see something like this screen:

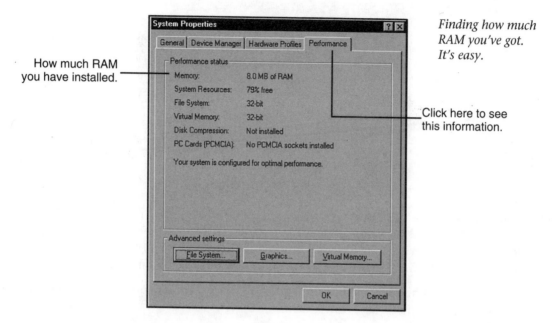

How much RAM you have installed.

Finding how much RAM you've got. It's easy.

Click here to see this information.

The first line of information, labeled Memory (and thank you for not singing that song from *Cats*), lists the amount of RAM installed on your computer.

You can also see how much RAM you have on the General tab, in the section labeled **Computer**.

Hard Disk Space—The Final Frontier

If you have two little icons on your desktop labeled *Microsoft Network* and *Inbox*, don't sweat this part. The software you need is already installed.

If you don't have those icons, or you just want to know how much hard drive space you have left, do this:

Double-click the **My Computer** icon on your Windows desktop. When the window opens, click the icon for your C: drive (indicated in the next figure).

The lower right hand corner of the My Computer window displays the available space and total capacity of your hard drive.

Checking out your C: drive.

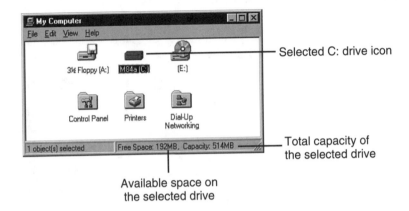

Selected C: drive icon

Total capacity of the selected drive

Available space on the selected drive

Monitoring Your Video

If you're running Windows 95 already, your video display is VGA (video graphics array) or, even better, SVGA (Super VGA).

If you want to know *exactly* what you have, open the System Properties dialog again, as described in the section "Say, How Much RAM Have I Got?"

This time, click the **Device Manager** tab (shown in the following figure). This action gives you a list of all the hardware devices attached to your computer. Locate the one labeled Monitor (indicated in the figure). You may need to click on the plus sign (+) in front of it. A list drops down showing all the monitors (if you've got more than one) you have installed. The one that's selected (that means it's the one you're using right now) should be called "VGA" something or "Super VGA" something. If it doesn't, don't panic—not yet anyway. Not all video adapter cards and drivers are as obviously named. Some are just a bunch of letters and numbers.

If you can't tell what kind of monitor you have, the only sure bet is to check the manual(s) that came with your computer: specifically, for the monitor and the video (display adapter) card.

If you want more information about your PC's video, select the monitor entry and click the **Properties** button.

First, click here. ——

Then click here. ——

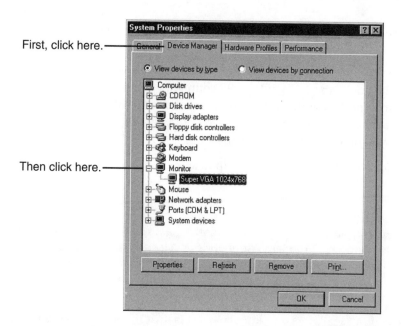

Checking out your video situation—this one's Super VGA, so it's fine.

What's That 1024x768 Mean?

That 1024×768 after "Super VGA" in the figure shows the highest possible *resolution* of the selected monitor. It means that the monitor (when set up with the Display Control Panel) can display an image that's 1024 *pixels* (short for *picture elements*—a fancy way of saying "dots") wide by 768 pixels tall.

The Display Properties dialog box is also where you set the basic color scheme for Windows 95, turn on the Windows screen saver, and wallpaper your desktop. See your Windows 95 manual or online Help for more information.

Modems Demystified

In addition to the basic hardware you need, as explained above, you also need a modem that's Windows 95-compatible.

A *modem* is a device that turns the information and commands from your computer into sounds that travel through telephone lines to another modem-equipped computer at a remote location. When the information and commands from your computer reach the other computer, the receiving computer's modem turns those sounds back into information and commands it can use.

Modem is a contraction of MODulating and DEModulating, which is science-speak for the process of turning information into sound and then back into information again.

In order to use MSN, you have to have a modem, preferably *Hayes-compatible* (but don't sweat it, most are). It should also be Windows 95-compatible (which means an external modem, or an internal modem with a UART chip). Beyond that, MSN isn't very finicky. If you already own a modem, make sure it's installed properly (check your manual for details). Otherwise, you may skip ahead to the next section.

If you're shopping for a modem, read on. I'll help take some of the mystery out of the process.

Hayes-compatible   A term that identifies a modem that conforms to the standard set of modem commands developed by the Hayes Corporation. Hayes compatibility is fairly standard among modems. I suggest that you don't mess with one that isn't—it complicates your life unnecessarily.

UART chip   You don't really need to know what it is, just if your internal modem has one. For the truly curious, though, it stands for Universal Asynchronous Receiver/Transmitter. It's a chip on an internal modem that makes an internal modem behave like a COM port. External modems don't require UART chips because they're connected to an actual COM port.

In-ies and Out-ies

Modems come in two varieties: internal and external. *Internal* modems go *inside* your computer. *External* modems sit on the desk near your computer, and you connect them to your computer with a cable that plugs into one of your COM ports (also known as *serial* ports).

Internal modems tend to be a little less expensive than external models because you don't have to pay for frills like a protective case and blinking lights. However, installing an internal modem means (oh, ack!) actually opening up your computer and tinkering with its innards.

For an internal modem, you need to know if you have an open expansion slot in which to put it. You also need to be sure that the internal modem you choose physically fits inside your computer, meaning that your PC's case is big enough to hold the sucker (generally that last bit is only an issue with laptop computers).

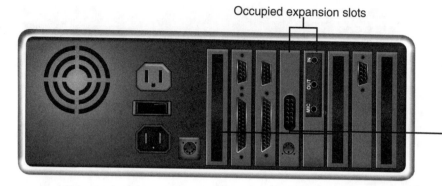

Occupied expansion slots

Check the back of your computer for an open expansion slot before you buy an internal modem.

Open expansion slots

Expansion Slots and Expansion Cards

An *expansion slot* is part of your computer that accepts an expansion card that adds new functions and/or features to your computer. An *expansion card* is a circuitry board that fits into an expansion slot inside your computer. An internal modem is an expansion card.

Generally speaking, an external modem is easier for timid computer users to set up and install—it doesn't feel like you're performing surgery on your computer.

All modems come with basic communications software, and fax modems (see "Other Bells and Whistles" later in the chapter) come with additional software that needs to be installed, too. The manual you get with the modem has details, but you install it using either the Run command on the Start menu, or the Add/Remove Programs Control Panel (which is shown in detail in the next chapter).

Speed Concerns

The other big concern when selecting a modem for use with MSN is its speed. Modem speed is often discussed in terms of *baud rate*, or *BPS* (bits per second). The baud rate measures how much information the modem can send. A *bit* is the smallest unit of information a computer can handle, like a molecule of information. Faster modems are more expensive, but can save you time while online, which may save you money in the long run.

Baud Rates and BPS

Even though you may see a modem's baud rate and BPS used as if they mean exactly the same thing (especially in mail order and other computer-type catalogs), they *are* two different things.

The good news is that the differences are actually so minor that only really, *really* anal-retentive computer geeks get annoyed when you use baud rate and BPS interchangeably. Try it and see.

A modem that sends information at 2400 BPS is much, *much* slower than a modem that sends information at 28,800 BPS.

28,800 BPS (sometimes written as 28.8) is currently the fastest modem around, but probably not for long. Most online services are upgrading their own systems (*they* have to buy new modems, too—a lot of them) to accept 28.8 speed communications. It won't be long before they're all, you should pardon the expression, up to speed.

You should think about getting as fast a modem as you can reasonably afford. Fast modems can always slow down if circumstances demand it, but slower modems can't speed up beyond their maximum capacities.

Other Bells and Whistles

You may also see modems that are *send fax,* or *send-and-receive fax* modems. These modems give you the ability to send documents from your computer to a regular fax machine. If it's capable, it also enables a regular fax machine to send a document to your computer.

If you know you never ever want to do anything but use MSN, and other online services, don't worry about fax capability. If you're the adventurous type, or a toy fanatic (like me), you may want to think about getting a fax modem. In either case, most modems you'll find these days will be fax-capable.

Fax capability doesn't increase a modem's price too much, and—if nothing else—faxing is a very techno-chic way to order a pizza.

Letting Windows 95 Know You Got a Modem

Once you install your modem and the software that came with it, you need to let Windows know you've got a new playmate on your PC. Windows 95 makes that very easy.

To start, click the **Start** button, and then select **Control Panels** from the **Settings** submenu. Then double-click the **Add New Hardware** icon. That starts up the Add New Hardware Wizard shown in the following figure.

Why do it yourself, when you can let the Wizard do it for you?

A *wizard* automates a Windows 95 process—in this case, by letting Windows know that you've bought a new toy.

Click **Next** to begin, and follow the simple instructions on screen. It's a piece of cake.

The Telephone Line

Man, I just got a flash of Glen Campbell singing "Wichita Lineman"—scary. I've got to lay off the oldies station while stuck in traffic.

Anyhow, in order for your computer and modem to work the magic that is MSN, you need to connect your computer to your modem, and you need to connect your modem to a telephone line.

If you can plug a telephone into a wall jack, you can connect your modem to your telephone line. No sweat. Beyond that, there aren't many concerns about your telephone line, you just need to know some information about it.

You need to know if your telephone line is *touch-tone*, or *pulse dial* (touch-tone lines beep once for each number you press, pulse lines sort of click the same number of times as the number you dial). You have to tell your Modems Control Panel so your PC knows what kind of noises to make to dial. Chapter 4 covers this.

Busy, Busy, Busy...

When you use MSN, your telephone line is busy—no incoming or outgoing calls—which can be traumatic if there are telephone junkies in your home. If you find it *is* traumatic, you may want to consider getting your local phone company to either hook you up with their call answer service (which takes messages while your line is busy), or put in another telephone line just for your modem. Both cost money, though, so consider the dollars-to-trauma ratio before you spring for either.

Another thing you need to know is that if you have call-waiting (that's when you're using the phone, and your phone beeps to let you know you've got another call coming in). It's a bad thing when you're online. Your computer tries its darndest to make sense out of those beeps, like they're part of the data stream coming in from MSN, and this can knock you offline—that is, disconnect you from the service.

The last thing you need to know is if you need to dial an additional number (usually a 9) before you can dial an outside phone number. Most home users don't have to, but many office workers do.

You'll put all of this telephone information to use in Chapter 4.

The Software You Need

The last thing you need to have on hand (well, on your computer—it doesn't do squat for you in your *hand*) is the proper software. To connect to MSN you need to install two pieces of software on your hard drive: the Microsoft Network software and Microsoft Exchange.

The Microsoft Network software includes all of the information your computer needs to call, connect, and enable you to do all the stuff there is to do online. You need to install the Microsoft Exchange software, because that's the software that handles e-mail. *E-mail* is short for electronic mail, and Chapter 12 covers it.

You must have both. The MSN software doesn't even look at you if you don't have Microsoft Exchange installed. If you've got two icons on your desktop named Microsoft Network and Inbox, don't sweat it. The software you need is already installed.

If not, hang out a minute while I wrap this up, and I'll show you how to install it in Chapter 3.

The Least You Need to Know

In order to get painlessly connected to MSN, you need to have the following hardware and software, and you need to know some basic information about it:

➤ You need to know your computer's configuration.

➤ You need a modem.

➤ You need a telephone line.

➤ You need to install the Microsoft Network and Microsoft Exchange software on your computer—and, it just so happens, that's what the next chapter covers.

CLACK

Clac

Chapter 3

No Stall Installation

In This Chapter

➤ Installing MSN while you install Windows 95

➤ Installing MSN later (or any other Windows 95 options you didn't add on the first go 'round)

➤ There is no third thing.

I've decided, after long years of observing humanity, studying philosophy, and just plain walking around, that there are only two kinds of people in the world. The first kind are those who see the dog poop just *before* they step in it. The second are those who see it just *after*.

The "just before" types are people who are in the moment, experiencing what they're doing, and (of course) watching where they're stepping.

The "just after" types are the ones who aren't in the moment. They're thinking about a destination or what they should or could be doing, and (of course) aren't watching where they're stepping.

You Gotta Install

As a sort of corollary to that observation, there are two finer distinctions to be drawn, two parallel types if you will: those who know (while they install Windows 95) that sooner or later they're going to get around to toying with the Microsoft Network; and those who don't.

Naturally, there is a third type, too. Those who install everything Windows 95 has to offer, right from the get-go. If you're one of these, you can blithely skip ahead to the next chapter (if you need to tinker with the settings for a new modem), or onto Chapter 5 (if you already installed and configured your modem, and it's working fine).

Whichever of the other two categories the rest of the readers fall into, you've got to install the appropriate software before you can play around with MSN. There are only two ways to install the necessary software: you can install it when you install Windows 95, or after the fact, using the Add/Remove Programs Control Panel.

While Installing Windows 95

If you still need to install Windows 95 on your PC, you can install MSN automatically along with everything else. It's practically a no-brainer, since the Windows 95 Setup Wizard really simplifies the process.

To begin, insert the first Windows 95 (Install 1) disk in your floppy drive, or the Windows 95 CD in your CD-ROM drive. The Windows 95 Setup Wizard may start up automatically (that's Microsoft's new AutoStart feature at work).

If it doesn't start on its own, select **Run** from the Program Manager's File menu. Then type the appropriate drive letter (typically **A:** for floppy disks, **E:** for CD-ROM drives, but your drive letter may vary, depending on your system configuration) followed by **Setup** in the text entry box. Click **OK**.

The Windows 95 Setup Wizard fires up. The process is very simple—just answer a few questions (and click the **Next** button when you're done) and follow the step-by-step instructions on-screen.

About halfway through the installation process, you see the screen below. This is where you tell the Setup Wizard if you want it to install some optional components, including (trumpet fanfare) the Microsoft Network.

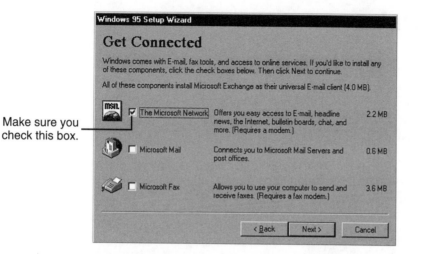

Installing MSN while installing Windows 95.

Make sure you check this box.

What About Microsoft Exchange?

Yes, I did say that Microsoft Exchange is required to use MSN, and that is still true. However, when you install MSN with the Windows 95 Setup Wizard, Microsoft Exchange is *automatically* installed when you add a component that requires it. As a matter of fact, installing any of the three options of the "Get Connected" screen installs Microsoft Exchange, too. Don't sweat it. It's in there.

Click the check box in front of **The Microsoft Network**, as shown in the figure above. (If it's already checked when the window opens, you've already installed MSN. You don't need to bother with it again.)

Only you know if you want or need the other two options (Microsoft Mail and Microsoft Fax). They aren't required to use MSN, so install them or not, at your own discretion. Proceed with the rest of the installation as the Setup Wizard directs you—swap some floppies, click some **Next** buttons, and sit back while the Wizard works its magic.

When all the disk swapping finishes (if you're using floppies), the Setup Wizard restarts your PC *twice*, automatically configuring itself to your system. Finally, you arrive at the desktop. First Time Help appears (you should probably go through it—it is actually helpful), and there is a brand new MSN icon on the left side of your screen.

Installing MSN Later

If you just got acclimated to Windows 95, and you decide you want to explore some of the optional features, you can add MSN (or any other optional items you skipped during the installation) by adding them with the Add/Remove Software Control Panel. Here's how.

Start with the Start Button

To begin, click the **Start** button as shown in the figure below. Slide the mouse pointer up the menu until it touches the **Settings** item. The submenu, also shown in the figure, pops up. Click the **Control Panel** item on the submenu.

Starting here, starting now...

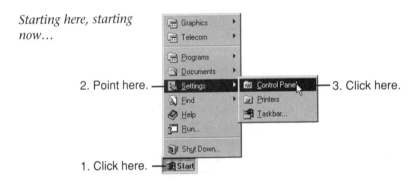

This action opens the Control Panel window shown at the beginning of the next section.

The Add/Remove Programs Control Panel

In the Control Panel window, scroll around until you find the icon called **Add/Remove Programs**. When you find it, double-click on it. This action opens the dialog box shown in the following figure.

Find the Add/Remove Programs Control Panel.

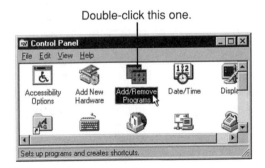

22

Click here first.

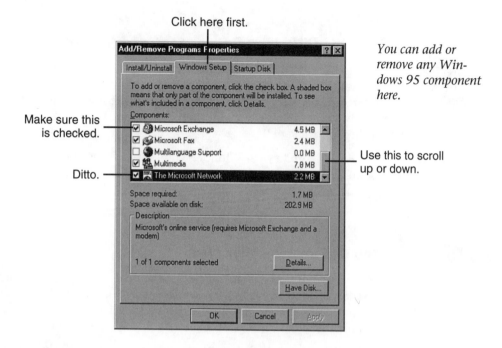

Make sure this
is checked.

Ditto.

*You can add or
remove any Win-
dows 95 component
here.*

Use this to scroll
up or down.

When the dialog box opens, click the **Windows Setup** tab to see the screen shown in the preceding figure.

In the center of the dialog box, there is a list box that shows all of the Windows 95 components that are installed (checked), partially installed (checked, but the check box is gray), or not installed at all (white check box, not checked).

Use the scroll bar at the right of the list box to scroll through the list until you find both Microsoft Exchange and The Microsoft Network. Click the check box in front of each application name to select the applications.

If you care to, you can click more check boxes to add the other options you skipped during your first installation. Personally, I recommend that you install Backup (under the System Tools heading) and use it to regularly back up your important files and application software—it's very easy and very handy.

Finally, click **OK** or **Apply**.

Windows asks for the appropriate floppy disk, or the Windows 95 CD (depending on which you used originally). Insert things as requested.

23

What's the Difference Between OK and Apply?

Good question! Glad you asked. Clicking OK starts the installation process and closes the Add/Remove Programs Properties window. Clicking Apply also starts the installation process, but it leaves the Add/Remove Programs Properties window open so you can make additional changes with this or one of the other tabs on the Control Panel.

If this is all you're going to do with Windows components, click **OK**. If you want to fool around some more, click **Apply** and carry on.

You Can Remove Junk, Too

While this Windows Setup stuff is handy, you can also remove any Windows features that you do not use. Just click the checked check box in front of the option you want to deep six. The check mark goes away, and the installed software does too, when you click OK or Apply, later.

If you want to be picky about it, click on the option name in the list box, and click the **Details** button. This shows you an itemized list of all the components under each heading. Click the check marks for the stuff you want out of there and click OK. Repeat the process until you remove all the fiddly bits you no longer want.

You can add and remove Windows components at the same time but you can't remove anything that's vital to Windows' operation, so don't worry. If you goof up, you can always put it back later.

When you finish, and depending on what you decided to install, Windows may ask you if it's okay to restart so it can use the new software. Click **OK** and Windows does the deed.

You're Ready To Roll

If you're just now installing MSN because you just bought your first modem, you may need some help getting your modem set up so Windows 95 knows where it is and what features it has. You can find out how to do this in Chapter 4.

With both MSN and Microsoft Exchange installed (and don't forget that modem), you're ready to set up the MSN software with your personal information so you can connect for the very first time. Chapter 5 covers this.

The Least You Need To Know

There. That wasn't too painful, was it? Barely broke a sweat in either scenario. Take five—but before you do, look over the following.

This is the absolute least you need to know before moving on:

➤ You can automatically install MSN (and Microsoft Exchange) when you install Windows 95. Just click the check box in front of The Microsoft Exchange on the Setup Wizard's Get Connected window.

➤ To install MSN and the Microsoft Exchange after you've installed Windows 95, use the Windows Setup tab on the Add/Remove Programs dialog box.

➤ You can also use the Windows Setup tab on the Add/Remove Programs dialog box to add any Windows options you opted out of while doing your original installation.

➤ You can also use the same tab (I'm not typing all that again) to delete any Windows 95 options that are just hogging up space on your hard drive because you don't use them.

➤ I guess that's why they decided to call it "Add/Remove Programs." *Duh.*

Setting Your Modem Properties

If you just installed a new modem, you need to provide Windows 95 with some pertinent information about it, and yourself, before you can use it. That's what this chapter is all about—so if your modem's already installed and working nicely, you may want to just skim this chapter (there are some interesting factoids here you may not be aware of) or skip ahead to the next. It's up to you.

Son Of "Add New Hardware"

The Add New Hardware Wizard, which you saw back in Chapter 2.

Back in Chapter 2, you saw how Windows 95 automates the addition of new hardware to your PC with the Add New Hardware Wizard (shown in the preceding figure).

By following its simple, step-by-step instructions, Windows checks your computer over from stem to stern looking for any hardware that you've added since the last time it looked. It then makes the appropriate adjustments to your system to accommodate the new bit of hardware.

In the case of adding a new modem, when it detects where you installed it, it launches another Wizard (the New Modem Wizard). The New Modem Wizard scans the modem for pertinent information: make and model, maximum speed, and any other additional features (like fax capability) that the modem has.

As thorough as the New Hardware Wizard is, there's just some things it can't learn about you from your modem. We're going to supply that information right now.

Back To The Control Panel

If you already closed the Control Panel window, you need to open it again. Select **Control Panel** from the Settings submenu on the Start menu. This action reopens the Control Panel window as shown in the following figure.

Scroll through the Control Panel window until you locate the **Modems** icon (it's the icon that's highlighted in the figure above) and double-click on it. This opens the Modems Properties dialog box.

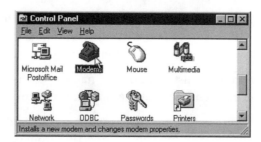

First, find and double-click the Modems icon.

Modems Properties

The Modems Properties (which sounds grammatically suspicious to me) dialog box is composed of two tabs: General and Diagnostics. When it first opens, the General tab appears, so let's look at that one first.

The General Tab

That sounds like a soft drink you have to salute, but it isn't. It's the place where you can review and change general information about your modem.

The dominant feature of the General tab of Modems Properties (shown in the following figure) is the list box labeled The following modems are set up on this computer. As you can see in the figure, mine has one (a U.S. Robotics Sportster 28800), and that modem is selected in the list box. If you have more than one modem installed on your PC (though why you'd *want* more than one is a mystery to me), you have two or more entries here.

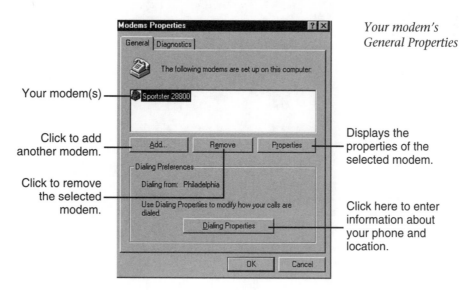

Your modem(s)

Click to add another modem.

Click to remove the selected modem.

Your modem's General Properties

Displays the properties of the selected modem.

Click here to enter information about your phone and location.

To add a new modem to the list, click the **Add** button, and Windows walks you through the process with the Add New Modem Wizard. The Add button, is a suitable alternative to the Add New Hardware Wizard, but only when adding a modem.

To remove a modem from the list, click on the name of the modem you want to remove. That selects it. Then click **Remove**, and that modem is history.

Chances are, you only use these two buttons when you upgrade to a new modem at some later date, or if you change your modem's connection from one COM port to another. If you do change your COM port connection, make sure you use the Add New Modem Wizard to let your PC know you've made the change. Then you'll have two modems listed here, with the same name: one for the old location, and one for the new. Then you may want to delete the old modem entry.

To find out which modem is which (or just to get more information about your one, lonely modem), click a modem entry, then click the **Properties** button.

Properties

When you click the Properties button, you see the dialog box shown in the following figure. Like the Modems Properties dialog box, it's made up of two tabs. The first shows the General properties of the selected modem (or, in my case, the only modem).

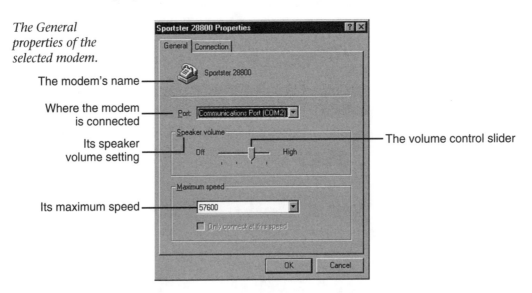

The General properties of the selected modem.

The modem's name

Where the modem is connected

Its speaker volume setting

Its maximum speed

The volume control slider

At the top of the General tab is the modem name ("Sportster 28800" in the figure). Below that is the port where the modem is connected ("COM2" in the figure). If you change your modem's connection, you can select the new port from the Port drop-down list.

At the center of the General tab is the modem's Speaker volume setting. This slider enables you to change the volume at which your modem plays your dial tone, dialing beeps, and connection tones when you use the modem. It isn't what I'd call music to the ears, so you may want to set it moderately low. Just click and drag the slider to move it to the new setting.

At the bottom of the General tab is the modem's Maximum speed setting. Windows receives this information directly when you use the Add New Hardware Wizard, so you don't have to change it.

On the off chance that you do need to change it (see the section "The Diagnostics Tab later in the chapter), select the new speed from the Maximum speed drop down list. If you click the Connection tab, you see a screen like the one shown in the following figure.

At the top of the Connection tab are your Connection preferences. There are three selections: Data bits, Parity, and Stop bits. The figures shows the standard settings. These settings are fine for MSN and most other online services. Don't mess with them.

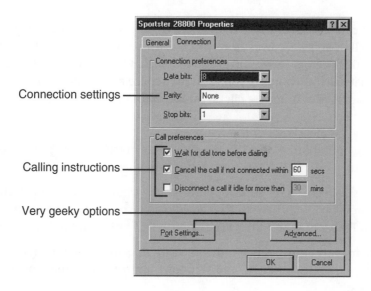

Your communication settings...okay, my communication settings.

Definitions Not Included

Normally, when I introduce new terms like *data bits, parity,* and *stop bits* I provide definitions for them. But you don't need to know what these mean. The only interesting thing about them is that a long time ago there were *two* commonly used sets of communications settings (the second set being: 7 data bits, Parity, and 0 stop bits). You probably won't need to use this second set. However, the option to change settings is still around—like the human appendix, the vestigial remains of a once-necessary feature.

Below the Connection preferences are your Call preferences. These give your modem specific instructions on what to do in certain situations. They are:

Wait for dial tone before dialing   Make sure you check this one if you also use the modem's phone line for regular telephone calls. That way, no one gets an earful of modem squeals if the phone is in use when you try to connect to MSN.

Cancel the call if not connected within X secs   In the figure, this is set to 60 seconds. You can adjust this number higher or lower (just double-click on the number to select it, and type in the new number) to suit your own level of impatience.

Disconnect a call if idle for more than X mins   This one can save you money on your phone bill. If you walk away from your PC (to get a beverage, go to the bathroom, or hitchhike across the country) and forget that you're online, checking this option automatically disconnects you from the service after your computer idles (meaning no keystrokes or mouse clicks) for the amount of time you enter in the text box.

To turn a preference option on or off, click the check box in front of the preference. If it's already checked (turned on), a click turns it off. If it isn't checked, a click turns it on.

The last two buttons (labeled "Very geeky options" in the figure) are for some techno-geek settings you probably don't have to change. I'll show you what these do in the section called "You Probably Won't Ever Need This, But..." at the end of the chapter.

When you're done making adjustments to the selected modem's properties (either General, Connection, or both) click **OK**, and Windows returns you to the Modems Properties dialog box.

Dialing Properties

If your PC is a desktop model that never goes anywhere, you can skip this section. The default Dialing Properties will work fine for you. Portable owners, and people who move a lot, read on.

When you're back at the Modems Properties Control Panel, click the Dialing Properties button and you see the screen shown in the following figure. Here is where you provide Windows (and therefore MSN) with information about your location and your telephone line.

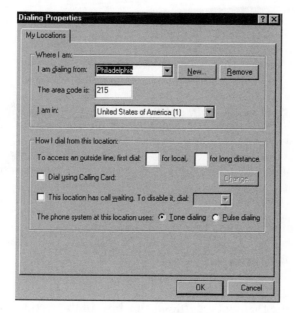

Dialing Properties tells Windows where you are and what kind of phone line you're using.

At the top of the Dialing Properties screen, in the box labeled Where I am, is where you enter the city you're calling from, your local area code, and your country.

If this is the first time you've seen your dialing properties, all this information is blank. To enter the necessary information, do the following:

1. Click the **New** button. This action gives you the small, Create New Location dialog box shown in the following figure.

2. Type the city name, or whatever will help you remember what this location file is for, in the text box (where it says "Scranton" in the following figure).

Creating a new location entry for your Dialing Properties.

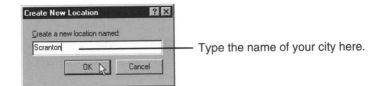

Type the name of your city here.

3. Click **OK**. This returns you to the Dialing Properties dialog box. The city name you enter appears in the text box labeled I am dialing from.

4. Double-click in the **The area code is** text box.

5. Type in your area code.

6. Click on the drop-down list box labeled I am in, and select the country you're in from the list. You're done!

You Can Keep Several Sets Of Location Settings

If you use a laptop or other portable computer, you can keep several location settings for cities you frequently visit. Just repeat the process described here for each city. I have settings for Boston, Philadelphia, Scranton, New York, and San Francisco on my laptop, because these are the cities I visit most often.

Before you use your modem in one of these cities, just call up your Dialing Properties and select the appropriate city from the I am dialing from drop-down list. Chapter 20 has more tips and tricks for using MSN on the road.

The bottom half of the Dialing Properties dialog box, in the section labeled How I dial from this location, is where you provide information about the telephone line you're using. (This information is usually different for each location you create.)

If you're calling from work, a hotel room, or any place where you need to dial a 9 or other number to place an outside call, click in the text box in front of for local and type the appropriate number (9 is the most common, but your dial out number may be different).

Likewise, if you need to dial a special number before you make a long distance call, click in the text box in front of for long distance and type the appropriate number (for most, it's a 1).

Below that, if you use a personal and/or company Calling Card(s) for phone calls made on the road, click in the Dial using Calling Card check box. This calls up the Change Calling Card dialog box shown in the following figure.

Drop-down list of popular
calling card companies.

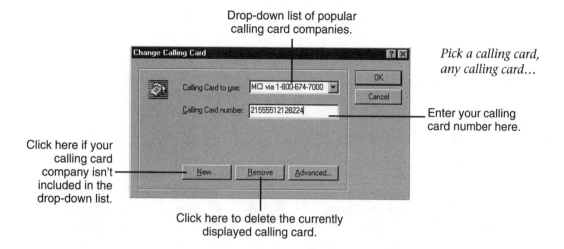

*Pick a calling card,
any calling card...*

Enter your calling
card number here.

Click here if your
calling card
company isn't
included in the
drop-down list.

Click here to delete the currently
displayed calling card.

Select your calling card from the Calling Card to use drop-down list. It contains most of the popular calling card companies. (If yours isn't in the list, click **New** and enter the name of your particular calling card.)

Enter your calling card number in the Calling Card number text box. You can also keep several calling cards on file here, which is convenient if you have one for personal use and another for business. To switch between calling cards, click the **Change** button on the main Dialing Properties dialog box, and select the calling card you want to use for this session.

To delete a calling card you've already entered (if you change long distance carriers, for instance), select it from the Calling Card to use drop-down list and click **Remove**.

The Advanced button calls up a set of dialing rules that are particular to each calling card company. You only need to mess with them if you don't use a calling card in the drop-down list—and you have to contact your calling card company to find out what you need to enter. Only they know what this gibberish means.

When you're done tinkering with the calling card information, click **OK**, and you go back to the Dialing Properties dialog box.

The last two items in the How I dial from this location section are the ones most folks need to use. If your phone has call waiting service, click in the check box labeled This location has call waiting. Then select the appropriate method to block call waiting from the drop-down list labeled To disable it, dial. Most people use either the *70, (for touch tone lines) or 1170, (rotary dial lines) options, as these are the most common ways to disable call waiting.

If you have call waiting, you must disable it. The tones an incoming call makes disrupt the flow of information between MSN and your PC, and probably end your online session abruptly. Not fun.

Naturally, if you don't have call waiting, you shouldn't mess with these settings.

What The Comma Means

The commas after *70, and 1170, aren't punctuation, but a command to your modem to wait a moment before it continues to dial the telephone number. It gives your phone a chance to accept the command before feeding it a phone number to cope with, too. To make your modem wait longer, add another comma (*70,,).

Finally, you need to tell Windows whether your telephone is touch-tone, or pulse dial. Click the appropriate phone type.

When you enter all of the information, click **OK** and you go back to the Modems Properties Control Panel.

You can have as many sets of How I dial from this location information as you have location entries in the Where I am section. That way, you don't have to re-enter all this stuff every time you travel to a city for which you've already entered Dialing Properties.

The Diagnostics Tab

When you're back at the Modems Properties Control Panel, click the **Diagnostics** tab, and you see information similar to that shown in the following figure.

Driver A bit of software that tells Windows 95 how to deal with a particular piece of hardware. Printers require printer drivers. Modems require modem drivers. Many common drivers are built into Windows, and hardware that requires a driver usually comes with a disk of driver software.

Windows 95 checks the modem's COM port by asking the modem for information about itself. The following figure shows the information it turned up. You'll notice is shows that the modem's maximum speed is 115 K Baud, and not 57,600 as displayed on the Modems Properties General tab earlier. That's also why I explained how to change the maximum speed setting at the end of that section—it's important that these two match, or you won't get the best performance out of your modem.

The Driver button enables you to see which driver(s) Windows is using to control your modem.

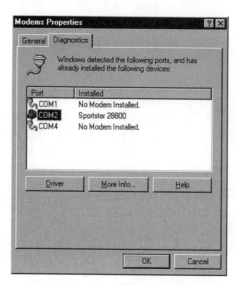

Diagnostics checks your communications port by chatting with your modem.

The More Info button sends a standard set of commands to your modem to find out all the picky technical details about the port it's connected to and what the modem can do. You can see More Info about my modem in the following figure.

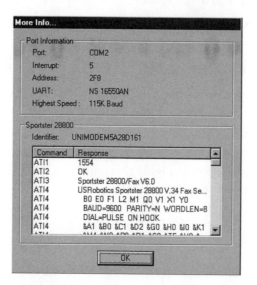

More Info about a modem than most humans ever need.

The top half of the More Info dialog box shows information about the port your modem is connected to. The bottom half (labeled with your modem's name—Sportster 28800 in the figure) contains your modem's response to the standard set of *AT commands*.

AT commands
The standardized set of modem commands (referred to as the AT Command Set) that most modems use. They're called "AT Commands" because each command begins with the letters "AT" (for "ATtention"), telling your modem that an instruction is coming.

You probably only need this information if your modem is somehow conflicting with another piece of hardware in your PC. If your modem isn't working, you can use Windows 95's Modem Troubleshooter to help figure it out.

Select **Help** from the Start menu and double-click **Troubleshooting** in the Contents list. Finally, double-click the entry **If you have trouble using your modem**. The Modem Troubleshooter asks you a series of questions about the problem you're having in order to help you resolve it.

There's also additional troubleshooting information in Chapter 25.

When you're done ogling this super-geeky information, click **OK** to return to the Diagnostics tab.

When You're Done Tinkering...

When you're done tinkering with the Modems Properties Control Panel, click **OK** at the very bottom of the Control Panel. This action closes the Modems Properties dialog box and puts any changes you made into effect.

If you don't want to use any of the changes you made, click **Cancel** instead.

You Probably Won't Ever Need This, But...

Back in the section on the Connection tab of your modem's properties (the following figure is a reminder), I brushed past two very geeky buttons at the bottom of the dialog box: Port Settings and Advanced.

You probably won't ever need to fiddle with these settings (at least, not with MSN), but in case you do, this section explains what they are. If you're following along by looking at them on your own PC, just look. Don't change anything.

Port Settings

To get at the Advanced Port Settings dialog box shown in the following figure, click the **Port Settings** button on the Connection tab of your modem's Properties dialog box.

The Advanced Port Settings tell Windows to use FIFO buffers with your modem. FIFO is a term borrowed from retail accounting that stands for "First In First Out." The first information Windows stores in the *buffer* is the first information it sends out.

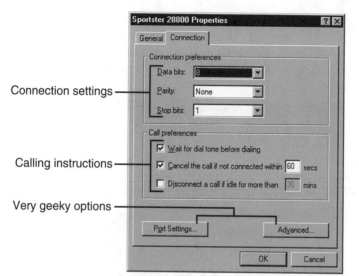

Remember me?

Connection settings

Calling instructions

Very geeky options

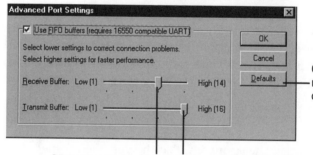

The very techno-geeky Advanced Port Settings.

Click here to revert to the original settings.

Click-drag these sliders to change the settings.

If your modem uses FIFO buffers (many don't), this option is automatically on. If your modem doesn't use FIFO buffers, these options are grayed out.

If you're using FIFO buffers, but find yourself frequently having connection problems (you can't connect, or can't stay connected), you can adjust the settings for the Receive and Transmit buffers.

Higher settings increase the speed at which the modem sends and receives data. Lower settings decrease the speed, but increase the stability of your connection.

Buffer A section of memory (RAM) set aside to hold information a modem sends or receives . Since computers and modems often cannot handle the same amount of information at the same speed, buffers enable the computer to store surplus information until the slower piece of hardware is ready to deal with it.

39

Advance Connection Settings

To get at the Advanced Connection Settings shown in the following figure, click the **Advanced** button on the Connection tab of your modem's Properties dialog box.

The Advance Connection Settings—they affect your modem's speed and reliability.

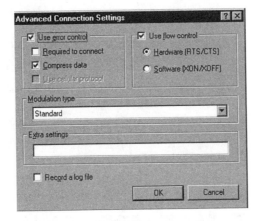

Most folks don't realize that today's very fast modems (28800 BPS and faster) really work at the same "speed" as 14400 BPS modems. They send more data in the same amount of time by compressing it. The Advanced Connection Settings enable you to change some of the features that give you that extra burst of speed.

Again, you probably don't have to alter these for use with MSN, but you may for other services.

The check box labeled Use error control at the upper left corner of the dialog box controls your modem's error checking routine. When checked, as it is in the figure, your modem double-checks that the information you're sending was not damaged by the compression process.

If you turn off error control, you may wind up with a less reliable connection. The error control options, listed in the section below Use error control are:

> **Required to connect**   When checked, it only enables your modem to connect to another modem or service that supports error correction. It forces a reliable connection.

> **Compress data**   When checked, this option enables your modem to work at its very highest speeds.

> **Use cellular protocol** (grayed out in the figure)   Enables your modem (if it's capable) to connect via a cellular phone. Mine isn't cellular capable, which is why the option isn't available to me.

Beside the error control settings are the flow control settings, in the box labeled Use flow control. Flow control (strangely enough) controls the flow of information from the modem to your computer. In the figure, I selected the Hardware (RTS/CTS) option because my modem is an internal model that optimizes the flow of data. (External modems not only coordinate the flow control, but also require a special cable as well. Check your modem's manual to see if your cable can handle hardware flow control.)

The Software (XON/XOFF) option turns flow control over to the communications software. Not all communications programs handle flow control (MSN can, by the way), turning control over to software that can't handle it can result in a less reliable connection.

At the center of the dialog box is a drop -down list box labeled Modulation type. In the rarest of circumstances (like you're trying to connect with a 10-year-old or older online service that hasn't updated it's hardware in all that time) you may need to change the modulation type to one other than Standard. The only other option here is Non-standard, and it will probably be a cold day in you-know-where when you need to select it.

The Extra Settings text box is where you can enter additional commands to your modem. It's another case of new hardware (yours) running into old hardware (theirs), and you need to tell your modem how to deal with theirs. You enter these settings as a line of gibberish-looking numbers, letters, and characters, and the service that is causing you grief normally provides you them.

Finally, you can click the check box in front of Record a log file to create a text file (called *Modemlog.txt*) of everything your modem does during the connection process. It's a handy tool to help solve a modem problem. You can open and print the log to have handy when you call the modem manufacturer's technical support line, if you're having trouble. Their technicians should be able to tell, from the record, what went wrong where, and what you can do to fix it.

The Least You Need To Know

Windows 95 can gather a lot of information about your modem when you use the Add New Hardware Wizard. However, some information only you can provide. In this chapter, you saw how to use the various parts of the Modems Properties dialog box to:

➤ View and change the properties of your modem (with the Properties button on the General tab of the Modem Properties dialog box).

➤ Supply Windows with information about your location, telephone line, and any calling cards you may use (with the Dialing Properties button on the General tab of the Modem Properties dialog box).

➤ Use Dialing Properties to store information about several locations you (and your computer) travel to frequently, so you can access MSN on the road.

➤ You also looked at some highly technical settings that you probably don't need to change, but you should know about...just in case.

Set Yourself Up

In the last chapter we provided Windows 95 (and, at the same time, MSN) with information about our modem, telephone line, and location—all to simplify the process of connecting with MSN—and any other online services you choose to use.

In this chapter, we're going to launch (a fancy way of saying "start") MSN and provide it with a pile of information so MSN can set up your personal account. I suggest that you read through the chapter *first*, then actually do the registration stuff with the book nearby for reference.

You need to have a credit card handy, and decide on a member ID and password. It simplifies your life if you have these ready *before* you do the actual registration. Afterwards, you can sign on at will, and do all those fun, informative, and downright bizarre things I promised you. I promise.

Launching the MSN Software

To start, we need to launch the Microsoft Network software we installed in Chapter 3. There are a couple of ways you can do that.

Double-Click the MSN Icon on Your Desktop

This is the easiest method: Locate **The Microsoft Network** icon (shown in the figure below) and double-click on it. (Windows places this icon on your desktop when you install the software.)

Launch MSN from your desktop—just double-click to start.

My Computer

Inbox

Recycle Bin

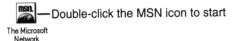
The Microsoft
Network
—Double-click the MSN icon to start

Bingo! You're off and running.

Use the Start Button

The next easiest method of launching MSN is to use Windows 95's fabulous new Start button.

To do so, click the **Start** button. The Start menu pops up, as shown in the figure below (yours looks different—I've been tinkering with mine).

Drag the mouse pointer up until it touches the **Programs** command, and a submenu pops up. Click **The Microsoft Network** option on the submenu.

You're off and running again.

You can also launch MSN from the Start menu.

Starting the Registration Process

However you start the MSN software, the first thing you see is the screen shown in the figure below.

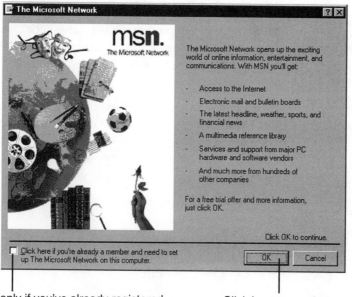

Registration begins here.

Click here only if you've already registered.   Click here to continue.

45

If You've Already Registered Once...

If you've already gone through the registration process once, but you are installing another copy of MSN on, say, a laptop computer, or reinstalling it on your desktop PC, you can breeze through the registration process. Just click on the check box at the lower-left corner of the screen. It's the one labeled Click here if you're already a member and need to set up The Microsoft Network on this computer.

MSN asks you for your member ID and password, signs you on to the service, and copies your registration information from the MSN computer to your own.

This screen explains a little about MSN, and what it can do for you. Read the information, and then click **OK** to continue.

You can click **Cancel** at any time to end the registration process, too.

What's Your Area Code?

Most of the registration process is a series of questions you need to answer. They aren't "Two trains leave Chicago at 8 a.m. One is traveling at 75 m.p.h...." type questions. MSN just wants some basic information about you.

Local Access Number
MSN's central computers are located in Seattle, Washington. Calling into Seattle is a long distance call for most people. Instead of socking you with long distance charges, you access MSN by calling (usually) a local phone number, and the computer at that location (called a *node*, if you care) connects you to MSN.

The first questions are "what's your area code?" and "what are the first three digits of your phone number?" They help the MSN software track down the best *local access number* for you to use.

Enter the information in the appropriate box. Click to place the cursor in the Your area or city code box, and then type your area or city code. Repeat the process in the box labeled The first three digits of your phone number, but enter the (duh) first three digits of your phone number.

Click **OK** when you're done.

Getting the Latest Scoop

Since MSN is brand-spanking new, there's a pile of new information available about the service, including new access numbers. To get the latest news, click **Connect** on the Calling dialog box.

Your computer dials into MSN, retrieves the latest information about the service, and disconnects. It only takes a few moments.

If you have trouble connecting, click the **Settings** button. That calls up the Connection Settings dialog box shown below. With it, you can select a new access number. Just click **Access Numbers** in the dialog box and select a new access number from the list of available access numbers in alphabetical order by state.

Pick a new access number.

These are the same options you saw in Chapter 4.

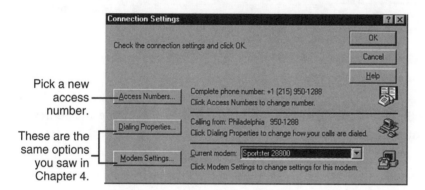

Changing your settings for a better connection.

The Dialing Properties and Modem Settings buttons call up those parts of the Modems Properties dialog box you looked at in the last chapter (so check there for the details on what these do).

In most cases, you won't have any trouble getting through. If you do have trouble, and you're completely confused about what to do about it, click the **Help** button, and the MSN software makes some suggestions.

After your computer connects to MSN and retrieves the latest information, you'll automatically be disconnected. Then you'll see the screen shown next.

The rest of the registration process on one easy-to-follow screen.

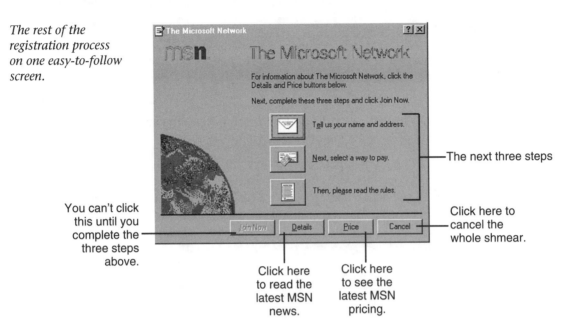

You can't click this until you complete the three steps above.

Click here to read the latest MSN news.

Click here to see the latest MSN pricing.

The next three steps

Click here to cancel the whole shmear.

This screen covers the rest of the registration process: filling in your name and address; selecting a payment method; and reading the rules for using MSN. The next few sections cover each of these steps.

However, this screen also enables you to take a peek at MSN's late-breaking information.

To read the latest news about the service, click **Details**. To get the latest pricing information, click **Price**. After you satisfy your curiosity, click the **Tell us your name and address** button.

Tell Us Your Name, for the Record...

When you click the Tell us your name and address button, it calls up the screen shown on the next page. Click in the **First name** box and type in your first name.

Press the **Tab** key, and the cursor jumps to the next box. Type in your last name. Repeat the process until you fill in all of the information. If a line doesn't apply to you (Company, or the second Street Address line), just leave it blank.

When you get to the box labeled Country, instead of typing, you can select your country from the Country drop-down list. Click on the downward pointing arrow and click on the appropriate country (you may have to scroll through a few until you find yours).

After you enter all that information, click **OK**. MSN returns you to the last screen, and there is a check mark beside the Tell us your name and address button, indicating that you completed that step.

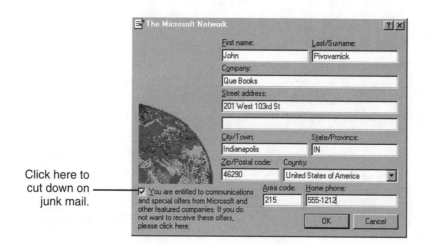

Just fill in the blanks.

Click here to cut down on junk mail.

Click on the **Next, select a way to pay** button.

You Got to Pay the Piper

When you click on the Next, select a way to pay button, you call up the screen shown below. Here you tell MSN how you're going to pay for the use of the service.

Select a credit card from the scroll box at the top of the screen. MSN accepts Visa, MasterCard, American Express/Optima, and the Discover Card.

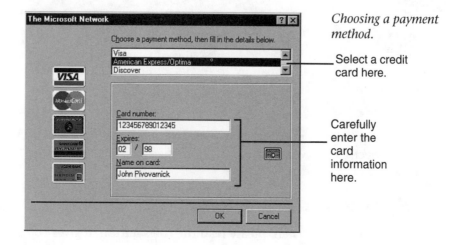

Choosing a payment method.

Select a credit card here.

Carefully enter the card information here.

How Much Does MSN Cost?

As of this writing, there are three MSN pricing plans. The first is a special trial offer that may expire before you read this. It gives you 10 free hours of use during your first 30 days as a member of MSN. Additional hours are $2.50 each. After the first 30 days, your account automatically switches over to a Standard Plan account.

The Standard Plan costs you $4.95 per month and includes 3 hours of online time each month. Additional hours are $2.50 each. For real online addicts, there's a heavy user plan that costs $19.95 a month. It includes a whopping 20 hours of online time, and additional hours cost $2.00 each. You can change your plan and payment method online. Chapter 6 tells you how.

At the bottom of the screen, click in the box labeled **Card number** and carefully type your credit card number. Hit the **Tab** key and type in the card's expiration date. The Name on card box already contains your name. If the name on the credit card is different, click and drag over the name to select it, and type the name as it appears on the credit card.

Safety Alert! Safety Alert!

This is the only time that MSN asks you for a credit card number, unless you, yourself change your method of payment (Chapter 6 explains this).

Never, never, *never* give out credit card information (or any other personal information) to anyone online. You may as well just hand your wallet over to a stranger. See Chapter 8 for more online safety tips.

Click **OK** when you're done. This screen goes away, and there's a check mark next to the Next, select a way to pay button. Only one step left: Click the button labeled **Then, please read the rules.**

The Rules of the Online Road

When you click the **Then, please read the rules button**, it gives you a text box that contains the Microsoft Network Member Agreement. These are the rules that MSN expects you to follow in all of your dealings online.

These rules cover what is and is not acceptable behavior online, as well as acceptable and unacceptable online activities. After you read them (and really read them, now), if you agree to follow them, click **I Agree**. If you don't agree to follow them, click **I Don't Agree**.

Heed this warning: if you don't agree, you can't join MSN. And, if you don't follow the rules while online, MSN may terminate your membership.

Sign Me Up!

After you agree to the Membership agreement, MSN returns you to the screen shown below. Now that you've completed the three registration steps, you're ready to join up. Click **Join Now**.

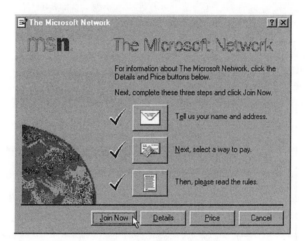

Registration mission accomplished!

When you click Join Now, MSN presents you with the screen shown below. It shows the two access numbers MSN selected for your use. MSN chooses the two numbers (a Primary and a Backup number, in case the Primary number is busy) it *thinks* are closest to where you live. Sometimes it guesses wrong.

Your access numbers.

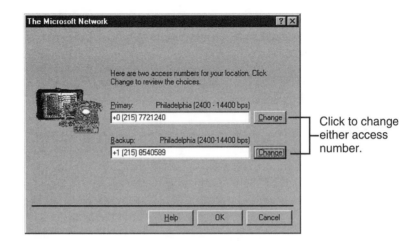

Click to change either access number.

If one or both of the numbers aren't actually local calls for you, click the **Change** button beside the bogus number. MSN presents you with the screen below.

Changing your local access number.

Select your country here.

Select your state/region.

Select a new local access number.

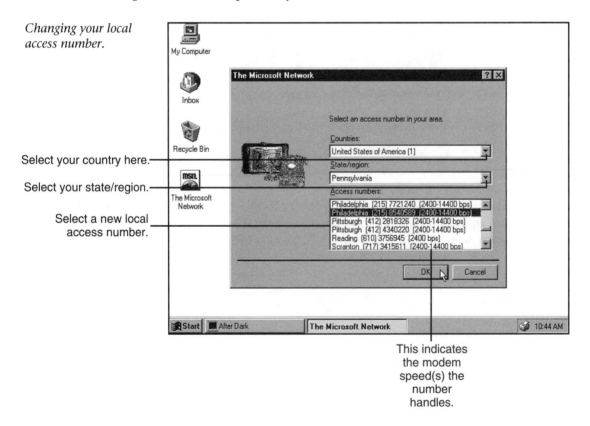

This indicates the modem speed(s) the number handles.

To select a new local access number, do the following:

1. Select your country from the **Countries** drop-down list.

2. Select your state or region from the **State/region** drop-down list.

3. Click on a new local access number from the **Access numbers** drop-down list box to select it.

4. Finally, click **OK**.

MSN lists the access numbers alphabetically by city. After each access number, the bracketed numbers that appear indicate the modem speed(s) the access number handles. For instance, one that says (2400-14400 bps) handles any modem speed from 2400 baud, up to and including 14,400. Make sure the number you select is capable of handling your modem's top speed.

When you're satisfied with both of your local access numbers, click **OK**.

Check Your Phone Bill!

If MSN doesn't offer an access number that is a local call for you, don't leap to the conclusion that a long distance call within your state will be less expensive than a long distance call to another state. Very often what they call intrastate long distance charges (for calls in the same state) are much higher than calls made to another state (interstate). Check a recent phone bill to compare costs, or call your long distance carrier for pricing information.

Next you see a Calling screen, like the one you saw earlier when you retrieved the lastest information on MSN in the section called "Getting the Latest Scoop."

Your computer dials the Primary access number and connects you to MSN for the very first time.

Pick a Member ID and Password

When you connect, your PC sends all your registration information to the MSN computers so MSN can create an account for you. Next, MSN asks you to choose your member ID (the name that other members identify you by) and a password (so no one else can access your account).

The password is...

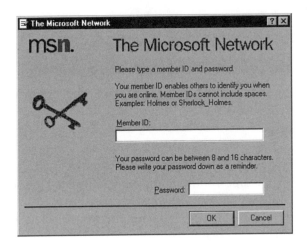

Your member ID can be your name, a nickname, or even a favorite character name from a book or movie. There are no minimum or maximum letter rules, so you have a lot of latitude to create your online handle. Just keep it clean, and remember that it can't contain any blank spaces. Try and be original, since only one member can use any given member ID.

For mine, I chose CompleteIdiot because that's what I am, and what I do. I could have also entered it as Complete_Idiot.

Choose an ID that's representative of you and your personality. To enter your member ID, click in the **Member ID** text box, and type your member ID. Press **Tab**, and the cursor jumps down to the Password text box.

Your Password is important. It needs to be something you can remember easily, that no one else can figure out. It has to be at *least* 8 characters long, and can't be more than 16 characters. Don't use your phone, or Social Security number. Don't use your cat's name. Don't use anything that anyone who knows you could guess is your password. That defeats the purpose.

Type your password in the Password text box. Then, click **OK**.

If no one else uses the member ID you enter, it's yours for ever and always. If someone is already using it, MSN asks you to select another. It's a good idea to prepare a couple of choices in advance, just in case. Great minds think alike, and all that.

You're All Set

Once MSN accepts your member ID and password, it disconnects and presents you with the screen shown below. This is the standard Sign In screen you use every time you connect to MSN.

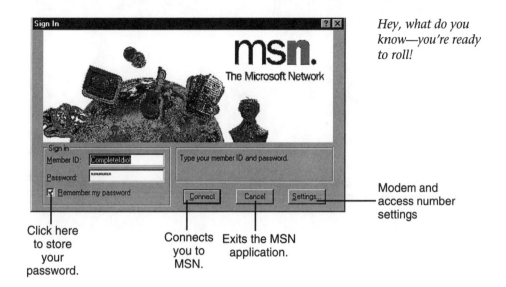

Hey, what do you know—you're ready to roll!

Click here to store your password.

Connects you to MSN.

Exits the MSN application.

Modem and access number settings

In the box labeled **Sign in** at the lower-right corner are your member ID and password (the Password is shown as asterisks, so no one can see what it is). If you click in the **Remember my password** check box, you don't ever have to worry about forgetting your password. MSN stores it for you—but then it doesn't offer any protection, either. Anyone with access to your computer can sign on with your MSN account, so think before you click.

The next chapter gives you a guided tour of the main parts of the Microsoft Network. You can read and cruise at the same time.

If you're ready to take a break, you can click **Cancel** or the Sign In screen's close box, and the MSN software shuts down.

The Least You Need to Know

The registration process is simple enough: there are step-by-step instructions on every screen. You probably don't need much help from me. That being the case, the least you need to know are these three things that you need to have or think about before you begin the registration process for real:

➤ You're going to need a credit card, so have it with you when you start.

➤ Think of a member ID that you can live with, and then think of a few spares, in case somebody has already used your first choice. (Sadly, it happens.)

➤ Think of a password (from 8–16 characters) that you can remember easily, but not one so obvious that anyone who knows you can figure out.

55

Your First Time Online (I'll Be Gentle)

Here comes the moment you've been waiting for—I hope you've been waiting for it. You haven't been skulking around online behind my back, have you?

In this chapter we're going to sign on to MSN, have a quick look around, and then beat a hasty retreat. I don't want to overload you on your first go round.

Before You Begin

Before you begin this, or any online session, you should prepare yourself. It's not like jogging where you can pull a muscle if you don't warm up beforehand. It's more like a long car trip. Since you're going to be sitting in one spot for a long while, you may want to do one or all of the following, before you sign on:

➤ Take a bathroom break. That way you don't have to stop in the middle of something interesting online. It also keeps me from having to say "You should have thought of that before you signed on."

➤ Change into comfortable, loose-fitting clothes. Personally, I don't wear any other kind, but I know some folks do. As with a long car trip, tight, restrictive clothing is annoying and uncomfortable after a while. No one sees you online, so dress for comfort, not for looks.

➤ Grab a beverage. I know liquids at the computer are a real no-no (having just spent a day trying to get all of a sticky soda spill out of my numeric keypad), but you're human and may get thirsty. If you decide to have a beverage, put it in one of those spill-proof travel mugs.

➤ Hang out the "Do Not Disturb" sign. You pay for online time. Don't waste part of your pre-paid 3 hours, or spend $2–$2.50 an hour explaining to your kid why he has to do his homework, or why she can't play video games.

When you're ready:

Enter and Sign In, Please

To start, launch the MSN software by your favorite method (I pointed out two different ways in the last chapter, if you're skimming around the book).

When MSN starts up, the Sign In screen below greets you. If your member ID doesn't show in the Member ID box, click in the **Member ID** box to place the cursor there and type in your member ID.

The ever-popular Sign In screen.

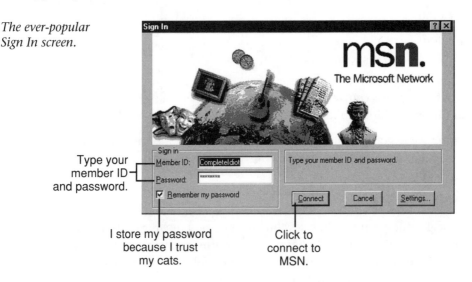

Type your member ID and password.

I store my password because I trust my cats.

Click to connect to MSN.

If you opted not to store your password (I store mine because, aside from the cats, I live alone—and my cats are more interested in the *other* kind of mice), you need to enter it before you sign on. Click in the **Password** box to place the cursor there and carefully type your password. I say "carefully" because you only see a series of asterisks (*) on-screen, not the characters you're typing.

After you enter your member ID and password, click **Connect**.

You see a little status display that tells you what your software is doing. It says "dialing" and (if your modem's speaker is set at an audible volume) you hear a dial tone and then dialing. When your local access number answers, you hear a high-pitched squeal, and your PC answers with a similar one.

The squeals (which sound for all the world like known gossips meeting with incredible dirt to share) are your modem and MSN's modem saying "Hi, how you doing? What can you do?" They negotiate the best connection possible with those squeals.

After the modems connect, your PC sends your member ID and password to MSN's computer. MSN's computer verifies your account, and (if you check out okay) enables you to enter its online world.

Sorry, Wrong Password

If you accidentally mistype your password, when you try to sign in MSN politely tells that you entered an invalid password. MSN then unceremoniously drops your connection, and you have to try again. Type your password *c-a-r-e-f-u-l-l-y*.

The very first thing you see is the MSN Central screen, shown below, but that doesn't appear for long. In another moment you probably see a blank window open (named "Online Viewer"). Things churn for a moment, and then you see the MSN Today page.

Since MSN Today is already in your face, let's take a look at that. We'll come back to MSN Central in a bit.

Welcome to MSN Central—but don't blink, or you miss it.

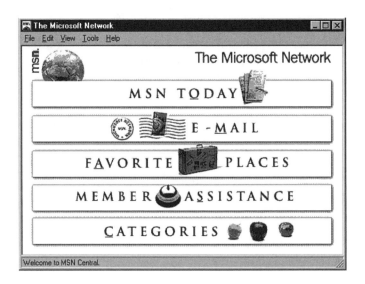

Getting Around on MSN

The next chapter covers all of this, but I don't want you floundering around like a digital carp when you get online.

MSN is organized much like the files on your hard drive. When you first sign on, you're at the root (C:\) level. As you do stuff, you're going deeper into the service (like opening a folder on your hard drive), and still deeper (opening another folder that's inside the folder you just opened).

However, every time you go to an new area online (open a new folder) you *don't* open a new window. One window stays open, and changes to reflect the new area you're visiting. To get back to the last area you were in, select **Up One Level** from the **File** menu. To get *quickly* back to where you started, select **MSN Central** from the **Go to** submenu on the **Edit** menu.

Remember these two simple things, and you'll never get lost and start crying like a misplaced 3-year-old in a mall.

MSN Today

The MSN Today screen you see only looks something like the one shown here because it changes daily. MSN Today is a listing of all the main events happening online today (hence the name—get it?).

You are here.

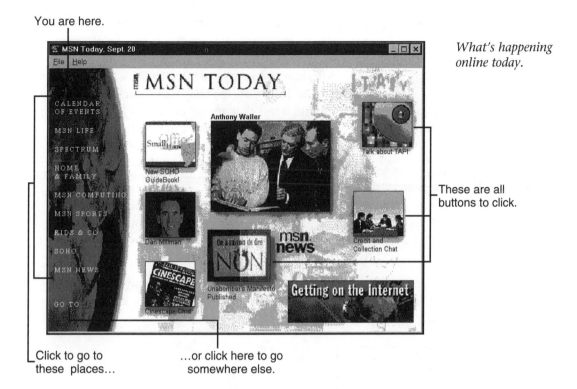

What's happening online today.

These are all buttons to click.

Click to go to these places...

...or click here to go somewhere else.

Each item on the screen gives you a little text display, explaining the "Who, what, when, where, why, and how" of the event. To see the explanation, click on the picture near the entry that interests you. The text box looks something like the one shown here.

A shortcut that takes you right there—just click on it.

An MSN Today info box with a shortcut.

Now, when you cruise MSN on your own, if you're really intrigued by the event, you can click on the little icon in the box, and it takes you right to the appropriate area online. It's a *shortcut*.

However, for the sake of our little guided tour, don't do that right now (I'll turn you loose to explore on your own in a bit). For now, just read the information and then click anywhere on the MSN Today screen to close the window to return to MSN Today.

Shortcut A tiny icon that appears on your desktop (and some other places) is a shortcut. When you click on it, it takes you to a particular area on MSN. You can create your own, or receive them from friends who use MSN. Chapter 25 tells you how.

Down the left side of the MSN Today screen are a couple of titles. These are buttons you can click, too. MSN Today is colored because that's where you are right now. If you click **Calendar of Events** the MSN Today screen becomes a calendar-like listing of *everything* happening online in the weeks ahead. Items that appear in cyan (a $2 word for "light blue") are shortcuts, too. Click on them, and the shortcuts take you to the appropriate area online—but again, for the sake of the tour, don't. Just know that you can.

If you click on **MSN Life**, you open a new window that displays the online magazine. Chapter 14 covers the Calendar of Events, MSN Life, and the rest of these little goodies in detail.

Finally, if you click **Go To** at the bottom of the screen, you get the handy little Go To Menu shown here. Click on an item, and it takes you right there (which is why it's called "Go To," I'm guessing).

Click any entry to "Go To" it.

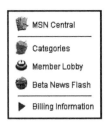

As long as we've got the Go To menu right there, let's use it. Click **MSN Central** on that funky little Go To menu.

MSN Central

As you can see in the figure here, MSN Central is the heart of the network. Each of the five bars is a big ol' clickable button; each button takes you to the area named on the bar. At the top is MSN Today, which we've already seen, so let's look at the others.

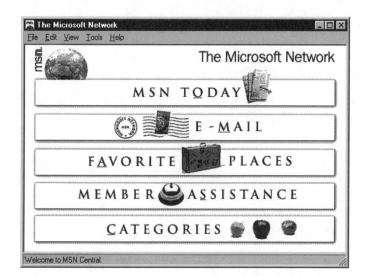

Déjà view: MSN Central again.

E-Mail

When you click the E-Mail button on **MSN Central** you launch your copy of Microsoft Exchange, which MSN co-opts to be your own, personal postal worker.

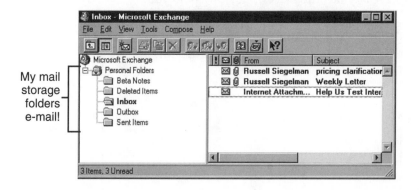

Microsoft Exchange handles e-mail.

On the right side of the Microsoft Exchange window (shown above) is where you see a listing of the mail you've received. All the messages have little envelope icons in front of them because they're all mail. But there are some other icons you may see here, too.

Items with an exclamation point (!) in front are messages the sender marked as urgent. That *doesn't* mean you'll think it's urgent, though. It may be urgently annoying junk mail.

Items with a paper clip icon in front have something attached to them. The attachment may be a file you need to download, or a shortcut included in the body of the message. (Don't panic if all this is G(r)eek to you right now. It all becomes clearer with time, practice, and some simple definitions.)

All of the e-mail entries are in bold type because I haven't read them yet. After I read them, names of the messages revert to normal, not-bold type. It's an easy way to tell what you've read and what you haven't.

On the left side of the screen are all of the folders you have available to store the mail you receive. Four of them are standard (Deleted Items, Inbox, Outbox, and Sent Items), but you can create any other folders you want (as I did with Notes). Inbox is highlighted because that's the folder that's open, and it appears in bold because there's unread mail in it. Chapter 12 covers e-mail and Microsoft Exchange in detail.

You can click either the close or minimize boxes on the Microsoft Exchange window to get it out of your way, and get back to MSN Central.

Favorite Places

When you click the **Favorite Places** button on MSN Central, the window changes to the one shown above. And, hey! Guess what? It's empty. That's because this is your first time online, so you don't have any favorite places yet. How could you?

Hello? Hello? Hey, there's nothing here!

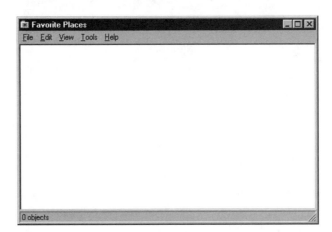

Favorite Places is literally a blank slate that you can customize to your liking, adding only the things you like. Chapter 27 tells you how to create and use Favorite Places, as well as some other really fast ways to get around online.

To get back to MSN Central, select **Up One Level** from the **File** menu.

Member Assistance

Click the **Member Assistance** button on MSN Central, and you see a window like this. Member Assistance (shown below) is where you come to get help with problems, change your password and billing information, and even visit the MSN Gift Shop.

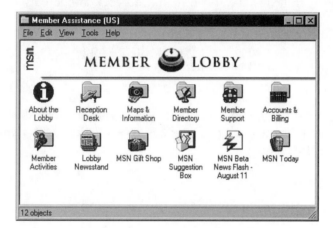

Member Assistance: That means HELP!

This is your first actual glimpse of how most areas online are set up. Chapter 9 gives you more details, but briefly:

➤ The artwork across the top of the window ("Member Lobby" in the figure) identifies the area.

➤ The Information Kiosk is in the circle "i" icon—which sounds like a '90s dude ranch. Double-click on it to read it. Here you find a text file describing the area and its contents.

➤ Sometimes there's so much information, the Information Kiosk is actually a folder containing *many* bits of news you can use. In that case, a double-click opens the folder. Then, you double-click individual items to read them.

➤ The folder icons contain different departments. Open a folder by double-clicking on it.

➤ Occasionally, there's some additional text files available, too. You double-click on one to read it.

Reading Online Text, or, Word Says "Boo!"

You may (or may not) be surprised when you double-click on an Information-tion Kiosk or another text file. MSN sends (downloads is the geeky word for it) the text file to your computer and launches your word processor so you can read the file. Yup. It's true.

MSN doesn't have a built-in text editor. Instead, it relies on WordPad, NotePad, or a larger word processor (for me, it's Microsoft Word) that can handle the format of the online text.

You can treat the text file just like any other file on your computer: save it, print it, or do whatever you like with it. If you don't save it, it goes away when you quit MSN (it deletes the temporary file). When you're done reading it (and after you save it, if you want to keep it), close the document window and minimize your word processor. That puts you right back where you were online.

Don't get too wrapped up in Member Assistance yet. There's so much stuff here that there's a whole chapter devoted to it (Chapter 23). To get back to MSN Central, select **Up One Level** from the **File** menu.

Categories

Meanwhile, back at MSN Central…

Click on the **Categories** button, and your window changes to resemble the one shown below. The categories are just that: categories, broad subject areas to help classify and organize the different forums they contain.

Categories out the wazoo.

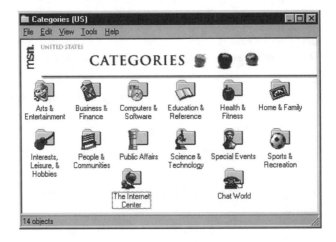

MSN has 16 categories: Arts & Entertainment; Business & Finance; Computers & Software; Education & Reference; Health & Fitness; Home & Family; Interests, Leisure, & Hobbies; News & Weather; People & Communities; Public Affairs; Science & Technology; Special Events; Sports & Recreation; The Internet Center; MSN Passport; and Chat World.

Each category is chock-full of *forums* that relate to the topic at hand. To open one, double-click on its icon.

> **Forum** MSN has 16 basic categories. Within each category there are dozens of individual areas geared to a specific aspect of the general category. Each individual area provides an assembly place for the discussion of the subject at hand. Members can speak out, learn from each other, and generally kibitz about their mutual interest—which is why they're also called *forums*.

I'm Letting Go of Your Hand Now...

This is where I turn you loose to explore on your own.
Don't worry that you don't know what's what, or what's where yet. There's plenty more informative stuff like that coming up in subsequent chapters. It all make more sense to you if you have a good look around first.

In the next chapter, you'll look at each of the MSN menus and learn what they do. I'll also show you how to change how MSN displays itself (that sounds lewd) so if you'd rather have a pile of windows open on your desktop rather than just one that's constantly changing as you open stuff, I'll show you how. Also, I'll make some suggestions of unaccompanied "things to do" for you adventurous souls out there.

In Part 2, we'll look at all of this stuff again, and in more detail, so there's very little you actually need to memorize or even vaguely recall (except for "The Least You Need to Know," of course).

Signing Out, Now

When you're done looking around, Sign Out. Here's how:

Wherever you are online, when you want to leave, select **Sign Out** from the **File** menu. MSN says "Thank you for using MSN. OK to disconnect?" Click **Yes** to exit the service. Click **No** if you want to hang out and explore some more.

You can also:

➤ Click the MSN Central Close button.

➤ Double-click the MSN icon near the clock on the Taskbar.

➤ Click with your right mouse button on the MSN icon near the clock on the Taskbar, then click Sign Out on the sneaky little menu that pops up.

In all cases, MSN will ask the same, polite "OK to disconnect?" question before it dumps your butt offline.

For now, go, explore, poke your nose into shadowy corners, have fun. You can't get but a little lost. If you do get lost:

The Least You Need to Know

A trail of bread crumbs for you, in case of emergency:

➤ To return to the last place you were, select **Up One Level** from the **File** menu.

➤ To get *quickly* back to MSN Central, select **MSN Central** from the **Go to** submenu on the **Edit** menu.

➤ When you're ready to leave MSN, select **Sign Out** from the **File** menu. When MSN asks if you really want to disconnect, click **Yes**. You are home again, home again, jiggedy-jig (and you don't have to kiss a pig, either).

Chapter 7

Your Second Time Online: MSN's Menus and Options

In This Chapter

➤ A quick spin through the MSN menus

➤ Customizing MSN

➤ An "extra credit" assignment

Last time you signed in on MSN and took a look around, you got a peek at MSN Today, MSN Central, Microsoft Exchange, and stuff like that there. Now that you've seen the service, I think you can better appreciate some of the menu information you'll see here, especially the options that enable you to customize MSN to your liking. First, let's cruise through the menus, then we'll put some of them to use.

For this chapter, I recommend you read it first (to familiarize yourself with things) and then sign on to MSN to try out the things you read about (because you can't use the menus offline). That way you don't waste expensive online time reading. Fair enough?

The MSN Menus, at Your Command

The menus shown below are from the Categories window (if the *Categories (US)* in the title bar didn't give that away), but these menus are the standard assortment you find in all MSN windows. In some locations (MSN Central springs to mind) the menu names remain the same, but the contents are a little different. For example, MSN Central's File menu contains fewer menu items than it does in the average forum.

Your typical set of MSN menus.

As with all Windows 95 menus, some menu items aren't available all the time. You need to select an icon in an MSN window, for example, to have some menu items available to you (Copy and Open, to name two).

Window Control Menu

MSN's windows behave like all Windows 95 windows. You can move them around the screen; shrink (or minimize) them down to little bars at the bottom of your screen; enlarge (or maximize) them to fill the whole screen; or close them altogether.

Click here.

This menu gives you control over your MSN window(s).

If you choose to work with only one MSN window that changes to show you each folder you open, you probably aren't going to be doing much with this menu. The commands are the same as for every other Windows 95 window you've ever used, so I'm not going to club you to death with them.

The File Menu

In most Windows applications, the File menu gives you access to all of the basic file-related commands: Open, Close, Save, Save As, Print, and so on. With MSN, the File menu (shown in the following figure) is a little different. Let's see how:

Open   Displays the selected file or Category/Forum folder on-screen.

Explore   Opens the selected Category/Forum folder into an easy-to-browse dialog box like the Windows Explorer. If you're comfortable using the Windows Explorer to dig through data on your hard drive, this may be a good tool for you to use to dig through the vast amounts of information in forums.

MSN's very different File menu.

Create Shortcut Makes a shortcut for the selected category or forum and places it on your desktop—you just have to click the shortcut to go there quickly. Chapter 25 covers shortcuts.

Add To Favorite Places Adds a shortcut for the selected item to your Favorite Places list (the big empty thing in the last chapter). Chapter 25 covers Favorite Places, too.

Properties Gives you detailed information about the selected icon. The properties for the People & Communities category are shown below.

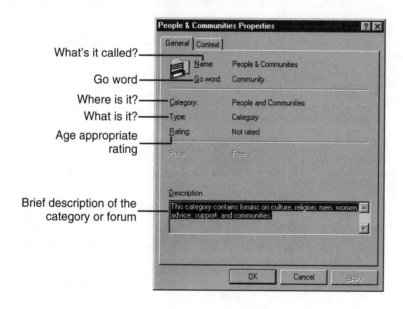

People & Communities General Properties—does that make it community property?

71

People & Communities Properties in Context.

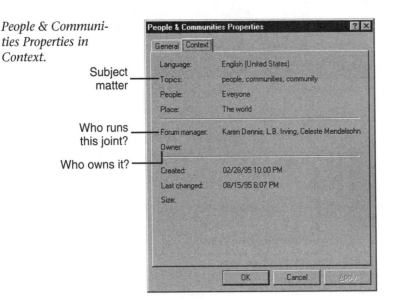

Subject matter

Who runs this joint?

Who owns it?

Grabbing Go Words As you explore, if you like a place online, check its properties and jot down its Go word. You can keep a piece of paper near your PC, or save a NotePad or WordPad document to disk just for this purpose. Pretty soon you'll have a major collection of Go words at your disposal, and you'll be the envy of your online friends.

To view both pages of a category or forum's properties, click the tabs at the top of the screen (General and Context, as shown).

The Properties give you some important information about the selected category or forum, including its rating (important if kids are using MSN in your home), the forum managers, its Go word (if you want to get there quickly—Chapter 25 tells you how), and more.

Up One Level You used this one in the last chapter. It works just like the Up One Level command in all Windows 95 Explorer, Save, and Save As windows. It takes you to the folder that contains the folder you're presently in. For example, if you select Up One Level in the People & Communities Category, MSN returns you to the general Categories display. Select it again to return to MSN Central.

Sign In This command is grayed-out because I'm already signed-in; it's only available when you're offline.

Sign Out Disconnects you from MSN.

Close Closes the MSN window. If you're only working with one window, this is a bad thing to do. It doesn't sign you off of MSN, but now you have no windows with which to work. If you do this accidentally, click on the **MSN** icon (on the toolbar, next to the clock) with your right mouse button to call up a menu of places to go to on MSN. You can at least get back to MSN Central.

Personal Preference Time Again

Personally, I don't like the one window option. I think it makes it too tough to remember where you are, where you were, and where the Up One Level command will take you.

I like to have a pile of windows open on my desktop that I can control just by clicking on them. I'll show you how to change that one window deal into a multiple windows extravaganza a little later in this chapter. You, of course, can do whatever you like.

The Edit Menu

With one exception, MSN's Edit menu, shown below, behaves exactly the same as the Windows Explorer's Edit menu. Since I'm operating on the assumption that you're familiar with the major Windows 95 concepts, I am not going to rehash Cut, Copy, Paste, and the other editorial commands here.

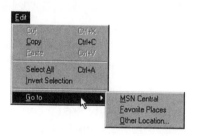

MSN's Edit menu only has one real surprise.

I am going to point out, however, the last item on the Edit menu: Go to. As you can see in the figure above, touching Go to with your mouse pointer brings up a submenu that quickly takes you to MSN Central, your Favorite Places display, or Other Location.

When you select Other Location, MSN asks you to enter a Go word for where you want to go. I showed you where to find Go words in the last section, and I'll show you again in Chapter 25.

A Menu with a View

MSN's View menu (seen in the figure below) works exactly the same as the View menu in any Windows 95 window. The only two differences here are:

The View menu—
you've seen these
options before.

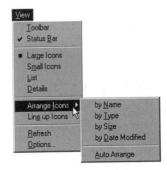

1. The View menu *works* with MSN windows (you can use the icon size and arrangement options with windows online).

2. The Toolbar command (the first command on the menu) gives your windows a toolbar with MSN-specific buttons on it (you can see what I mean, below).

MSN's toolbar
variation.

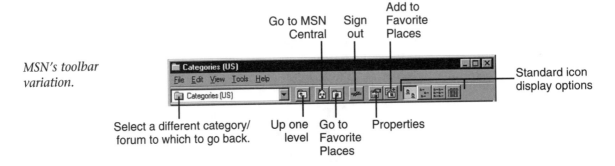

As with the regular Windows toolbar, the buttons on the MSN variation give you easy access to several of the more regularly used menu commands (they're labeled in the figure). They make navigating MSN much simpler, even for the squeamish. Check 'em out.

The last option on the View menu (coincidentally called Options) has a section all to itself, "Changing Your Options," later in this chapter.

Tools for Days

The Tools menu (shown in the following figure) gives you access to some pretty powerful...well, *tools*, you can use online. In order of appearance, they are:

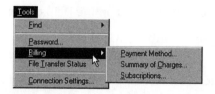

It's Tool (menu) Time! (Grunt, grunt.)

Find   Gives you a submenu that enables you to search for Files or Folders on your computer, or On The Microsoft Network. Chapters 10 and 11 both demonstrate using the Find command.

Password   Enables you to change your MSN password whenever you want. For the sake of security, you should change your password regularly—once a month, or so. (Chapter 22 walks you through the process.)

Billing   Presents you with a submenu with three options:

➤ **Payment Method**   Changes the credit card you use to pay for MSN.

➤ **Summary of Charges**   View your bill for the current, or even past, months.

➤ **Subscriptions**   Want to switch to another billing plan? Select Subscriptions.

File Transfer Status   When you send or copy an attached file from e-mail, or download one from a file library, MSN places the file in a *transfer queue*. You can display the status of files waiting to be transferred and change the order, options, and status of files in the queue. Chapter 11 de-babble-izes all this gobbledy-gook.

Connection Settings   Calls up that dialog box (last seen in Chapter 5) that enables you to fiddle with your local access number, modem properties, and dialing properties. You saw every square inch of them in Chapter 4.

Help! (A Nice Menu, a Great Movie)

A Help menu is a standard feature of all Windows applications. MSN is no different. The figure below shows you the three help options available.

Help is just a mouse-click away.

75

Help Topics   Opens standard online Help dialog box.

Member Support Numbers   Gives you a worldwide list of MSN technical support phone numbers you can call if online Help isn't helping.

About the Microsoft Network   Opens a dialog box that displays the version number of the software you're using, the name of the person to whom the software is registered, and copyright information.

Cheap Trick!

Not the band, the kind that saves you money.

You may get the impression that you can only use MSN's online help files while online—because you only see the Help menu while online. That's *soooooo* bogus I can't stand it.

You can run Help while you're offline and save yourself the shekels. Here's how:

Click the **Start** button, and then click **Run**. When the Run dialog box opens, type **C:\WINDOWS\HELP\Msn.hlp** in the text box. Click **OK**. The Microsoft Network Help fires right up.

Chapter 23 covers online Help and other help sources in detail. Be there, or be square.

A Sneaky, Invisible Menu

While you're mousing around online, you can save yourself the extra steps of clicking on an icon, a menu, and then a menu command. Instead, do this: point your cursor at the category or forum icon and click on it with the right mouse button. The tiny menu (shown below), a sort of an abridged File menu, pops right up. All the commands work the same as described earlier in the chapter.

The old right mouse button click trick. Third time I fell for that this month.

Changing Your Options

Back in the section on the View menu, I mysteriously alluded to the Options command. When you select **Options** from the View menu, you open the dialog shown below. It enables you to customize several MSN options, including whether you want to work with one or several windows while online. Let's tinker.

Options too geeky to be believed

Auto sign off

Turns off MSN Today

Pick a language.

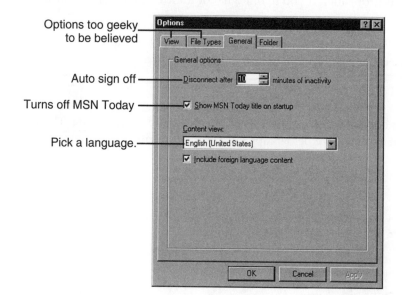

The General Options.

General Options

When the dialog box opens, the General options are in front. The first two tabs (View and File Types) are too geeky to be believed. Look at them if you want, but they even give *me* a headache.

The first option in the General options box enables you to tell MSN when to automatically disconnect you from the service. Whatever amount of time you enter in the text box (where it says 10 minutes in the figure), MSN disconnects you after your computer has been idle that long—idle meaning no keystrokes or mouse clicks at all.

To change the amount of idle time, double-click in the **Disconnect after X minutes of inactivity** text box. Then type in the time limit (in minutes). You can also click on the teeny-tiny up- and down-arrows next to the number. Each click increases (up-arrow) or decreases (down-arrow) the time by one minute.

Below that, there's a check box called Show MSN Today title on startup. This is the option that automatically opens MSN Today when you sign on. It's already checked, so if you like seeing MSN Today first thing, leave it alone. If *you* want to decide when you read the MSN Today screen, click on the check mark to remove it. Forever after, you don't see MSN Today unless *you* click on it in MSN Central.

The drop-down menu labeled Content view enables you to select an alternate language for the contents of MSN. It is automatically set to the same language as your Windows 95 Regional Settings Control Panel. If you're bilingual or multilingual, make your brain happy.

The Include foreign language content check box enables MSN to show you online stuff that's in a language other than the one selected. *Quelle surprise!*

Folder Options

To get at the Folder options, click on the **Folder** tab at the top of the dialog. The Browsing Options (shown in the figure below) appears front and center.

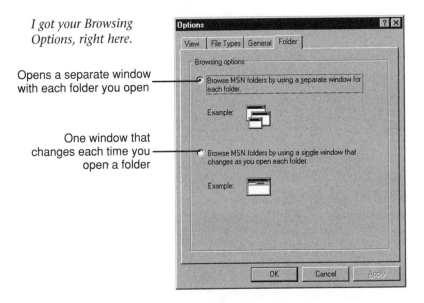

I got your Browsing Options, right here.

Opens a separate window with each folder you open

One window that changes each time you open a folder

There are only two options on this page: whether MSN opens a another new window every time you open a folder (the top option, and my personal choice); or whether MSN is stingy and only gives you one window that changes to show you the contents of the folders you open.

Click the one you want.

Apply Those Options

When you're done tinkering with your options, you apply them by either clicking **OK** or **Apply**.

If you click OK, MSN makes your changes, and the dialog box closes.

If you click Apply, MSN makes the changes, but the dialog box remains open.

If you aren't sure you want to keep the changes you've made to your Options, keep your options open: click **Apply**. You can always change things back once you get a look at the final effect on your windows.

My Recommendations and Extra Credit

You've only been online once, so it may be tough for you to decide whether you want to use the toolbar (on the View menu), have one or several windows open (your Browse Options), or anything. Here's my two cents worth:

Change your options. Try them all ways (with toolbar and without; with one window and with several; and all the various combinations). Work with them for a bit. Try them on for size. Then decide.

It's not like any changes you make are set in stone. You can change them whenever you like, and as often as you like (as long as you're online).

While you're trying out your custom settings, earn yourself some extra credit by exploring Member Assistance—there's lots of new and useful information there that is hot off the press (and more current than some of the information in here).

If you need help sorting out Member Assistance, check out Chapter 23. It covers Member Assistance in detail.

The Least You Need to Know

Most of the menu commands and options are at least somewhat familiar to you from working with them in Windows 95. If you're also very new to Windows 95, rest assured that using the menus in both becomes second nature in no time. All it takes is a little practice.

Since all of these menus appear over and over throughout the course of this book, you'll have them down quickly. Don't sweat it.

Part 2
Cruisin' MSN

Now that we've got MSN installed and configured, and we've had a chance to poke around online (if only in a limited way), it's time to pull out all the stops and tour this sucker from stem to stern.

In this section, we'll get a look at all the categories, how the forums work, e-mail, chatting, and all that good stuff. There's even a chapter on online etiquette (which is required reading, because politeness counts).

Fasten your seat belts, everybody, it's going to be a whirlwind tour. (You thought I was going to say "bumpy night" didn't you? Well, I don't do Bette Davis impersonations. Sorry.)

Chapter 8

Aunt Effie's Guide to Online Etiquette

In This Chapter

➤ Safety tips

➤ Public and private behavior

➤ Rules for gracious living in the digital world

Aunt Effie is a lovely woman with whom I sometimes consult over Earl Grey tea and finger sandwiches. She mediates the complexities of the life online the way Emily Post and Miss Manners do for the non-digital world. The following letters and responses from the Aunt Effie Archives deal with some of the more common issues of etiquette online.

Safety First!

Dear Aunt Effie:

It seems like every few months I hear horror stories on the news about people who are victimized by way of online services. Credit card scams, child pornography, and even stalking. Is this stuff really happening, or is the media just trying to scare us?

Signed,

Afraid to turn on my computer

Dear Afraid:

Is this stuff happening? Yes. Is the media trying to scare you? Yes again.

Do you notice how you only hear these stories during ratings, or sweeps, periods? Any excuse to get sexually explicit or frightening matter on the news, that's what I think.

But, dearie, the digital world is just a smaller version of the rest of the world (I was going to say "real" world, but I'm not sure what that means anymore). There's crime in the streets, child abuse, neglect, discrimination…you name it, it's out there. And it's also online.

All the same folks who do dastardly, unkind, rude, or misguided deeds out *there* also do these things online. Just because you use an online service (any one, not just the Microsoft Network) from the safety of your own home, or another location in which you're comfortable, you should behave just as you do when you travel the streets of any large city. Protect yourself by following some basic safety tips:

You don't have to avoid talking to strangers (that would take away half the fun), *but* you shouldn't give out any information online that you don't want people offline to have, like phone, calling card, or credit card numbers; home address; work address—anything that you don't want generally known.

If someone harasses you in any way (sexually, emotionally, or because of gender, ethnicity, sexual orientation, disability, or whatever), and by any means (live chat, e-mail, bulletin board postings), you don't have to take it. Report the offending person to the nearest Host or Forum Manager, or to Member Assistance (there's more about Hosts in Chapter 13; Member Assistance in Chapter 23). Get the offender's member ID, the name of the chat room in which the incident occurred, the time the offense happened, and a sample (as distasteful as it may be for you to repeat it, it *must* be done) of the offensive language or behavior.

After you've gotten all that together (and it's very easy if you know how to Copy and Paste), you may want to ignore the offensive person with the Ignore button (that's in Chapter 13, too). Don't allow yourself to be a victim—it's just no fun.

Signed,

Aunt Effie

Be Polite and Courteous

Dear Aunt Effie,

I was online the other night with my buddy, and we were goofing around the way we usually do, you know, calling each other names (booger breath, doody brain) when suddenly other people in the chat room started getting on our cases, calling us names that really hurt. It felt like we were being ganged up on. Why? We were just fooling around.

Signed,

Not a booger brain

Dear Boog:

When you talk to someone in person, people can tell whether you're kidding by your tone of voice, the look in your eyes, or the smile on your face. These are all *visual clues* that help people figure out what you're really trying to say.

Online, no one can see you, so that rich source of visual information is cut off from innocent bystanders. The ones who picked on you may have thought there was a real fight brewing and either wanted to stop it, egg it on, or join right in. That's probably why you got the response you did.

The rule of thumb online is the tried and true golden rule: treat people the way you want people to treat you. Politeness counts, as does courtesy. If you and your buddy have a thing for calling each other "doody brains," you need to learn how to let other folks online know that you're having harmless fun with shorthands and smilies (see Chapter 13). It gives chat, which otherwise sounds mean-spirited or malicious, the "just kidding" spin you normally add with a nudge or wink.

However, I feel I must comment on the use of words like "doody" in general. Even sanitized scatological references may give other chatters pause, and this may lead to a warning from a Host (depending on the usage) and subject you to being "ganged up on" again. I suggest refraining from using such language in open chats—or, if you can't resist, confining it to private communications, like e-mail (Chapter 12 discusses this). Just as you can't see the visual clues that let you in on a joke online, neither can you tell how old other chatters are, nor whether your ever-so-slightly off-color comments are embarrassing or angering them. When in doubt, don't.

Signed,

Aunt Effie

NO SHOUTING!!!!

Dear Eff, bubeleh,

I'm an older, recently widowed gentleman of comfortable means, but with poor eyesight. I occasionally use MSN to rendezvous with a certain Alaskan lady friend, to chat. She's a retired person, also with eye trouble. When we are in a chat room, we type IN ALL CAPITAL LETTERS so we may easily pick each other's chat from the general chat. We've been repeatedly asked not to type in all capitals. Why?

Signed,

SHLOMO S.

Dear Shlo, my little kugel:

TYPING IN ALL CAPS IS CONSIDERED SHOUTING, AND IS RUDE. You and your lady friend's visual concerns are legitimate. Unfortunately, the first version of MSN's software doesn't give you much control over the display of text in chat rooms (or anywhere else). Maybe concerned users will drop a note into a suggestion box online. There are, however, some things you can do to ease the strain on your peepers.

You can increase the spacing between lines of chat in a chat room (to give you a little more time to spot your lady friend's messages). Chapter 13 tells you how.

You can also use Windows 95's Accessibility Options Control Panel to make using your computer generally easier. It doesn't help in the chat rooms on MSN, but it does make icons, windows, and other options (like the taskbar) easier to see and use.

And, Shlo, darling, should anything (God forbid) happen to your lady friend, call me—we'll talk.

Signed,

Aunt Effie

P.S. *Wink, wink.*

Public Behavior

Dear Aunt Effie,

I'm a twelve-year-old girl. I was in a chat room the other night—don't remember the name—and all the other teens (at least I think they were teens; grown-ups don't act like this, do they?)

wanted to talk about was, like, oh, you know—mushy and dirty stuff. Like, kissing and making out. And someone kept calling me a "MorF"! Geesh. If I wanted that stuff, I'd go to the mall! What gives?

Signed,

Sweet Polly Pureheart

Dear Sweet PP,

I know some fifty-year-olds who act like randy teens. Don't assume they were all teens, and don't assume that one who speaks like a grandmother is a grandmother either. You just can't tell for sure. That's one of the nice things about being online: not being able to "see" puts everyone on a level playing field, but it's one of the hazards, too.

I suggest that if you don't care for the general conversation in a room, that you move on until you find one that you *do* like. If it's really offensive (people using words they can't say on television), you may want to report it to a Host or Member Assistance.

As for people calling you a "MorF," they weren't *calling* you a name, my pet, they were asking your gender. "MorF" is one of those typing shorthands I mentioned earlier. MorF is short for "Male or Female?" MorF is easier and faster to type. Most people prefer to flirt with a specific gender, and the MorF in question wanted to be sure you were his/her type before the eyelash batting began.

Some folks, myself included, with genderless screen names get awfully tired of being "MorFed," as it is called, or the seemingly endless "Age and location checks" some members seem to delight in. Then everyone is expected to state their name, gender, age, and location for general consumption.

I think it is perfectly acceptable to avoid answering the question if you don't care to disclose your gender—a simple "yes" is the most evasive answer. When someone asks me my age, I generally say it's "Under the speed limit—except in a school zone." However, I think it is *totally* inappropriate to chat under an assumed gender (or age, ethnic background, or anything). Either don't say anything, or be honest.

Signed,

Aunt Effie

Privacy, Please!

Dear Aunt Effie,

The other night online, someone I didn't know asked me if I wanted to have a private chat. I don't know what that means, so I said "No, thank you." Did I miss out on something fun?

Cautious in Carlisle

Dear CC:

You've discovered, all on your own, one of Aunt Effie's favorite mottos: "When in doubt, don't." Good for you!

About whether you missed out on something fun, well, I don't know. It depends on how old you are and what your idea of "fun" is. Here's how it works.

The somewhat strict, but fair and necessary, membership agreement that everyone should have read when they first joined MSN regulates chatting in public rooms (where anyone can walk in and observe or join in the conversation). That means strictly G- or at most PG-rated conversations except in adults-only areas (which are all clearly labeled, and which a 12-year-old shouldn't be in anyhow). Hosts and other members keep the conversations on track, and you can be fairly sure that you won't encounter anything too offensive for too long. That's in a public room.

When someone asks you to "go private," they're asking you to begin what's known as a private conversation, where only the select people can follow the conversation. These chats are not moderated, and pretty much anything goes.

There are people who use private conversations as a sort of 900-number to talk in explicit sexual language to each other. Depending on how you feel about such conversations, you may want to politely refuse invitations to "go private," or you may not. Aunt Effie is stridently non-judgmental about such things (as long as everyone involved is over eighteen, and a willing participant). Though I do not care for such chat myself (I blush too easily), I won't say "Boo" about it if you do.

If you care to, Chapter 13 tells you how to enter into a private conversation. If you are concerned about young people getting an eyeful in a chat room, or private conversation, Chapter 22 tells you how to restrict their access to chat rooms and other parts of MSN.

Signed,

Aunt Effie

Father Knows Best

Dear Aunt Effie,

I am a teen-aged MSN user with a problem.

I wanted to visit the Comedy area online, and I was dismayed to discover that MSN's restricting options and the power of a 46-year-old man kept me out. I am STEAMED!

I want to know if restricting access online is even legal, and if there's a way to get around it.

Signed,

Steamed in NJ

Dear Steamy,

Sorry to hear you got steamed, and then fried. I'm guessing that "the power of a 46-year-old man" is the power of your father or other guardian. That's an awesome force to reckon with, even when you get to be Aunt Effie's age (thanks for not asking).

The power to restrict access to certain areas of MSN is not only legal, but also I happen to think it's good idea. Parental-types really *do* need to monitor what their children are doing online.

What ages should be monitored, and what areas should be restricted, well, I don't know that you'd find any two people who agree completely. I, however, will not presume to stick my two cents in with your father/guardian. That's strictly between the two of you.

If you aren't happy with the arrangement, you should try sitting down and discussing it with him calmly and rationally. He's doing what he thinks is best. Ranting and raving and dragging outsiders (like myself) into the fray only goes to show him that you lack the maturity to deal with things in an adult manner. I'm sorry if that sounds unfair to you.

Signed,

Aunt Effie

E-Mail Mania

Dear Aunt Effie,

I met someone online who I really, really like, and now we correspond regularly through e-mail. The problem is that Doug (not his real name) is always doing fancy stuff to his e-mail. He uses fonts that I don't have and colors I can't see on my gray-scale monitor, and he always makes the e-mail window twice the size of my screen. It makes it very difficult for me to read his letters to me. I don't want to embarrass him (or myself) by complaining, but what else can I do?

Signed,

Hates to Whine

Dear Whine,

No you certainly don't want to embarrass the dear boy. That could put undo strain on your blossoming relationship. What you can do (and without whining—that's *very* unattractive) is send him a note the next time he sends you an illegible piece of e-mail. It should say something like:

> *Dear Doug:*
>
> *I just received your lovely note. I can tell you put a lot of time into it because of all the different fonts and color pictures (or whatever), however, your embellishments don't translate well on my computer, and I can't really make out what you're trying to say. My computer isn't nearly as big and powerful as yours.*
>
> *Could you please send me a plain copy? As much as I appreciate your efforts to pretty up your note, I'm much more impressed by what you have to say...*

Trust me, he won't ever do it again.

In general, you shouldn't mess too much with your e-mail unless you know the recipient's computer and what it can do.

If you're sending e-mail to an Internet address, or to someone using a laptop computer, you should definitely keep your text plain, and the window size smaller than your desktop computer's monitor is capable of showing. Otherwise your mail looks all screwy when it gets where it's going. There are many more tips on e-mail etiquette in Chapter 12.

Signed,

Aunt Effie

E-mail is not the only area where you should not make assumptions about the recipient's computer. Read on.

File Foibles

Dear Aunt Effie,

I have an acquaintance online who is forever sending me files that she thinks I will find interesting. I don't know if I'm interested or not—I can never open the files because I don't use the same software as she does. What should I do?

Signed,

Interested in Being Interested

Dear IBI,

For goodness sake, *say something* to your friend! Send her a note on the order of the one in the e-mail section above, telling her that you *might* be interested in what she sent if only you could open it. Send her a list of the software you own (a word processor or graphics program, or whatever is appropriate to the files you exchange) and ask if she has that program, or one that can *export* a file in a format you can open, or at least *import* into a program you *do* own.

Export and Import

Exporting is the capability of an application to save a file in the format of another application (or one that another application can *import*, at least). For example, with Microsoft Word you can save files in a number of formats (like WordPerfect) for both Macintosh and IBM-compatible computers. You can usually exporting files with the **Save As** command, but check your manual.

Importing is the capability of an application to open a file created in another application with a minimum of fuss. In the process, the application translates the file into its own format, so you never have to bother with it again.

Generally, when you want to send someone a file, there are a few things you can do to make the process as painless as possible for the recipient:

1. **Ask.** Ask the recipient what file format they want. It's the easiest method all-around.

2. **Stick to basics.** If you're sending a word processing document, send it as a plain text or RTF file (check your word processor's manual for details on saving as text). If the file is short enough, you may want to use Windows WordPad or NotePad.

3. **Use standard formats.** If you're sending another type of file, say a picture file, stick to a basic format like the GIF, because just about any computer can open a GIF file created on any other computer.

Chapter 11 covers the details on how to e-mail a file to someone. Chapter 10 covers files in general.

The Least You Need to Know

Generally, all of the advice given here boils down to a few basic tenets, *or* Aunt Effie's "Guide to Gracious Living":

➤ *Always* be polite. "Please" and "Thank you" go a long way in this world.

➤ Public behavior should be kept above board and appropriate to members of all ages and sensitivity.

➤ Private conversation behavior can be whatever the participants decide it to be, as long as everyone knows and agrees to it beforehand.

➤ Never make assumptions about the people you meet online. Don't assume anything about them personally (race, creed, gender, and such), or about their computers (hardware, software, or other peripherals).

➤ When in doubt, ask. That applies to new terms, new situations, or anything of which you're unsure.

➤ If you're still in doubt, *don't*.

Broadstrokes: The Categories at a Glance

If you look at the following figure, you see our old friend, the Categories window, again. MSN uses these sixteen broad categories as a handy organizational tool to group related materials together so you can find what you're interested in, as quickly as possible.

Within each of the sixteen categories, there's about a dozen individual things to look at: forums, information kiosks, *bulletin boards* (that MSN calls *BBSs*), and other stuff. (If you want to be picky, a rough count turns up over 150 folders, files, and forums in the sixteen categories—not including the stuff inside those folders and forums. By the time you read this, there are probably even more.)

Techno Talk

Bulletin Board
Like its cork cousin, a bulletin board is a place where you can read and post messages. On MSN, however, the bulletin board is online, and you read and post messages to and from other MSN members.

blah blah
blah blah
bl b
b

The categories, again.

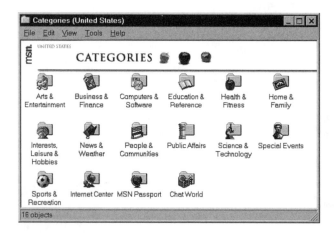

The point of all this is to say that there's no *way* I can show you (in the confines of a smallish book) *everything* there is to see and do online. This chapter introduces you to the main contents of each category. The next chapter shows you how a typical forum works (and they're all fairly similar, in terms of how you use them). Then, you're on your own to explore and find the forums that interest you.

Let's look at each of the categories in the fractured alphabetical order in which they appear in the figure, starting with Arts & Entertainment.

Kiosk

A fancy word for "booth." Some of MSN's information folders are called Information Kiosks, though that seems to be changing in favor of InfoCenters. Maybe they don't think any of us own dictionaries. Whatever they're named, they're easy to spot: just look for the file or folder icons with an "i" in a blue circle.

Arts & Entertainment

You probably guessed from the category's name that this area contains information and member discussion about movies, theater, television, books and book genres, and music. You're right.

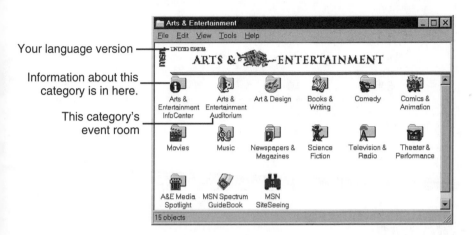

Your language version —

Information about this category is in here.

This category's event room

Expose yourself to the arts...

Of particular note (to *me*, anyway, I don't know what you're interested in) are the areas devoted to Comics & Animation (my godsons are into comics, and I love animation) and Theater & Performance (I dabble; I'm a dabbler). These are a few of my favorite things—*don't do it!* Don't sing that song!

If you're the kind of person who picks up the occasional copy of *Entertainment Weekly*, for a dose of Hollywood news (all right, gossip), or likes to leave copies of *Architectural Digest* on your coffee table, there's information here for you. Check out Movies and Television & Radio for your entertainment news needs. Sketch your way through Art & Design to get your fill of sculpture, painting, and other plastic arts.

To get back to the Categories window, select **Up One Level** from the **File** menu, or, if you're working with multiple MSN windows, just close the Arts & Entertainment window.

Business & Finance

Oh, everything's a song today. Now it's Monty Python's "The Money Song." Well, this is a good place for it. The Business & Finance category (shown on the next page) is where you can learn everything you need to know about earning, keeping, and investing your cash.

There are areas here devoted to businesses both large and small, as well as directories of services and job postings. You can get tips on investing like a Wall Street tycoon, or just balancing your own little budget (mine *never* seems to balance). If there's an entrepreneur in you that's just fighting to get out, here's the category that may just inspire you to financial greatness.

The Business & Finance category can help you decide what to with the forty-thousand French francs in your fridge.

Computers & Software

Here's the category where you find everything you've ever wanted to know about computers, but were afraid to ask. And, thank goodness, there are no really catchy computer songs. Not yet anyhow.

One of my own personal favorites: Computers & Software.

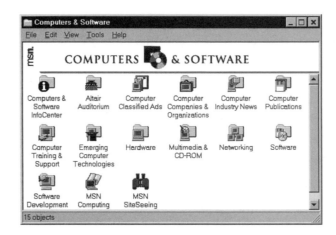

In Computers & Software you find areas devoted to the hardware and software you have, plus stuff developers are creating; you also learn how to create brand new computer software of your own.

Additionally, there's a classified ad area—Computer Classified Ads— where you can sell and buy computer doodads to and from other MSN members (of course, the old "Let the buyer beware" adage is in full force when you buy things sight unseen from strangers).

Computers & Software also features two news forums: Computer Industry News and Computer Publications. Since MSN gets industry news almost immediately upon its release, there's no waiting around for columnists and magazine writers to figure out what they think about the latest innovations. You can make up your own mind.

If you're yearning to pore over the pages of your favorite magazine online, there's no waiting for the post office to deliver (or your newsstand to stock) the latest issue. This is one of my personal faves (you may have noticed). I spend all of Chapter 16 babbling about it.

Education & Reference

Don't know much about history? Don't know much of biology? You can find some of it out here, in Education & Reference (check out Fields of Study, maybe).

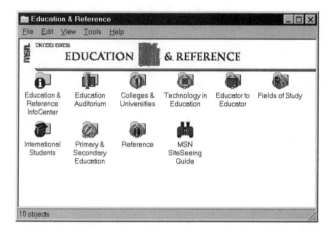

Education & Reference: Can I find a definition for "pore" here?

Here you find areas devoted to all levels of schooling, from Primary and Secondary Education, through Colleges and Universities and beyond to Continuing Education. You also find areas devoted to educators themselves (Educator to Educator), and to International Students (who have the daunting chore of dealing with a new culture, in addition to actually learning stuff). There's so much here that Chapter 15 is completely devoted to this category.

Health & Fitness

If you are one of the folks who got hooked on the fitness craze (the one that started way back when Olivia Neutron-Bomb's "Let's Get Physical" was a hit), this category is right up your StairMaster.

Health & Fitness, where you can exercise your mind, too.

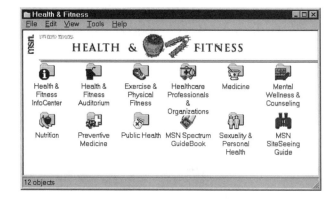

There are areas devoted to Nutrition, Exercise & Physical Fitness, Public Health, Medicine, and Healthcare Professionals. There's even an area devoted to human sexuality (Sexuality & Personal Health), which reminds me: I tell you how to check MSN's rating system a little later in the chapter. I also tell you where to find information on getting full adult access for yourself while limiting your children's access to adult material. Don't let me forget.

Home and Family

The Home and Family category contains areas of interest to anyone with children, a home, garden, or kitchen—whether your family fits the traditional definition or not. Of particular interest to teens, especially in light of all the challenges they face these days, is the Teen to Teen area. Here teens can confer and exchange ideas with their peers about issues that are important to them.

The Internet tie-in may mean absolutely nothing to you right now—perhaps you think Internet is what you use before you spray on FinalNet? See Chapters 19 and 20 for the full scoop.

The Parenting area can help parents cope with all facets of child development, from terrible two (and before) to teen years (and beyond).

We are family ("Oooh, everybody can see we're together, as we stroll on by...").

Interests, Leisure, & Hobbies

Talk about a hodgepodge, catch-all, "all of the above" category. Interests, Leisure, & Hobbies covers a wealth of activities, so there's probably something here that appeals to you and yours.

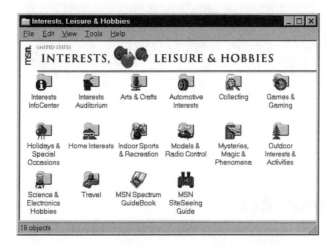

What do you do for fun? It's probably here in Interests, Leisure, & Hobbies.

Like to fish? Check out Outdoor Interests & Activities. Ham radio operator? Dial up Science & Electronics Hobbies. Interested in the latest on alien abductions and UFOs? Want to whip up a batch of Love Potion #9? Materialize yourself inside Mysteries, Magic, & Phenomena.

If people do it, study it, collect it, or argue over it in their spare time, it's probably here. If it isn't, it probably will be shortly—or you can start it yourself.

You Can Make Suggestions, You Know...

I'm not just blowing sunshine up your skirt when I say that you can start a forum yourself. Every category and forum has a BBS where you can post messages. All of the bulletin boards I browsed through had messages from forum leaders asking for suggestions and help developing new areas.

If you have an idea for something you want to see online, post it in the appropriate forum's BBS (Chapter 10 tells how) and watch what happens.

News & Weather

The News & Weather category consolidates all of MSN's news resources (oh, *duh*) into one handy location. It's very cool—a lot of fun for the news addict in you. It's completely covered in Chapter 14.

All the news you can use, and then some.

People & Communities

People & Communities is a celebration of the richness of life. Here you find areas devoted to ethnicity and culture. Socialize with people in the Cultures, Genealogy, Men, Women, and People to People areas.

There are two very interesting features of this forum. One is a very cool feature, and the other demonstrates the rapid change you'll see as MSN grows and expands. The very cool feature is the Advice and Support area. No one ever claimed life was easy, so you can pop in here, commiserate, and ask advice from others in your same circumstances (whatever they may be).

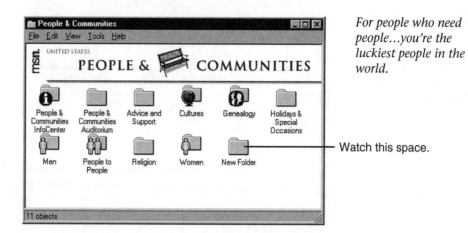

For people who need people...you're the luckiest people in the world.

Watch this space.

The demonstration of growth is the New Folder (look for it in the People & Communities screen). Every now and then you see one: a folder with no real name (just New Folder) and nothing inside it yet.

This is a new area waiting to happen. Stop back every now and then to see what it will be when it grows up.

Public Affairs

Public Affairs covers issues involving Politics, Government Agencies & Departments (if you've ever wanted to gripe to the Secretary of the Department of the Interior), Media Affairs, and Consumer Services and Information. Politics is always a good topic to get a, ahem, discussion going (at least that's what we call them in my house).

Public Affairs also shows you one of the other features of MSN: how one forum can wind up in two or more categories. You may think, for example, that you've seen Public Health before. You have. If you flip back, you see it's also in the Health & Fitness category. Public Health fits into both categories, so you find it in both.

That's a good thing. If you're looking for Public Health because you want to comment to the government about the insurance crisis, you logically think to look in Public Affairs, because it deals with government. Someone else, however, may want to find the latest statistics on the spread of tuberculosis in the nation. That's a health issue, and they are more likely to look in Health & Fitness first. Neither of you are disappointed.

Heard something through the grapevine? Let your government know what you think in Public Affairs.

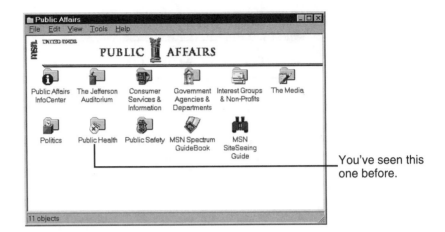

You've seen this one before.

Science & Technology

If your professional life, or one of your hobbies, involves science and technology, you can find scads of information here.

MSN blinds you with science.

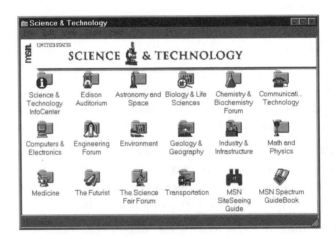

For me, I usually turn on the NASA Channel as soon as a shuttle takes off and leave it on until it lands again. I can't get enough of that space stuff. Astronomy & Space is one of my regular hangouts.

You, however, may be fascinated by science shows like "Mr. Wizard," "Beakman's World," and "Bill Nye The Science Guy." You can explore information you see there in more detail in forums like Chemistry, Physics, and Geology & Geography.

Whatever your area of scientific curiosity, you can learn more about it in Science & Technology.

Special Events

I won't babble too much about the stuff you see in the following figure. By the time you read this, the Special Events category will look different; it changes quickly.

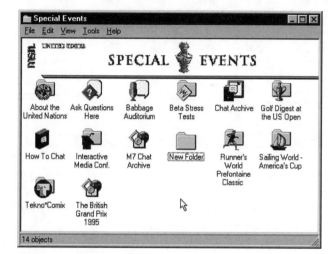

An ever-changing kaleidoscope of Special Event areas.

If there's something special going on in the world, you find online coverage of it here. This is Special Events, after all. You notice in the figure that there's an area devoted to Sailing World—America's Cup, Golf Digest at the US Open, and even one for the British Grand Prix 1995.

When these special events are over, you can find a record of everything that happened in the Chat Archive, but MSN replaces the areas with new, hot and happening special events. I'll wager there will be an area here soon for the '96 Olympics in Atlanta, and probably another for the Papal visits to New York City.

Sports & Recreation

Most sports aren't really my thing—bowling, sure (it's an ethnic stereotype, but I do it); fishing, sometimes; swimming when I can; and maybe volleyball and badminton at picnics, but that's about it. Oh, and miniature golf. Give me a putter and a windmill any day of the week.

However, you may be nuts for football, soccer, baseball, or one of a hundred other sports. Whether you're an armchair jock or a real player, you find discussions and coverage of the latest sporting events here.

All sorts of sports.

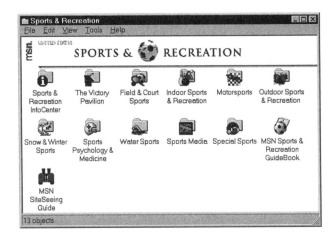

MSN breaks this category down by type (indoor vs. outdoor sports) plus extra categories for Field & Court Sports, Snow & Winter Sports, and Water Sports (water polo, anyone?). There's an area devoted to Sports Psychology & Medicine (if you *really* become a sports nut, or accidentally brain yourself in a batting cage).

The Internet Center

Unless you've been living under a rock for the last year or so, you've heard all sorts of stuff about the Internet. Here's where you can find out, first hand, what all the buzz is about.

Internet An *International network* of computers that enables people to exchange information, files, e-mail, and bad, bad jokes with each other.

The Internet has been around for years, but until recently was the private domain of students, research scientists, and a handful other education, government, and industry types. Now it's the latest rage among all computer users, giving you immediate access, literally, to a whole world of information.

MSN's Internet Center gives you access to newsgroups (the Internet version of BBSs), file libraries, mailing lists (like newsgroups, but they show up in your e-mail), and World Wide Web (WWW) pages.

WWW Acronym for World Wide Web, a hyper-text-based system where informa-tion appears graphically on *pages*. When you click on an icon, or a highlight word or phrase, the WWW page auto-matically takes you to another page (that's what makes it *hyper*text) with related information.

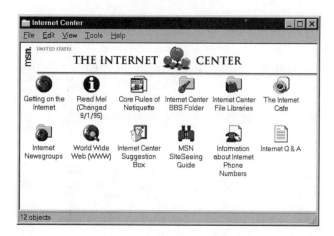

The Internet Center brings the world to your PC.

The Internet (sometimes called the Net) is a wonderfully strange and complex beast, so it's got *two* chapters all to itself. Chapter 19 covers newsgroups, mailing lists, and retrieving files and information from the Net. Chapter 20 covers reading WWW pages with Microsoft's Internet Tools. Put on your propeller beanie, we're going super geek (he's a super geek, super geek, he's super geeky—yow).

MSN Passport

As you may expect, something involving a passport also involves crossing national boundaries. The MSN Passport category is devoted to visitors from outside the good old US of A, including the French, German, British, Australians, and Canadians. It contains information of interest to foreign visitors and provides a way for same-language folks to meet each other quickly. Pretty neat.

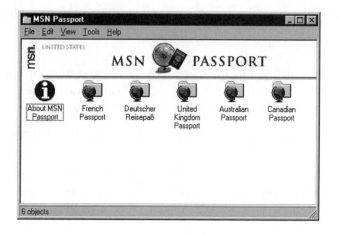

MSN can say "Howdy" in several languages. Look for more as the service expands to more countries.

Chat World

Chat World is a collection of chat rooms with various themes (like the Chat Garden, Pool and Spa, and Atrium Restaurant) where members get together to talk to each other (via the typed word).

Welcome to Chat World. Talkers, start your motors.

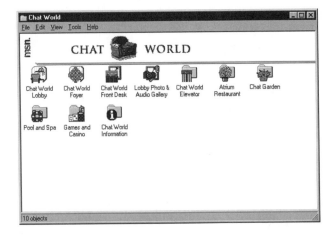

Chat is a great social outlet, especially for folks who (for whatever reason) have trouble meeting and talking with folks in the real world. It's the major social component to any online service, MSN included. As such, it gets a chapter all to itself, Chapter 13, where you'll learn where all of the chat rooms are, how they work, and how to find out about with whom you're talking.

Parental Guidance Suggested

Those are the basic categories. You notice, if you flip back through the categories, that even with this cursory glance, there are some areas online you're probably not sure you want your children to visit.

Your children may be a little young for some of the frank discussions in the Human Sexuality forum, for example. (To be fair, though, there are educational materials in there that can be a help when you sit down to have "the talk" with your son or daughter.)

Before you let your children visit an area online, you can check MSN's rating for the area. Here's how:

1. For the sake of this example, in the Categories window, double-click on the **Health & Fitness** icon. This opens the Health & Fitness category you looked at earlier in this chapter.

2. Click on the **Sexuality Forum** icon.

3. Select **Properties** from the **File** menu. This opens the Sexuality Forum's Property display, as shown in the next figure.

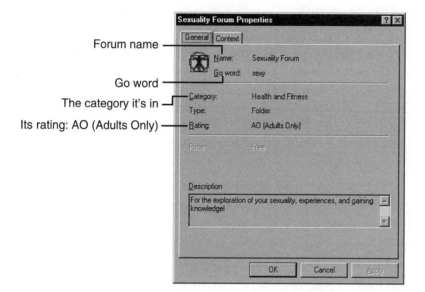

Forum name

Go word

The category it's in

Its rating: AO (Adults Only)

Is this forum appropriate for kids?

4. Check MSN's rating for the forum. It's in the line labeled Rating. The Sexuality Forum is rated AO, for Adults Only.

MSN's rating system, like the motion picture association's rating for movies (you know, G through NC-17), and the rating system for video games, is merely a guideline. You may find nothing wrong with your child reading discussions in the Sexuality forum.

Alternatively, an area that's rated GA (General Audiences) may contain some items that you may not find appropriate for your children (for instance, some of the movie gossip in Arts & Entertainment).

The ratings signify that an area contains a majority of adult information, or not. It doesn't judge every last thing that's posted in every single BBS in the area, and it doesn't take your own personal standards into account (how can it?).

For your own peace of mind, I recommend you explore the service before you allow your children online to make sure that your children aren't exposed to items you find objectionable.

Chapter 22 explains all of your options, from creating and limiting a child's personal account, to getting full access for yourself.

107

The Least You Need to Know

There's a lot of stuff online. The categories are a convenient way to, well, *categorize* all of it. While we will be looking at some areas in greater detail (Computers & Software, Education & Reference, The Internet Center), we won't have the opportunity to examine all the areas online in the same sort of detail.

Now that you know what's available, after you learn to navigate and use the various forums and features, you should feel free to explore areas that may be of interest to you.

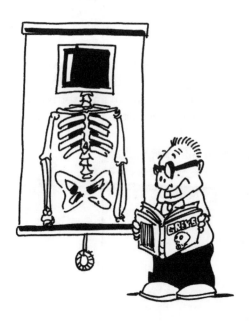

Chapter 10

Anatomy of a Forum

In This Chapter

➤ What's a forum?

➤ Elements common to all forums

➤ What BBSs are, and how they work

Now that you've had a quick look through all the various categories of information you find online, let's zero in on a forum and see how one is put together, how it works, and how to use it.

If you're going to follow along online, make sure your PC is on with the MSN software up and running. To start, you need to sign on (see Chapter 6 if you need a refresher on this).

When the MSN Central window opens, click on **Categories**. When the Categories window appears, double-click on the **Interests, Leisure, & Hobbies** category.

So, What's a Forum?

Within each main category there are dozens of subcategories that further break down the category into easy-to-digest chunks. The following figure shows the subcategories in the Interests, Leisure, & Hobbies category. The subcategories, in turn, contain an assortment of areas geared to a single aspect of the category it falls under. These areas are the forums.

The Interests, Leisure, & Hobbies subcategories.

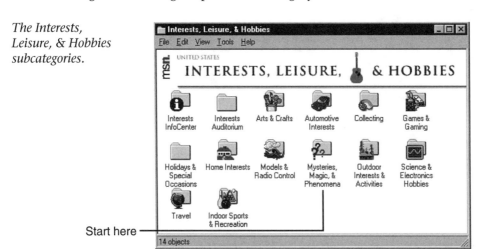

Each forum provides an assembly place for discussion, information files, and BBSs about the subject at hand where members can speak out, learn from each other, and generally kibitz about their mutual interest.

Find the icon for the Mysteries, Magic, & Phenomena subcategory (it's indicated in the figure) and double-click on it. The subcategory opens and shows you forums like those shown in the next figure (except there may be *more* forums by the time you read this).

The forums in Mysteries, Magic, & Phenomena.

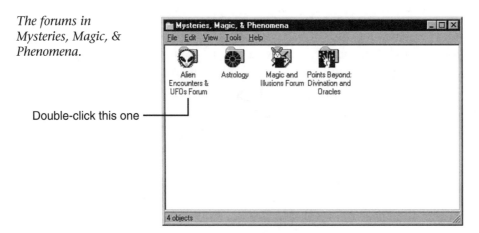

In the figure, Mysteries, Magic, & Phenomena contains four forums: Alien Encounters & UFOs; Astrology; Magic and Illusions; and Points Beyond: Divination and Oracles.

As the sample forum, we're going to take apart the Alien Encounters and UFOs forum, so double-click on its icon.

Elements Common to All Forums

Even though you're looking at a forum in the next figure, it looks pretty much the same as a category or subcategory window: it's a window with a title bar and a pile of folders and documents below. The difference is that everything in the window is directly related to the subject of the forum: alien encounters and UFOs.

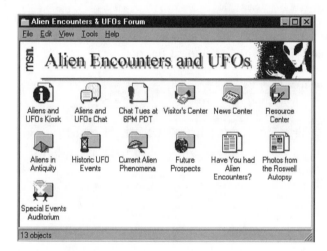

A pretty standard forum (even for a not-so-standard subject).

The icons in this window represent elements you find in most forums, so let's take a look.

Click and Read Text Files

In every forum, you usually find a handful of document icons that you double-click to read. Some are text (with the occasional shortcut thrown in); others are more complex documents that include photographic images.

The common text file icons are these:

 Information Files   These information files usually contain "About This Forum" type of information.

 News Items   These news items are usually about an upcoming Forum event.

Special Information Files   There are two in the figure, with slightly different icons. They contain interesting news bits and change regularly. Double-click to read one.

There are some other variations, as well. News item icons also appear with lightning bolts—these are news flashes. Get it?

Regardless of the extra graphic accessories, all text files in all forums are built off of the same basic icon: a blank piece of paper with one dog-eared corner. It's an easy icon to spot.

When you double-click a text file (like most information files), MSN *downloads* the text to your computer, launches your word processor, and displays the file.

With the more complicated documents, like the Photos from the Roswell Autopsy, double-clicking the icon opens the document in a window that looks like an online Help window (you can see what I mean in the next figure).

Complex online documents appear in windows that look like Windows Help files.

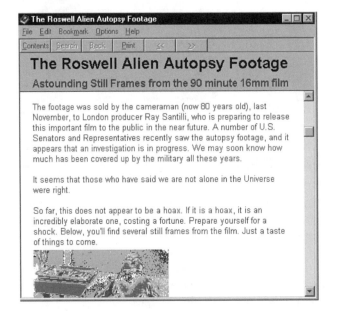

You can return to the previous forum window by clicking the Close button (X) in the top right corner of the screen.

Download
Retrieve a file from a remote computer for use on your own computer.

Save Some Time and Some $$$

If you tend to read text files, like those discussed here, online, launch the application that MSN uses to display the files (Word, WordPad, NotePad) *before* you sign on to MSN. That way you don't waste valuable online time waiting for the application to launch.

Many of the online text files are RTF (Rich Text Format) files. In RTF format, a file keeps its formatting (fonts, margins, colors, etc.) regardless of the word processor you use to view them.

Make sure the word processor you launch can handle RTF files. Check its manual or online Help files to be sure.

Meeting and Chat Rooms

Most online forums also provide one or more areas where visitors to the forum can get together to discuss the topic at hand. The Alien Encounters forum has two such rooms.

 Regular Chat Rooms   They're "regular" because they're open all the time. These chat rooms can hold about 20 participants at one time.

 Auditoriums   MSN uses auditoriums to host special events (celebrity appearances, and such) because auditoriums hold hundreds of people.

Chapter 13 covers the ins and outs of chat rooms, etiquette, and actual chatting.

The icon for the Special Events Auditorium is also the last sort of icon you find in a forum: a folder icon.

Forum Folder Folderol

Folder icons in a forum, like the Special Events Auditorium shown in the last section, and those discussed below, indicate there's more to the forum than meets the eye. For example, the Chat Room icon, shown in the last section, is *not* a folder icon. When you double-click on it, you go right to the Aliens and UFOs chat room.

With a folder icon, if you double-click on it, you open another window that shows you the folder's contents. Folder icons indicate that there's more to look at inside. Double-click the Special Events Auditorium icon shown in the last section, and you open a window like the next one.

Folder icons contain more stuff to see.

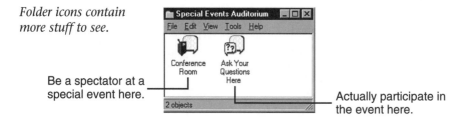

Be a spectator at a special event here.

Actually participate in the event here.

Chapter 13 gives you an explanation of why there are two ways to get into a Special Events Auditorium. The short version is because one icon gets you into the auditorium as a *spectator*, where all you do is watch, and the other gets you in as a *participant*, where you can ask questions of the special guest.

All of the remaining icons in the Alien Encounters and UFOs forum are folder icons. Each folder icon enables you to access information related to a particular aspect of the UFO phenomena. For example:

 The forum's Resource Center

 A subtopic folder

 The forum's News Center

Resource Centers usually contain shortcuts to areas that contain related information online or on the Internet. From the Alien Encounters and UFOs forum, you can access the Astronomy and Space forum by double-clicking its icon, or go to related topics on the Internet (Chapters 19 and 20 show you how to use MSN's Internet features).

Typically, Resource Centers also contain a *file library* of text and application files that you can download to your computer for your own edification and enjoyment. The next chapter explains file libraries and the whole downloading deal in detail.

This particular forum (Alien Encounters and UFOs) doesn't have a file library at this time. It probably will have one by the time you read this, though.

Folders like the ones shown, may contain additional text files you can read, and many have BBSs where members share their thoughts on the subject at hand. The News Center icon contains a text file and three (count 'em) BBSs. Because message boards are such an integral part of visiting a forum, let's see how they work.

Treading the Boards: Forum BBSs

If you're still following along online, double-click the **Alien Encounters and UFOs News Center** icon. A window like the one shown in the next figure opens.

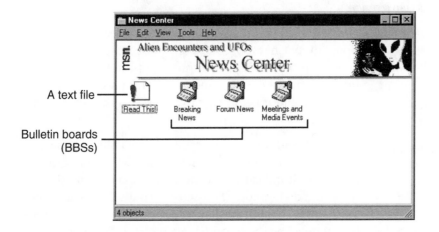

A text file

Bulletin boards (BBSs)

The Alien Encounters and UFOs News Center—complete with three BBSs.

Double-click the **Forum News** icon. This opens the BBS display, and it looks something like the one in the following figure (though there are bound to be more, and different, messages when you go looking).

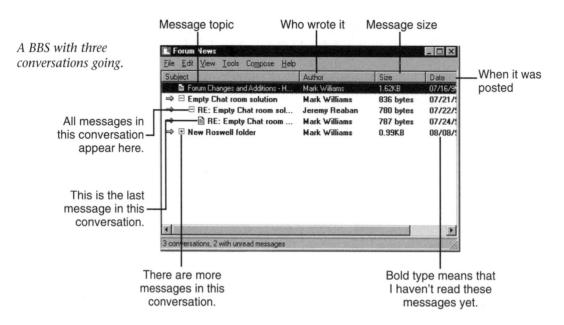

A BBS with three conversations going.

Message topic | Who wrote it | Message size

When it was posted

All messages in this conversation appear here.

This is the last message in this conversation.

There are more messages in this conversation.

Bold type means that I haven't read these messages yet.

In the figure, you can tell I've read the first message, Forum Changes and Additions, because it isn't in **bold** type. The little document icon in front of it indicates that it's the only message in this *conversation*.

Conversation
A group of BBS messages on a related topic is a conversation. Like a regular conversation, you can follow the series of messages from start to finish, and anyone is free to put in their own two cents worth.

I haven't read the message that starts the second conversation, Empty Chat room solution. Notice that the message appears in **bold** type. The minus sign (-) in front of it indicates that there are responses to this message, and the responses appear below (the two messages that start with **RE:**).

The third, and final, conversation on this BBS begins with a message about the New Roswell folder. The plus sign (+) in front of it indicates that there are responses, but the responses do not appear on-screen. To display them, click on the plus sign. The responses appear below and to the right of the original message (like those below the second conversation). The plus sign turns into a minus (does that mean it's pregnant?).

116

Message thread   Old-timers like me sometimes refer to "conversations" as "message threads." They mean the same thing; they just use different metaphors.

RE   Abbreviated form of "regarding," borrowed from business memos. All responses to BBS messages are automatically named "RE:" followed by the name/subject of the first message in the conversation.

Reading Messages

To read a message, double-click on it. This opens the message in a window like the one shown in the next figure. The body of the message appears in the text box at the bottom of the window. Just read it, scrolling as necessary to see the whole thing.

When you're done reading the message, you can use the toolbar (indicated in the figure) to do a number of things. Some of the buttons on the toolbar are familiar to you (you use the similar ones with Windows 95 as well as other applications); other buttons are new to you.

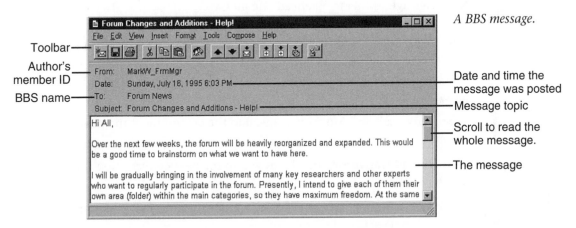

A BBS message.

Don't Sweat Memorizing These Buttons, Though...

If you happen to forget (or, like I do, get confused) which button is which, simply point at it with your mouse cursor. A short message pops up to remind you what the button does.

New Message   Creates the first message of a whole new conversation

Save   Saves the current message to disk.

Print   Prints the message.

Cut   Removes selected text from the message and puts it in Windows Clipboard.

Copy   Copies selected text from the message and puts it in Windows Clipboard.

Paste   Places whatever is in Windows Clipboard in the message.

Reply to BBS   Creates a response to the message.

Previous Message   Takes you back one message.

Next Message   Moves you ahead one message.

Next Unread Message   Takes you to the next message you haven't yet read.

Previous Conversation   Takes you back to the beginning of the last conversation.

Next Conversation   Moves you ahead to the beginning of the next conversation.

Next Unread Conversation   Takes you to the next conversation that you haven't read.

File Transfer Status   Opens the MSN window that enables you to monitor file transfers. (See Chapter 11).

After you read a message, you may want to post your own thoughts on the subject, so read the next section to learn how to respond to messages.

Responding to Messages

To post a response to another user's message, click on the **Reply to BBS** button (you have to be reading a message for this button to work). This opens a dialog box like the one shown in the following figure.

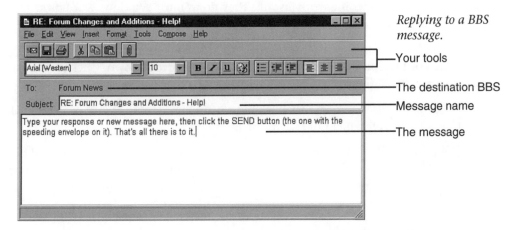

Replying to a BBS message.

—Your tools

—The destination BBS

—Message name

—The message

MSN automatically enters a Subject in the text box. It is "RE:" plus the subject of the message to which you're responding. In the figure, it's "RE: Forum Changes and Additions—Help!" You can edit it, if you care to, so it better suits your message, or not. It's up to you. To enter your reply, simply click in the large text box at the bottom of the dialog box—this places your cursor there—and type your message.

You can use the toolbar buttons (explained below) to alter the appearance of your message text. When you're happy with it, click the **Send** button (it's the one with the speeding envelope on it).

Speaking of those toolbar buttons, there are a few here you haven't seen before (well, not on MSN). They are...

 Send   Posts your message to the BBS.

 Insert   Places the contents of a saved text file in the body of the message.

 **Font** and **Font Size**   Enables you to select the font(s) and font size(s) for your message.

B *I* <u>U</u>   **Bold**, **Italic**, and **Underline**   Use these to apply styles to your message text.

    Font Color   Select a color for your message fonts.

Bold, Italic, and Underline work just like they do in most Windows word processing software. Select the text and click the button for the style you want to apply.

Font Color works like the other style buttons. Select the text you want to colorize and click the **Font Color** button. A menu of color choices drops down. Click on the color you want to use.

You've probably used the next toolbars buttons in your favorite word processor. These buttons alter the placement of text in the message.

The first three mess with the text's indentation: add bullets to a list, move indent left, and move indent right. The last three change the alignment of the text: right align, center, and left align. Check them out while you're composing a message—they don't hurt anything.

Starting a New Conversation

After you read the BBS messages for a while, you probably work up the nerve to start a new conversation of your own. Good for you.

There are three ways to begin a new conversation:

➤ From the list of conversations in the BBS, select **New Conversation** from the **Compose** menu.

➤ From the list of conversations in the BBS, press **Ctrl+N**.

➤ While reading any message on the BBS, click the **New Message** button.

Any of the three methods opens a dialog box like the one you used earlier to respond to a BBS message. There's just one difference: because this is a completely new conversation you're starting, you need to type a subject in the Subject text box. Just click in the text box and type one. Other than that one little thing, the process is exactly the same as the one for responding to someone else's message.

Hey! My Message Didn't Show Up!

If you go looking for a message you just posted (either a response to a message, or one starting a whole new conversation), you won't find it.

When you click the Send button, MSN actually sends your message to one of the forum managers who reads it to make sure it's suitable for the area (and stays within the terms of MSN's Member Agreement). Then, the forum manager posts the message for other members to read.

It may take as long as a day or two (depending on the volume of messages the area gets) before your message finally appears. Don't panic. It hasn't disappeared forever.

Don't Make a Mess with Messages

As a public service, here are a few tips you should keep in mind when you're posting anything to a BBS online.

Read Before You Respond

Make sure that someone else hasn't beaten you to the punch with a comment. Nothing annoys BBS readers more than reading the same comment over and over from various members. If you don't have anything new to say, don't say anything.

Likewise, it's annoying to have someone ask a question in a BBS that's already been asked and answered. Keep in mind that everyone online is paying for the privilege of reading these postings. Reruns are as tiresome here as they are on television.

Stay on the Subject

Reading the previous postings in a conversation, especially the early ones, helps you keep to the actual subject on hand.

If a conversation starts out being about the effects of a heat wave on pets, a posting about how your cat eats your houseplants isn't really appropriate (unless your tabby only eats the plants during a heat wave). Keep the conversation on track.

Don't Take Things Personally

When you post a message stating your point of view, you *will* get responses. Some of them may seem to be unkind, mean-spirited personal attacks. (For example, the marital status of my parents has been called into question in some responses to my messages.)

This is called *flaming*, and it's a waste of time and money, except for the few who get giggles from inciting a flame war. To me, flaming is the last resort of small minds. They can't frame a convincing or persuasive argument, so they resort to name calling.

You find the most flames in areas where religion, politics, abortion, gay rights, or anywhere else an emotional hot potato gets tossed around, but you'll also find them in the most innocuous of areas (I saw a wicked flame in a technical support area on another online service that made *me* blush).

Argue, sure. Disagree, fine. State your case plainly and simply—that's lovely. Question someone's parentage, or IQ, and that's uncalled-for flaming. If you see some, don't get involved. If someone flames you, don't respond (or respond without fanning the flames).

If you *really* want to tick off a flamer, learn to construct solid arguments and hone your skills…on them.

It's Okay to Repeat Some Things

If you're responding to a message, no matter where it falls in the conversation, MSN adds your message to the end of the conversation.

It helps readers remember what the original message was about if you quote the important points you're responding to. Use the Copy and Paste buttons to quickly quote the original and set off the quotes like this (your new message is the stuff that's not in bold type):

> In your message of 8/24/95, you said:
>
> >>**They say you can always win at Free Cell, but I don't**
>
> >>**believe it. I lose more often than win.**
>
> I think you'll find…insert your words of wisdom here.

That way, latecomers to the discussion don't have to search through the whole conversation looking for the message you're responding to, or wonder what the heck you're going on about.

But Don't Copy the Whole Thing!

I've seen messages where some lazy bugger just copied an old, three paragraph message into their new message. I had to skim through the old stuff just to get to the point of their response.

Don't do that. Only quote the "good parts," a sentence here, a phrase there—the stuff that made you feel the need to respond in the first place.

Making folks re-read an entire posting is rude and wastes their money. Be considerate of other people's credit card bills. In the same vein:

Keep It Short and Sweet

A BBS is no place to post a doctoral thesis. Say what you have to say, succinctly (maybe with a touch of humor, if it's appropriate) and get on with your life.

Got the idea?

Save Time and Money

If you're really into a conversation, but don't want to spend hours online reading the whole thing, you can open each message and save it as a file on your hard drive. Just click the **Save** button. You get a standard Windows Save As dialog you can use to name and save the file.

You can open the saved files later with your favorite word processor, to read at your leisure, without paying by the hour.

Likewise, you can compose your message postings offline, too. Write the message with your favorite word processor and save it in its own file. When you're online next, go to the BBS and/or message you're responding to (or just the BBS if you're starting a new conversation). Click the **New Message** or **Reply to BBS** button, as appropriate.

When the message opens, click the **Insert** button (the one with the paper clip on it). It gives you a standard Windows Open dialog box. Use it to locate the saved BBS message you want to post. Click on the file name and click **OK**. MSN inserts the text from that file into the BBS message. All you have to do then is click the **Send** button.

Chapter 25 gathers this and other money saving tips together for you.

The Least You Need to Know

Even though we only looked at the components of one fairly simple forum here, the parts are standard in all the forums on MSN—only the names change.

Once you learn to work your way through one forum, you're ready to tackle all of them.

The BBSs, located in each forum, are some of the most heavily used areas online. Keep the simple message posting tips from this chapter in mind when you begin to post your own messages.

Chapter 11

Conan the Librarian: Dealing with File Libraries

In This Chapter

➤ Finding the files you want

➤ Downloading files

➤ Uploading files

➤ The joy of safe computing

➤ Files you gotta get

I don't know about you, but for me, one of the things I do almost every time I'm online (besides shmooze via e-mail) is scour the *file libraries* for new and exciting software. It's a passion for me, and it may become one for you. This chapter, I hope, will fire that passion in you and give you the tools you need to keep that fire going.

Check This Out...

File Library
As with book libraries, a file library is an online storage place for application, text, and graphics files. You can browse through the files, download files, and even upload files of your own to share with other MSN users.

There's One in Every Forum...Well, Almost

Can you spot the file library? (It's easier than playing "Spot the Loony" or "Spot the Brain Cell.")

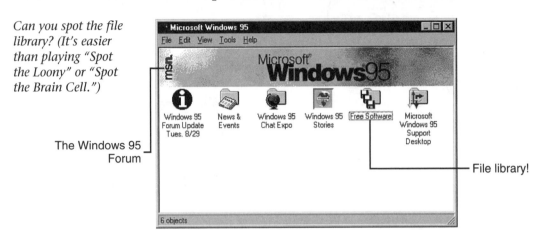

The Windows 95 Forum

File library!

Forums that don't have a file library (like Alien Abductions & Encounters in the last chapter) are rare exceptions. I attribute forums without file libraries to the newness of MSN; I don't believe that there are no appropriate files to share in these forums. Given time, there will probably be at least one file library in every forum.

In the previous figure, you see the Windows 95 Forum (Go word: WINDOWS). Its file library is called Free Software. It's a great place to find the latest add-ins for Windows 95 (like you hadn't figured *that* out already) as they're written.

You can generally spot a file library by its icon: there's usually a floppy disk on it, or several, and the name usually includes one of the "ware" words. (Does that make a voracious file downloader a ware-wolf?) The "ware" words are soft*ware*, share*ware*, and free*ware*. If they're a mystery to you, there's a section toward the end of this chapter that explains them. To get at the file library's contents, just double click on its icon in the forum window. This opens a familiar looking display like the one shown in the following figure.

If you look at the figure, you notice that a file library looks remarkably like a BBS message board—that's because they *are* BBSs. That means that all the BBS tips and tricks from Chapter 10 *also* apply to file libraries—so you don't have to learn a huge pile of new stuff. You already know a lot of this. Cool.

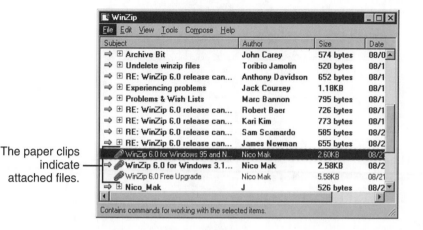

Looks like a message board, doesn't it? It is!

The paper clips indicate attached files.

Confusion Alert!

Because *I* get so easily confused...what was I talking about?...I assume everybody does. Since MSN's bulletin boards (BBSs) and file libraries are basically the same, you can find software posted to message areas, and messages (without software) posted in file libraries.

Finding Files

My favorite way to search for files is to just browse—sort of like window shopping. I cruise around online. If the forum I'm visiting strikes my fancy, I open its file library and see what it has to offer. That's a fun (if slow) way to do it.

Sometimes, however, you need a thought-out approach: you have a problem with your PC and you need a bit of software to fix it, or you have a job to do and another bit of software will help you do it. Whatever the situation, sometimes you need something specific—and you need it now. There are a couple ways to find what you need quickly.

Round Up the Usual Suspects

When you need a specific software program (say, a Windows 95 add-in to make your life easier), your easiest choice is to find a forum file library that's likely to contain what you need. If it's a Windows 95 thingy you need, check out the Windows 95 file library.

There's a pile of software in Computing & Software's Software Forums, all conveniently broken down by subject.

Publishing accessories   Kid stuff

SOFTWARE

UNITED STATES

Software

File Edit View Tools Help

msn.

Computer Games | Computer Design & Graphics | Desktop Publishing | Geographic Software | Kids Software | Operating Systems

Shareware | Software BBS | Software Chat | Management Software | Engineering Software

Distracting games

11 objects

If you're looking for software to keep the kids amused, complete a desktop publishing job, or kill time at work when your boss isn't looking, check out the appropriate file libraries in Computing & Software's Software Forums (Go word: SOFTWARE). They're shown in the previous figure.

For kid stuff, look in the Kids Software folder; for that DTP (desktop publishing) chore, check out the Desktop Publishing folder; and for down-time amusement, look in the Computer Games folder. As I said, look in the obvious places.

Go Words

If you're interested, the Go words for these software forums are:

Kids Software: KIDSSOFTWARE

Desktop Publishing: DESKTOPPUB

Computer Games: COMPUTERGAMES

To use Go words, select **Other Location** from the **Go To** submenu on the **Edit** menu. Type the Go word in the text box and click **OK**. Chapter 25 covers Go words and other speedy methods of getting around online.

Use the Find Command

Sometimes time to browse is a luxury you just don't have. If you need to find some software (or practically anything else online) you can use the Find command. Find works whether you're connected to MSN, or not—if you're not, Find connects you. We saw it, briefly, back in Chapter 10, in the context of looking for a forum; now we'll use it to find software.

Here's how it works:

1. Click on the **Start** button. (If you're already online, you can select **Find** from the **Tools** menu—then skip to step 3.)

2. Point at **Find**.

3. Click **On The Microsoft Network**. This opens the Find dialog box shown in the next figure.

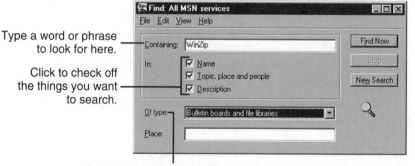

Type a word or phrase to look for here.

Click to check off the things you want to search.

Select where you want to search.

The Find dialog box—you found it!

4. Type a word or phrase to search for in the text box labeled Containing. In the figure, I've entered WinZip, which is the name of an excellent *compression* utility I'll be talking about later in the chapter.

Techno Talk

Hey, Pal—ZIP You!

Most of the files you find online are *compressed*. That means they've been smooshed down to take up less space, and therefore take less time to transfer from MSN to your computer (or vice-versa). You can identify compressed files by their file extensions. File names that end with .ZIP, .ARC, .LZH, and even (sometimes) .EXE indicate that the file is compressed, and you need to decompress the file before you can use it.

To compress a file, you need a compression utility, like the one I'm downloading here, *WinZip*, which is based on the PC compression standard PKZip, from PKWare. MSN can decompress files for you, but you need a utility to compress files yourself.

5. The In area of the dialog box contains three search options. Select how you want MSN to handle the search:

Name searches file, folder, and forum names for your search word or phrase.

Topic, place, and people isn't really appropriate for a software search (it is good for forums, however.

Description searches for your word or phrase in the description of files, folders, and forums.

6. Select what you want to search by selecting one of the **Of type** options. For a software search, I select **Bulletin boards and file libraries** because these are the two places software appears.

If you aren't sure *where* to look, select **All MSN services**.

7. If what you're looking for is files, folders, or forums relating to a particular city (I don't know how much city specific software there is, though), enter the city name in the Place box.

8. Click **Find Now**.

When you click Find Now, MSN searches in the areas you specified (of course, if you aren't connected to MSN yet, you have to sign in with the Sign In screen that automatically appears). Any matches show up in the list box that magically opens at the bottom of the Find dialog box (go back to the last figure to see what I mean).

The results are in!

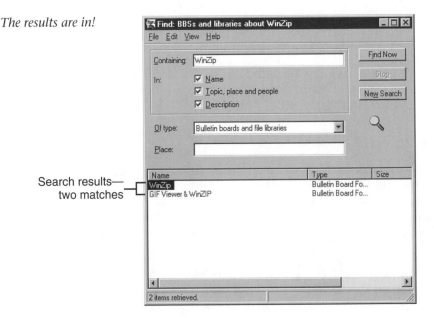

Search results—
two matches

To get a look at the files you turn up, double-click on an entry and MSN takes you to it. I double-clicked on the **WinZip** entry, and MSN magically transported me to the area shown in the next figure.

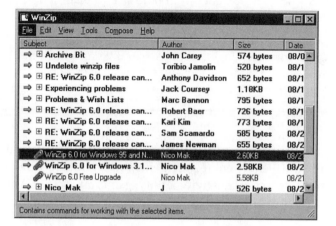

WinZip stuff for days...

Figuring Out If a File Is What You Want

Well, there's no sure-fire way to tell if a file online is exactly what you need, but you can get a pretty good idea before you download it to your computer.

Since the file libraries are pretty much the same as BBSs, every file has some descriptive information with it. To read it, double-click on the listing that strikes your fancy. In the last figure, I looked at the one called WinZip 6.0 for Windows 95 and NT (it's the one selected in the figure). When I double-clicked it, I got the description shown in the following figure.

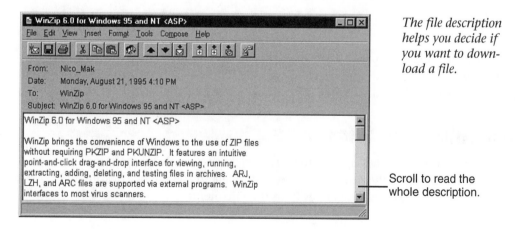

The file description helps you decide if you want to download a file.

Scroll to read the whole description.

131

If You Go Back to a File Later...

File libraries behave just like message boards. When you read a file description, its title goes from **boldface** to plain type, indicating that you've read it.

If, for some reason, you return to a file library to download a file you've already seen, *it isn't visible.* In order to conserve space in BBSs and file libraries, MSN hides messages you've read. If you want to re-read a message or file description, select **Show All Messages** from the **Tools** menu. This restores the messages you've read to the display.

File descriptions usually contain a brief summary of what the file is or does, what you need to have to use the file (system requirements), who wrote it, what it costs (if anything), and a basic category (productivity, utility, game, and so on). You can see that information for WinZip in the next figure.

Information about the author and system requirement for this file.

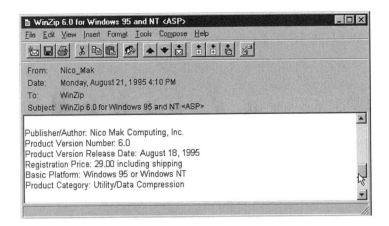

If your computer doesn't meet the requirements listed in the Basic Platform line, don't download it—you'll just waste your time and money. On the other hand, if your PC can handle it, and the file sounds like what you need, download away.

Downloading Files

At the end of the message, there is an icon that *is* the file. There's one shown in the next figure. You can get a little more information about the file by clicking on its icon to select it and then selecting **Properties** from the **File** menu.

Alternatively, you can use the right mouse button to click on the file's icon. In the shortcut menu that appears, select **Properties** from the **File Object** submenu.

Whichever way you choose to do it, the file's properties appear in the Attached Files Properties dialog box (see the next figure).

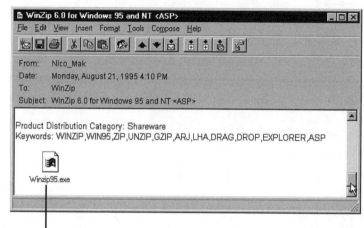

The icon is the file.

This is the file. Really.

File Properties

The information in the file's properties display is very helpful: it's good to know how big the file is (File size line), how long it takes to send it to your computer (Download time line), and whether or not the forum manager has approved it (Status line).

Additionally, you can also find out if downloading the file costs you anything beyond your normal online charges. In some forums, especially those operated by retail software companies (like Microsoft) you can download commercial products to your computer. MSN adds the price that you'd normally fork over in a computer store to your MSN bill (and your credit card). Don't confuse this price with a shareware registration fee. They aren't the same thing. Shareware is explained in the section called "File Types: Shareware, Freeware, and Public Domain," a little later in this chapter.

WinZip's properties display.

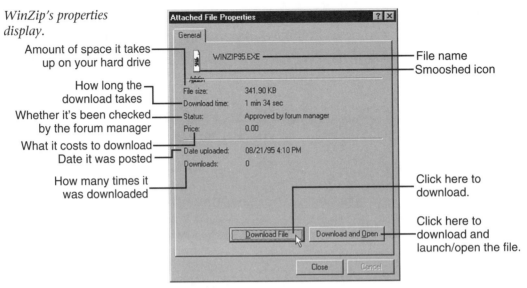

Amount of space it takes up on your hard drive

How long the download takes

Whether it's been checked by the forum manager

What it costs to download

Date it was posted

How many times it was downloaded

File name

Smooshed icon

Click here to download.

Click here to download and launch/open the file.

What's to "Approve" of?

When a forum manager approves a file, it's *not* the forum manager saying "This is a good file!" (Although that kind of approval is nice.) It means that the forum manager has scanned the file for viruses. See the section "A Word About Viruses" later in this chapter for more details.

Finally, you can see when the file was originally uploaded to MSN (Date uploaded entry), and how many people have downloaded the file since (the Downloads entry).

After scanning the file's properties, you can download it if you want it. If you don't want it, click **Close**. The file's properties display goes away.

Downloading: Send It to Me!

At the bottom of the Attached File Properties dialog box, there are two buttons: Download File and Download and Open. The Download File button sends a copy of the file to your PC. Download and Open not only sends you a copy, but also launches an application file, or opens a document file with an appropriate application (word processor for a text file, graphics program for a graphics file, and so on).

I don't recommend using the Download and Open option if you intend to stay online, unless you're *really* desperate to see the file in action. It runs up your online charges unnecessarily.

To download the file, click **Download**. MSN springs into action, opening the File Transfer Status window shown next.

The File Transfer Status Window

You can watch the status of your download by looking at the thermometer-type display in the status bar at the bottom of the File Transfer Status window.

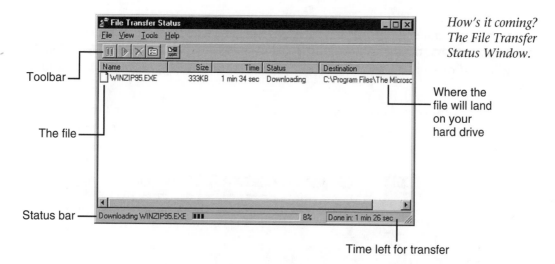

How's it coming? The File Transfer Status Window.

Toolbar

The file

Status bar

Where the file will land on your hard drive

Time left for transfer

You can use the toolbar at the top of the window to do a couple of things during the transfer:

 Pause   Pauses the transfer so you can finish it later.

 Resume   Continues transferring a file that's been paused with the Pause button. The Pause and Resume buttons are grayed-out unless you set your Transfer Options to Pause files as queued. I'll tell you how in a second.

 Delete   Removes a file from the list of files to download.

 Transfer Options   Calls up your (*duh*) transfer options, covered below.

 Transfer and Disconnect   Automatically downloads the files you've selected and then signs you off MSN. (This is the button to click if you've chosen the Download and Open option for a single file.)

135

To use these buttons, click on the file's name to select the file and then click a button. For example, to delete a file, click on the file's name and then click the **Delete** button.

File Transfer Options

If you try to download a file without fiddling with your File Transfer Options, this is what happens:

You click **Download**. The File Transfer Status window opens. MSN sends the one lonely file to your computer and stores it in MSN's Transferred Files folder (it's at the path: C:\Program Files\The Microsoft Network\Transferred Files). When the transfer is complete, MSN *decompresses* the file (if it's compressed) and sends you on your merry online way.

If you tinker with your transfer options, you can change all that. You need to be signed in to MSN to fiddle with these options. Let's look at them one at a time. Click on the **Transfer Options** button on the toolbar.

Here's where you change your file transfer options.

Your compression options

Where your files will land when downloaded

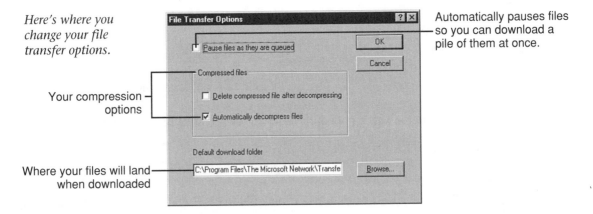

Automatically pauses files so you can download a pile of them at once.

The Pause That Refreshes

Downloading multiple files, one at a time, can be tedious as all get-out. If you click the **Pause files as they are queued** check box when you select files for downloading, MSN adds the files to the list in the File Transfer Status window, but doesn't begin downloading. That way, you can save up all of your files for the end of your online session.

When you're done poking around online, open the File Transfer Status window (select **File Transfer Status** from the **Tools** menu). Select all the file names and click the Resume button. Then you can click the **Transfer and disconnect** button (as described in the last section). MSN downloads the list of files to your computer and signs you off of MSN when it's done. You don't have to baby-sit your PC during the download. Instead, you can go have a refreshing beverage and check back later.

Compression Options

There are two options in the Compressed Files box: Delete compressed files after decompressing and Automatically decompress files.

Click **Delete compressed files after decompressing** to save some hard drive space. MSN deletes the .ZIP (or .ARC, or whatever) file, leaving you with just the usable, decompressed files.

When you click **Automatically decompress files**, MSN (you guessed it) automatically decompresses any compressed files you've downloaded.

You can select both options. If you remove the check mark in front of **Automatically decompress files**, MSN leaves your downloaded files compressed, and you need to manually decompress them with a compression utility (or you can turn this option back on, the next time you're online, and MSN decompresses the files after your next download).

Default Download Folder

Here you can type in a new path statement, telling MSN where you want all of your downloaded files to land. You can also use the Browse button to navigate to the folder you want to use for your downloads.

I think the *default* setting of MSN's Transferred Files folder is perfectly fine, but you can do what you like.

Finishing Up

Once you've tinkered with your options, and you're happy with them, click **OK**. MSN puts any changes you've made into effect right away. If you don't change any option, or don't want the changes you've made to kick in, click **Cancel**.

File Types: Shareware, Freeware, Public Domain, and Others

Generally, all the files you find online fall into a few common types—and I don't mean applications versus documents, though that's true too. Software you download tends to be one of four varieties: freeware, shareware, public domain, and demos.

Freeware is free—it's yours to have and hold, give to your friends, and pretty much do whatever you like with—except sell it, or claim it as your own. It's still the author's property.

Common File Extensions

Once you download a file and sign off of MSN, you're ready to use the file—just remember that compressed files have to be decompressed before you use them. For document files, you also need to have an application that can run the file. These are some of the common kinds files you find online (these are in no particular order):

.TXT	A text file
.RTF	A file in Microsoft's Rich Text Format
.DOC	A Microsoft Word, or other word processor file
.GIF	A graphic file in Graphic Interchange Format, often a photograph
.BMP	A graphic in Windows bitmap format
.JPG	A JPEG file, a graphic format that takes up very little space
.TIF	A graphic in Tagged Image File format
.PCX	A PC Paintbrush graphics file
.WMF	A graphic in Windows Metafile format
.WAV	A Windows sound file
.MPEG	A video file, live-action or animated
.EPS	An Encapsulated PostScript file that includes graphics, text, or a combination

There are also files that end with extensions specific to a particular application. Microsoft Works database files, for example, all end with the extension .WDB.

The important thing to know about all these file types is whether or not you own an application that can use them: check your manuals or online Help files to make sure.

If you don't have an appropriate application, you won't be able to do much with the downloaded document. Save yourself the time and money: don't download it until you know you can use it.

Shareware is software that the author chooses to distribute on a "try before you buy basis." You download it, try it out for a week or so, and, if you decide to keep it, send the author a registration fee. In the interim, the software's author may design the program to remind you that you're using an unregistered version, requesting you to please register it.

Sending in the registration fee usually gets you the latest version of the software (or a fully functional version; see demos below) and a code number which turns off the registration reminders. There's some great stuff available as shareware (WinZip is one, and it's practically cheap at $29).

Public Domain software is stuff that a company or author used to own, but the copyright lapsed or was waived. Now, technically, it doesn't belong to anyone (or it belongs to *everyone,* depending on how you look at it). It doesn't cost anything, and you can do whatever you want with it.

Demos are demonstration versions of software. They do enough to give you an idea of what the program does, but some vital options (like Save or Print) are disabled. There are demos for both shareware and the regular commercial software you'd normally buy in a store. You need to buy a fully functional copy in order to do anything meaningful with it.

A Word about Viruses: Eeeewwwww!

If you don't know about them, computer viruses are nasty little bits of programming that get hidden inside of application files. When you use an application that's been infected with a virus, the virus gets into your computer and usually wreaks havoc. MSN's forum managers scan all uploaded files for viruses before they get put into file libraries online. You don't really have to worry too much about those.

However, if you download files from the Internet (covered in Chapters 19 and 20), you really need to get and use an anti-virus utility. The Internet is so vast that no one, but no one, can check all of the files for all the viruses. You've got to check the ones you download.

You may already have an anti-virus program. They're part of many utility packages (PC Tools, for one), and others are sold in stand-alone versions (like Norton's Anti-Virus). If you don't have one, there are some really good ones available online. See the section "Files You've Gotta Get" later in this chapter.

Practice safe computing: get and use an anti-virus utility on a regular basis—especially if you're using files you've downloaded from the Internet.

Uploading Files

There may come a time when downloading files isn't enough for you. You want to share a creation of your own with the rest of the online world. You most certainly can. Here's how to do it (make sure your file is ready to go before you start):

1. Sign in to MSN and go to the **Shareware Forum** (Go word: SHAREWARE). At the moment, this is the only place on MSN where you can upload files—that may change, but check here first.

2. Open the **New Shareware File Submissions** folder.

3. Select **New Message** from the **Compose** menu.

4. Type the file's name in the Subject box and enter a description of the file in the message body (see the section "MSN Uploading Rules" below for details).

Check This Out...

You Can Prepare Your File Description Offline and Save Money

You can write your file description offline and save it as a text or RTF file. After you type the file's name in the Subject box, select **File** from the **Insert** menu. You use the Insert dialog box to navigate to the saved file on your hard drive and then click the file's name to select the file. At the bottom of the dialog box, click **Text Only** and then click **OK**. Your saved text appears in the body of the message. Cool.

5. Click to place the cursor at the point in the message where you want the file's icon to appear.

6. Click the **Attach file** button (the one with the paper clip).

7. Use the Attach dialog box to navigate to the file you're uploading on your hard drive and click the file's name to select the file. Click **OK**. An icon with the file's name appears in the message.

8. Check your message for embarrassing lapses in grammar and spelling, and when you're happy with it, click the **Post** button (the one with the speeding envelope) or select **Post Message** from the **File** menu.

You're done! Your computer sends the file to MSN's computer, and your message and file appear online after MSN's staff checks it for viruses and copyrighted materials.

MSN's Uploading Rules

This section is a summary of MSN's uploading rules. The full document is available online in the Shareware Forum (Go word: SHAREWARE). You should only upload shareware, freeware, or public domain files to the MSN libraries.

A lot of uploadable material is public domain (see the "File Types" section earlier in this chapter), and you can upload it without getting permission from the author. Other stuff, however, is usually owned or copyrighted by a company or author. You'll be breaking federal copyright laws if you upload (or just copy and give away) copyrighted materials without permission from the creator or owner of the material. If there is any doubt as to the legality of posting any material, don't post it. If you do have permission from the author or owner to post copyrighted material, say so in the file description.

If you're uploading articles or graphics files, consider the source. Most of this material created by others is automatically copyrighted on creation, even if there aren't any copyright notices on the article or graphic. Get permission from the author or artist to upload her work. If you are unsure, don't upload the material. (This also includes, for instance, scanned images from a magazine, or whatever, that you then assemble into a work of your own—the original copyright still applies.)

Your file description and title should tell MSN members what the file is and does. Don't upload files with a description that only says…"A great file, worth the download!" That doesn't tell anyone anything about the file. Forum managers do not post files that are uploaded without a full description. Instead, you get e-mail from the forum manager saying that the file was not accepted, and you have to post it again, with a proper description.

A good file description includes the following information:

➤ A complete description of what the files are and what they do.

➤ Publisher and author information, including whether you have their permission to upload.

➤ Product Version Number, for example WhizBang 3.0 for Win 95.

➤ Product Version Release Date.

➤ Registration Price: the shareware fee, if any.

➤ Basic Platform: what hardware you need to have to use the files.

➤ Product Category: a personal information manager, for example.

➤ Product Distribution Category.

➤ Keywords.

Files You've Gotta Get

In my humble opinion, you need to have these shareware applications to survive online:

WinZip 6.0   A fabulously simple and easy compression utility that integrates itself right into the Windows Explorer. I use it all the time. As I mentioned earlier, the registration fee is $29, and it's Windows 95 savvy, so it's simple to install with the Add/Remove Programs Wizard in the Control Panel window.

An anti-virus utility   The one the forum managers use to check uploads is McAfee's Scan for Windows 95, a commercial product you can find in stores for about $45. You can also find a number of good shareware anti-virus utilities. If you're going to download files from the Internet (or if your friends are always inserting strange floppy disks in your PC), you need some kind of anti-virus protection.

If nothing else, you should search for them online, using the Find On MSN option discussed earlier. It will be good practice for you.

The Least You Need to Know

This chapter covers a lot of ground. The absolute least you need to know is where to find this chapter when you want to down- or up-load a file for the first time. Otherwise, remember these few tidbits:

➤ Most forums have file libraries.

➤ To find files, you browse, or use the **Find On The Microsoft Network** option on your **Start** menu.

➤ File libraries are set up like BBSs, so you want to read Chapter 10 before experimenting—it covers BBS operations in detail.

➤ To download a file, click its icon, select **Properties** from the **File** menu, and click the **Download** button.

Chapter 12

E-Mail: Digital Love Letters

In This Chapter

➤ Getting and reading your MSN e-mail

➤ Sending your own e-mail

➤ Attaching files to e-mail

➤ Using the Address Book

Right up front, I need to tell you something: Microsoft Exchange, the application that handles MSN's e-mail for you, is a full-featured application in its own right. If you care to, you can use it not just with MSN, but with a fleet of online services including MCI Mail, America Online, CompuServe, and others.

Unfortunately, this isn't a book about Exchange and everything it can do; it's about MSN and the role Exchange plays with it. Some of the things Exchange can do, while very cool, don't fit the context of this chapter, or even the book. If you care to use Exchange with another online service, or explore its more esoteric functions, check out the instructions in its online Help files, available under the Help menu.

If You Want to Use Exchange with Other Services...

You need to configure it for the other services. You can use the Mail & Fax Properties display (double-click **Mail & Fax** in the Control Panel window), or select **Services** from Exchange's **Tools** menu. See Exchange's online Help for, well, help.

That said, let's talk about using MSN to e-mail the world through Exchange.

Starting Microsoft Exchange

Since Exchange is a stand-alone application, you can fire it up even if you aren't connected to MSN. That's a good thing, because that means you can compose, read, and respond to your e-mail offline, saving money. (Online, of course, you can just click the E-mail bar of MSN Central; it opens the same Exchange window.)

There are two ways to launch Exchange while offline (shown in the next figure). You can double-click the **Inbox** icon on your desktop. Or, you can click the **Start** button, point at **Programs**, and click **Microsoft Exchange** in the Programs submenu. Either method works, so use your favorite.

How you start Microsoft Exchange is up to you.

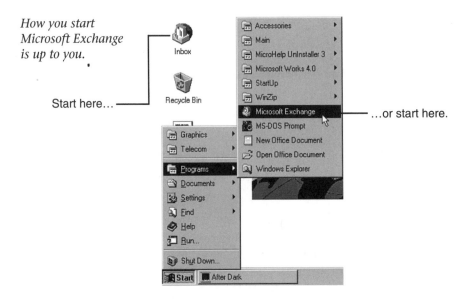

144

The Exchange Window

When Microsoft Exchange opens, it looks a little like the following figure. You may already have a piece of mail in your Inbox—some junk mail from Sprint. You can practice on that if you've got it, and if you care to.

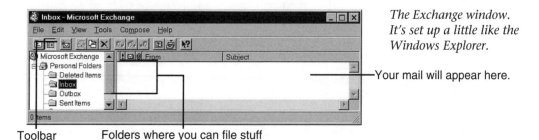

The Exchange window. It's set up a little like the Windows Explorer.

Your mail will appear here.

Toolbar   Folders where you can file stuff

You'll notice that Explorer's window looks vaguely familiar—it looks similar to the Windows Explorer. There's a toolbar with buttons that perform the most frequently used menu commands (we'll run through these in a moment). The pane on the right, the Folder List, shows your filing options and which file folder is open. The pane on the left shows you the contents of the selected folder. In the figure, the Inbox is open. This is where new e-mail lands.

Exchange's Toolbar

Since the toolbar is a speedy way of dealing with e-mail, let's take a look at the buttons here. That way you'll know what they are when you're called upon to use them. Some of them are already familiar to you from the BBS toolbars you saw in Chapter 10 and in the Windows Explorer.

Up 1 Level   The same as the Explorer's.

Show/Hide Folder List   Does just that.

New Message   Creates a new e-mail message.

Print   Prints open or selected message.

Move Item   Sends selected item to another folder (you can also just drag and drop to move stuff).

145

Delete   Deletes selected item.

Reply to Sender   Answers author of selected e-mail.

Reply to All   Answers to author and addressees of selected e-mail.

Forward   Sends a copy of letter to someone.

Address Book   Opens your Address Book.

Inbox   Opens your Inbox folder.

Help   Opens Microsoft Exchange Help when you click this and click an Exchange button.

The best way to get a handle on these tools is to write some mail, so let's do that.

I'm Gonna Sit Right Down and Write Myself a Letter

And you don't have to pretend it came from you; it does. To begin, click the **New Message** button. This opens the New Message window shown next. Look it over.

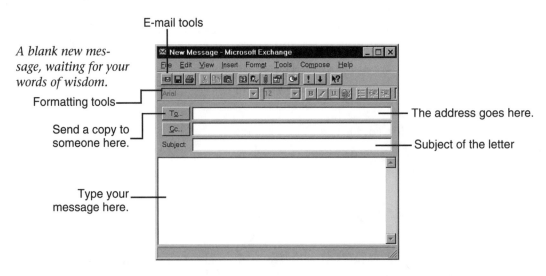

A blank new message, waiting for your words of wisdom.

Composing an e-mail message, in its simplest form, only takes a few simple steps:

---

1. Address it. Click in the **To** box and type the member ID of the person you want to get your mail. For this example, type your own member ID. (You thought that "write myself a letter" thing was a joke, didn't you?)

2. Carbon Copy? If you want to send someone a copy of your note, click in the **Cc** box and type their member ID. You can send e-mail without a Cc.

3. Slap a Subject on it. Click in the **Subject** box and type **This Is Only Test.** You don't have to type a Subject to send mail, but it's nice to let the recipient know what you're writing about.

4. Type your message. Click in the message box (the big one at the bottom of the screen). Type yourself a nice note. Say nice things about yourself.

5. Don't do this yet, but next you click **Send** (that's the button with the speeding envelope on it).

That's all there is to it. You've written your message and stored it for later delivery (if you're offline), or sent it (if you're online).

We'll complete the process and actually deliver your mail after we take a look at all of the tools at our disposal.

> **Check This Out...**
>
> **Quick Trick** If you're addressing e-mail to someone who's in your Address Book (covered later in this chapter), a click on the **To** or Cc boxes opens your Address Book. The window makes it easy to select one or more member IDs for both the **To** and Cc addresses. Check it out.

Techno Talk

Getting Fancy with E-Mail

If you want to get fancy with the mail you send, you can use the formatting buttons on the New Message toolbars. These should already be familiar to you because they're standard in most Windows word processors. (If they're unfamiliar to you, point at the buttons with your mouse, and their names pop up.)

The **Font** and **Font Size** buttons enable you to easily select a font and font size for your message text. The **Bold, Italic, Underline** buttons apply those styles to the selected text. The button with the painter's palette on it is the **Color** button; it colors selected text.

The remaining buttons are your paragraph formatting options; with these buttons you can add bullets, decrease and increase paragraph indentation, and align your text to the left, center, or right. To use them, select some text in your message (they don't work on the To, Cc, or Subject fields) and go click-crazy, applying one or more of these formatting options. Try them on for size; you can't hurt anything with them.

More Toolbar Buttons

The following buttons don't affect the appearance of your message, but they do enable you to fiddle with the contents of the message in some cool and convenient ways.

The first five buttons you've seen and used in most of your Windows applications, so I won't beat you about the head with them. They are (in order of appearance): **Send** (sends your message); **Save** (saves your message to disk); **Print** (prints a copy of your message); **Cut** (removes selected text to Clipboard); **Copy** (copies selected text to Clipboard); and **Paste** (places Clipboard contents in your message).

These buttons, however, are peculiar to e-mail and Exchange:

Address Book   Opens your Address Book.

Check Names   Compares the member IDs you enter to those in your personal Address Book entries. It makes sure you've entered the member IDs correctly and enables you to create a new entry.

Insert File   Places a saved file in your message.

Properties   Displays the message's properties.

Read Receipt   Requests or cancels the request for notification that you've read a message.

Importance High   Tells recipient your note is urgent.

Importance Low   Tells recipient your note is not urgent.

Help   Opens Exchange Help.

We'll use some of these in upcoming sections, but, because we're just starting out with a simple note, click the **Send** button.

Sending Mail

When you click Send, Exchange does a few things as a matter of course. First it checks the addressee's name in the To box to make sure you've entered it correctly, and then it checks the spelling in your message.

Check Names

When Exchange checks the addressee(s), it checks the member ID(s) against your personal Address Book. You're probably not listed in your own book, so you see a Check Names dialog box warning you: Microsoft Exchange does not recognize "Your Member ID."

In the Check Names dialog box, click **Create a new address for "Your Member ID"?** and then click **OK**.

The New Entry dialog box appears, asking you to specify what kind of entry you want to create. The Microsoft Network is already selected, so simply click **OK** again. This opens the New The Microsoft Network Member Properties dialog box, shown next. Click in the **Member ID** field and type your Member ID. Click in the **Name** field and type your name.

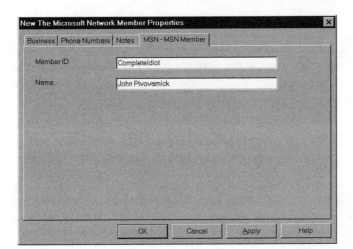

Adding a new member to your Address Book.

Click **OK**. This creates an entry for you in your personal Address Book. (Don't worry. I'll show you how to delete it later.)

More Info If You Want

The New The Microsoft Network Member Properties dialog box has several more tabs full of information you can supply about people in your Address Book. However, only the member ID and name are really necessary. The rest is purely optional.

If you know it, and want it stored here, you can click each tab in turn and type in the requested information. Click **OK** when you're done.

Check My Speeling

Next Exchange checks your spelling. If it finds something it doesn't like, it asks you about it with the Spelling dialog box shown next. It works the same as most word processor spelling checkers.

"Hiya" isn't a real word? Who knew?

Click on the **Ignore** button to skip the suspect word; click **Ignore All** to skip all occurrences of the word in the message. If the Spelling dialog box shows you a correct spelling (it doesn't always, as you can see in the preceding figure), click the correct spelling and click **Change** or **Change All**. If you spelled the word correctly to begin with, and it's just not in Exchange's vocabulary, click **Add** to add it to Exchange's dictionary.

Send Doesn't "Send" to MSN

> **Check This Out...**
>
> **Turn Off Spell Checking**
> I find the spelling check annoying for e-mail; don't ask me why. If you do too, and you want to turn off this feature, click **Options** on the Spelling dialog box. When the Options dialog box opens, click the **Always check spelling before sending** option, and spell checking stops.

After Exchange checks your spelling, it puts a little thermometer on the status bar at the bottom of the Exchange window that says Sending. Don't be fooled. It isn't sending your mail to the addressee; it's formatting your message for MSN and sending it to your Outbox for later delivery—*if* you're doing this offline, as suggested, that is. If you're online, it does send the message after formatting it.

If you click on the **Outbox** icon in the Folder List, you see the message. You can see mine in the next figure (I showed you mine, now you show me yours). The information under the To and Subject headings on the right side of the window are in italics to show you that you still need to deliver this mail. Let's do that now.

Mail, ready for delivery.

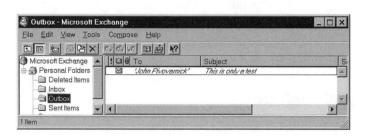

Special Delivery

To actually *deliver* this letter to yourself (if, again, you're doing this offline, as suggested), select **Deliver Now** from the Exchange's **Tools** menu. A couple of things happen:

1. A teeny-tiny window appears that says Checking for new messages. Exchange kills two birds with one stone whenever you send mail and picks up any mail that's waiting for you, too.

2. Your MSN Sign In screen appears. Enter your member ID and password and then click **Connect** to sign in.

3. Your letter disappears from your Outbox and goes two places: first, Exchange places a copy of the message in your Sent Items folder; then, Exchange places your note in your Inbox (you did, after all, send it to yourself).

4. To let you know you've gotten mail, your Inbox folder's name turns bold in the Folder List.

Mission accomplished! You can, if you care to, sign off from MSN now. (Or you can play around online. I don't care. Just come back here when you're done.)

Reading Your Mail

When you sign off from MSN, click on your **Inbox** folder in Exchange's Folder List. You see the mail you received neatly tucked inside. Its author's name and subject also appear in bold to indicate that you haven't read the message yet.

To read your new mail, double-click on it. Exchange opens the message in a window. At the top is your name after the From. Below that, the date it was sent. Your name also appears after the To. The Cc is blank, unless you decided to send a carbon copy to someone. Finally, the subject appears in a text box, and the message appears below that.

More of the Same

You can change the format and content of your message using the buttons in the toolbar, which should be very familiar to you by now. The only ones I haven't mentioned are:

The **Up Arrow**, which takes you to the previous message; the **Down Arrow**, which takes you to the next message; and finally, the **Help** button.

Getting Your Mail When You Sign In

If you don't happen to be sending any mail as described here, you can still retrieve it easily. Remember, I recommend starting Exchange *before* you sign in to MSN, because it saves you money in the long run, and I'm a cheap so-and-so.

When you sign in to MSN and there's mail waiting for you, you get a little message that says, "You have received new mail on The Microsoft Network. Open your inbox now?"

Click **Yes**, and Exchange springs to the front and shows you the mail you received. If Exchange isn't running, you have to wait for it to start up—at about four cents a minute. (Did I mention that I'm cheap?)

You can read and reply to your mail (but I recommend doing that offline—it's cheaper) and then proceed with your business online.

Answering Your Mail

To respond to your mail (this is generally speaking—I don't expect you to send yourself *another* piece of e-mail, unless you really want to), click the appropriate **Reply** button (**to Sender** or **to All**, depending on what you want to do). This opens a New Message dialog box just like the one you used to write the note, but with the To and Subject boxes already filled in for you. If you click **Reply to All**, the Cc box may be filled in as well.

All you have to do now is type your message in the message box. When you finish the message, click the **Send** button and proceed as described in the "Special Delivery" section.

Mailing Files, Addressing the Internet, and More Stuff

That takes care of basic e-mail sending, receiving, reading, and replying. If that's all you want to do right now, that's fine; you may want to skip ahead to "The Address Book" section. But be warned: there's lots *more* stuff you can do with mail, and the next few sections cover it.

Sending Files with E-Mail

If you want to share a story you've written or graphic you've created with an online friend, you can send it attached to a note. Here's how to do it:

1. Create and save the file.

2. Using Exchange, address e-mail to your friend's member ID.

3. You don't *have* to, but it is nice if you include a description of the file and the reason why you're sending it in the message box. It's the polite thing to do.

4. Click in the message box to place the cursor where you want the file to go.

5. Click the **Insert File** button (the one with the paper clip on it). This opens a standard Open File-type dialog box, only this one is called Insert File.

6. Navigate to the saved file you want to send. Click on it to select it.

7. Click **OK**. The selected file appears as a tidy little icon in your message that the addressee can then download and use.

About Those Insert as Options

At the lower right corner of the Insert File dialog, there's a box of options labeled Insert as. You should leave them alone (with **An attachment** marked) if you want to send the file "as is."

If you want to insert the contents of a text file into your message as *part* of the message, click **Text only**.

The Link attachment to original file doesn't work over MSN. That's an option for folks using Exchange on a network (in an office, maybe) where they can use an application on a remote computer as if it was on their own.

Send your mail as usual, and the attached file goes along for the ride.

Getting a File Attached to Mail

After you retrieve mail with an attached file, you want to use the file, right? In order to use it, you need to save the file to your hard drive. This detaches the file from the message.

Here's how to do it. With Exchange and the e-mail message open:

1. Select **Save As** from the File menu. This opens a Save As dialog like the one shown in the following figure.

2. Navigate to where you want to store the file on your hard drive.

3. Click **Save these Attachments only**.

4. Click **Save**.

You have to save a file attached to e-mail before you can use it.

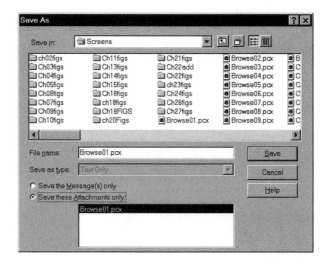

You can then open and use the file (with the appropriate application) just like any other file on your hard drive.

E-Mail to and from the Internet

If you have friends on the Internet or another online service (CompuServe, or America Online, maybe) and you want to write to them, you can. You just have to address your mail a little differently.

For example, if you want to send e-mail to me at my America Online account, you use this as the address in the To box:

piv@aol.com

This is what it means:

piv   That's my member ID (they call it a screen name on America Online).

@   Tells MSN's mail handling system that the mail is leaving MSN's computer.

aol.com   Tells MSN's computer (and any computers in between) that this mail is going to America Online. Technically, it's known as the *domain name*.

The process is the same for your friends on those other networks. If, for example, my friend Karen Razler, actress babe, sends me a note from America Online to my MSN account, she sends it addressed like this:

>   completeidiot@msn.com

The breakdown remains the same. If your friends want to send you e-mail from another service, make sure they address it:

>   yourmemberid@msn.com

It's important to note that there are no blank spaces or capital letters in an Internet e-mail address. Any dashes (—) need to be replaced with underline marks (_).

Internet e-mail addresses are tough to read and type, so be careful or your mail will come bouncing back to you as undeliverable—or worse, wind up in the e-mailbox of entirely the wrong person. It can happen.

Sending and Receiving Files to Internet Addresses

If you want to exchange files attached to the e-mail you're sending your Net pals, it means nothing different—for *you*. Count your blessings. You get to attach and send files as described above. When you receive files, you save and use them as described above, too.

Your friends, however, have to do a little work. When you send a file outside MSN's computers, any attached files are (get this) converted to text and inserted in the body of your message. This happens automatically; you don't have to do anything extra.

For the Internet addressee to use the file, however, they need to convert it back into a usable file form with an application called *uudecode*. It's available on MSN, most online services, and on the Internet.

To send you a file, that same Internet friend needs to turn the file into text (with the application *uuencode*) and insert that text into the e-mail message. When it hits your mailbox, MSN automatically converts it back into a usable file for you.

The upshot: it's no sweat if you want to share files with Internet pen pals, just make sure they know what they have to do to use the files you send (uudecode them), and what to do to send you usable files (uuencode them).

Remote Mail

Remote Mail is a particularly geeky option that some folks may not want to fool around with. In the name of completeness, I'm including brief coverage of it, just in case.

To save some time, and be a little picky about what mail you retrieve, launch Exchange offline. From the **Tools** menu, select **Remote Mail**. This opens a Remote Mail window.

With the Remote Mail window (and yes, *another* toolbar) you can briefly log on to MSN and see if there's mail waiting for you. You don't waste the time getting the mail itself; you just get the *header* information: the From, Subject, and Received date and time. You can then decide which mail you want to read, mark it for retrieval, and then tell Remote Mail to fetch only that mail for you. Pretty cool, a little teeny tiny bit intimidating, but very useful for e-mail junkies.

If you care to try it out, go ahead—it won't bite you. Read through the Exchange's online Help files (available on the Help menu) for detailed instructions.

The Address Book

Wait until you're connected to MSN before you tackle this section. You need to be online (with Exchange open) to look at the complete list of MSN members.

The Address Book is a very handy tool. You can use it to keep all the names and member IDs of people you know together in one easy place. You can also search through the listing of every last MSN member to look for friends, relatives, or even strangers with similar interests.

E-Mail Addresses You Can Use

There's another Address Book available, called E-mail Addresses You Can Use. It contains three addresses for MSN employees (the French Forum Manager, the MSN Editor, and MSN's Postmaster) if you feel the need to drop any of them a note.

While online, and with Exchange running, click the **Address Book** button. This opens an Address Book window like the one shown next, with the names from your personal Address Book showing. Unless you've been adding names behind my back, you only have one: your own. That isn't very exciting, so click on the **Show Names from the** drop-down list and select **Microsoft Network**. Names for days.

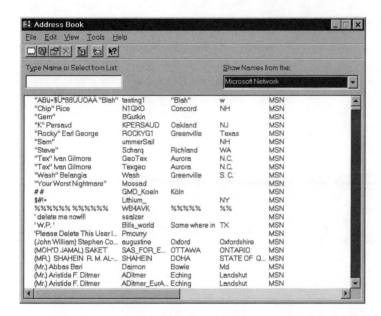

The names of every MSN user on the planet. Wow.

This is an alphabetical (by first name) listing of all the MSN members there are. Pretty intimidating. You can browse through it, looking for friends, but this is tedious and time consuming. You can use the toolbar tools to sift through them quickly.

(Oy! Stop with the buttons, already!)

 New Entry   Enables you to manually create a new personal Address Book entry. The process is the same as described in the "Check Names" section earlier.

 Find   Searches the Address Book for members that meet your search criteria (more on that in a moment).

 Properties   Displays the properties of the selected name. Online, that's the member properties, offline, it's the additional personal information you may have entered in your personal Address Book.

 Delete   Deletes the selected entry from your personal Address Book—you can't use it with the complete MSN list.

 Add To Personal Address Book   Adds the selected name to your personal Address Book.

 New Message   Opens a new message form, so you can write e-mail.

 Help   Opens online Help.

157

I'm Trying to Find Myself

You can winnow out unwanted member names from the MSN list by using the Find button. For example, I wanted to find all of the MSN members who listed "writer" as their profession.

This is what to do:

1. Click the **Find** button. This opens the Find dialog box (which is a blank MSN Member Properties display).

The Address Book's Find dialog box.

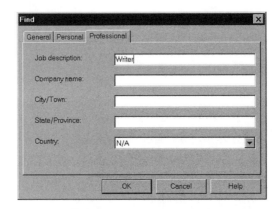

2. Click the **Professional** tab.

3. Enter **Writer** in the Job Description field.

4. Click **OK**.

MSN thinks about it for a minute and then shows you a list of all the MSN members who have the word "writer" in their job description. I scrolled through the list until I found myself and then clicked on my name to select it. Then I clicked the **Properties** button. What I turned up is shown next.

You Can Search for Anything

The Find dialog has three tabs with a total of 16 different fields. You can search by any or all of these fields, just enter the appropriate word or phrase in the field(s). To find yourself, enter your name in the First name and Last name fields and click **OK**. When you find yourself, click the **Properties** button. You can then read and change your own member properties display. Enter only the information you want to share with the world. The rest is optional. Naturally, you can't change someone else's properties. MSN doesn't let you, so don't even try it.

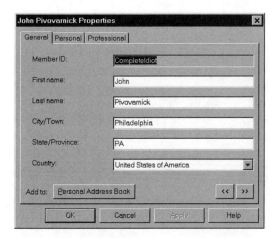

These are my properties—and here I thought it meant real estate.

Adding Your Finds to Your Address Book

If you turn up the names of friends in your search, you can add them to your Address Book easy as pie. Just click on your friend's name in the Search Results list and click the **Add To Personal Address Book** button.

Offline, you can add friends to your personal Address Book, too, but you need to know their real name and member ID.

Click the **New Entry** button. In the dialog box that pops up, click **The Microsoft Network Member** and click **OK**. Enter your friend's name and member ID in the text boxes on the New Member Screen (you saw this one earlier in the "Check Names" section above). You can also add any additional information you have on the other information tabs, but this information isn't required. When you finish, click **OK**.

To add an Internet friend to your Address Book, the process is the same, with minor variations (it does help if you've read the section "E-Mail to and from the Internet" earlier in the chapter):

1. Click the **New Entry** button. In the dialog, click **Internet over The Microsoft Network** and click **OK**. This opens the next dialog box.

2. In the E-mail address box, enter your friend's e-mail address. For me, it's **piv**.

3. In the Domain name box, enter the domain portion of your friend's e-mail address. For me, and other America Online users, it is: **aol.com**.

4. Enter your friend's real name in the Name box. You can enter any additional information in the appropriate tabs. When you're done, click **OK**.

159

Adding an Internet address to your Address Book.

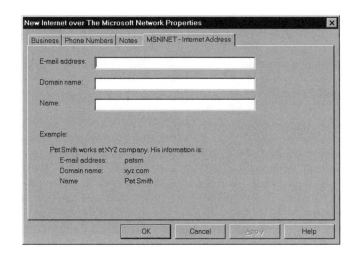

When you address e-mail to your Internet friends using your Address Book, you don't have to deal with entering addresses like whoever@whatever.com. The Address Book assembles the address for you from the information you just entered.

The Least You Need to Know

Man, that Exchange does a lot of stuff! I don't expect you to memorize any of it, really. The parts you use will become second nature to you with a little experience. The important points to remember are:

➤ You save money if you launch Exchange before you sign in to MSN.

➤ You also save money if you compose, read, and reply to your e-mail offline.

Chapter 13

Talking the Talk Online

In This Chapter

➤ Finding places to chat

➤ How chat rooms work

➤ Getting the scoop on other chatters

➤ Wink ;), wink ;)

Of all the things to do online, chatting is one of the more pleasant and, perhaps, the most sociable. Where else, save for a soiree at the United Nations, can you find people from all around the world, gathered peacefully in one place, sharing the news and views from their little corner of the world?

If you're about to take the plunge into the world of online chat, I suggest you read this chapter *before* you sign in to MSN—that way there won't be any surprises. Online, later, you can refer back to this chapter if you get puzzled by the goings-on.

Chat Is...

In case you were wondering, online chat is the same as chatting face-to-face or by phone, except with a couple of computers and a few more miles between the chatters.

When you chat, you *type* your part of the conversation. Your computer sends the message to the MSN computer, and the MSN computer shoots it out to all the other members in your chat room. The other members then read what you've "said" and respond.

All this happens so quickly that there's usually no noticeable delay between when you hit the Enter key and when your statement appears on the other member's screen. That's why it's sometimes referred to as *real-time* chatting.

Unreal Time Stuff

This has nothing to do with "The Twilight Zone" or time warps, or even Stephen Hawking and the effects of traveling faster than the speed of light.

Online, some things just don't happen in real time. These are exchanges where there's a delay between the time you send a message and when the recipient responds. E-mail, BBS postings, and regular postal mail are all examples of conversations that don't happen real-time.

To participate in online chat, you need to find a chat room—but that's not a problem because there are chat rooms all over the place. You may remember, when you looked at forums and how they work back in Chapter 10, that I pointed out how most forums have their own chat areas, sometimes two or more.

The first sort of chat room is where forum visitors (about 30 or so) gather to discuss the topic at hand, thrash out new ideas, or just get to know each other. The other kind are the event rooms where hundreds of MSN members congregate to meet a special online guest. Both kinds of chat rooms are usually moderated by a host who keeps the conversations civil and (if there's a specific topic being discussed) on track.

There are also smaller clutches of chat rooms scattered around where two or more members can meet in privacy for some unmoderated chat. Unmoderated means there's no host around, so folks can say pretty much whatever they want to whomever they want. Talk can get fairly adult in nature, and so unmoderated rooms carry a Mature Audiences (MA) rating.

If You've Got Concerns...

If you have concerns about your children and the adult nature of unmoderated chat rooms, you might want to check out Chapter 22, "Kids and MSN."

If you're concerned that you don't know how to behave in public chat areas online (I'm like that—you can dress me up, but you can't take me out), you may want to check out Chapter 8, "Aunt Effie's Guide To Online Etiquette."

Finding Chat Rooms: Looking for Chat in all the Right Places...

As with all things online, there are a couple of ways to find chat rooms, depending on the sort of chat you want to have.

Chat on a Particular Subject

Say you're a world-class collector of, oh, blue glass. You want to compare notes with other collectors. Where to go?

You may want to try tracking down a chat room in the Interests, Leisure, & Hobbies Category. Likewise, if your interest is in sports, try Sports & Recreation.

The point is this: if there's a forum you visit regularly because you're interested in its subject matter, check out the associated chat room(s). You're bound to find somebody that shares your interest.

Chat for Chat's Sake

If you're just looking for conversation and company, with no other expectations, check out Chat World (Go word: CHATWORLD). You see it in the following figure.

As the name suggests, it's a category devoted to chatting. Like any category, there's a library (Lobby Photo & Audio Gallery), an Information Kiosk, and a BBS (Chat World Front Desk), all of which you can also visit. The rest of the category is chat rooms, nothing but chat rooms, and each set operates on a different theme.

If you're just looking for company and general chat, check out the Chat World Lobby. It's the room where some folks meet before they break off into groups to use the smaller rooms, like those discussed below.

First there was "Westworld," then "Futureworld," now there's "Chat World."

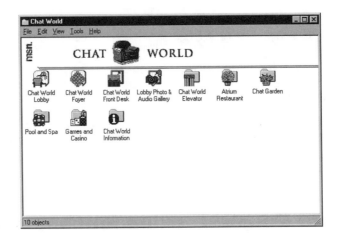

Chatting for Two (or More)

If you already have one or more buddies lined up for a chat, you may want to check in to one of Chat World's theme areas. The Chat Garden (shown here) has a (*duh*) garden theme.

"I went to a garden party to reminisce with my old friends..."

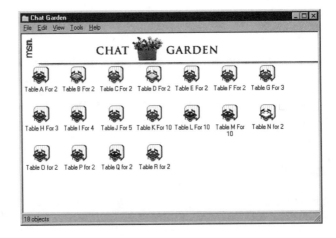

Imagine a picturesque garden, arranged so there are private little corners set with tables and chairs where you can have a secluded rendezvous, and you've got the idea of the Chat Garden. As you can see in the figure (well, maybe if you scrunch up your eyes or use a magnifier), the chat rooms come in assorted sizes for two to ten chatters.

You, and a select group of online friends, can congregate in a private room to discuss whatever you care to discuss, without the distraction of other MSN users barging in—as long as you fill the room to capacity.

Use the Find Command

You can use Find to locate more chat rooms, too. You've already used the Find command back in Chapters 10 and 11, so I won't beat it to death again here. Check out those chapters for the details on using the Find command.

When entering your search information, you can enter a word or phrase that describes the subject in which you're interested in the Containing text box. Then select **Chat Rooms** from the **Of type** drop-down menu.

> **More Rooms**
> The rooms you find online are all the rooms there are. Unlike some online services, you can't create your own on MSN—but don't panic, there's plenty to go around.

Check This Out...

When Find turns up chat rooms that match your entry in the Containing text box, you can go to a room by double-clicking its entry in the list box at the bottom of the Find dialog box. Find doesn't guarantee that there's anyone *in* the room, but now you know where it is, and you can check it on a regular basis.

Techno Talk

How To Be in Two Places at Once

If you want to keep an eye on an interesting, but empty chat room, you can watch for others to enter and still do other things online. To do this, however, you need to have your options set so MSN opens a new window for every folder you open online. Chapter 7 tells you how.

With your options set, you can open a chat room window, minimize it, and go anywhere else online. Just maximize the chat room window every now and then to make sure you aren't snubbing a recent arrival who's trying to talk to you.

Are You a Spectator or Participant?

If you want to chat, you have to go into a chat room; that much should be apparent by now. What may not be so obvious is that with *some* chat rooms, you have a decision to make before you even enter.

This Doesn't Apply to Regular Chat Rooms

The information in this Spectator/Participant section doesn't apply to garden-variety chat rooms like those in Chat World. This only applies to the special event auditoriums, like the one in the Alien Encounters & UFOs Forum (shown here), or the Altair Pavilion, and the other huge meeting rooms online.

Even though the big special event-type auditoriums are exactly the same as their small-scale cousins, there is one difference: you can either watch the special event as a *spectator*, or you can take part in it as a *participant*.

As you may have guessed from the names, a spectator can only *watch* an online event happening on his or her screen. A participant can actually ask questions and, well, *participate*.

This is the Special Events Auditorium for the Alien Encounters & UFOs Forum.

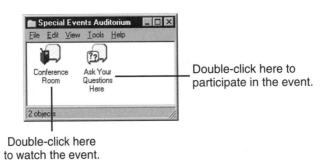

Double-click here to participate in the event.

Double-click here to watch the event.

When you've decided on which role you want to take, entering is a simple affair: just double-click the appropriate chat room icon: in the previous figure, you'd double-click **Conference Room** to be a spectator, or **Ask Your Questions Here** to participate.

Okay! Okay! So One Thing Applies to Regular Chat Rooms, Too. So Sue Me.

You enter *any* chat room online the same way: double-click the chat room's icon to enter.

When you double-click a chat room icon, you get a little message from MSN that says: "Chat is starting. Please wait...." In a moment or two, the chat window appears. There's one shown in the figure in the next section.

Anatomy of a Chat Room

Just about every chat room you enter online looks like the one shown here. Let's look at the main parts.

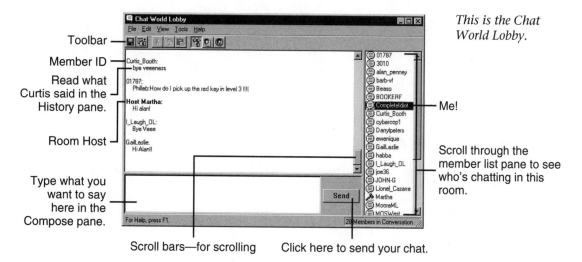

This is the Chat World Lobby.

Toolbar

Member ID

Read what Curtis said in the History pane.

Room Host

Type what you want to say here in the Compose pane.

Me!

Scroll through the member list pane to see who's chatting in this room.

Scroll bars—for scrolling   Click here to send your chat.

What a Pane!

Who knew? Somebody at Microsoft has a sense of humor! The major portions of the chat window are all referred to as "panes." Window. Pane. Windowpane. Get it?

The large text display (the one that shows the actual chat) is called the History pane. This is where you read what's being said (preceded by the member ID of the person saying it). It's called the History pane because it keeps the record (or history) of everything everyone has said in the room from the moment you enter. You probably won't do anything more than read what's in this pane, although you can copy any or all of the chat and paste it into a word processing document, if you care to.

You can also save the history (if this is an especially memorable chat or special event) so you can relive it later. I'll tell you how in a moment or two.

Below that is the Compose pane. This is where you type your contribution to the conversation. You click in the Compose pane to place your cursor there and then type what you

167

want to say. When you're done (or you run out of space—it can happen if you're long-winded), click **Send**, and MSN sends your message to all of the members in the room—it also appears in the History pane.

Finally, to the right, there is the vertical list of members who are in the room with you. This is the Member List pane.

Depending on how you set your chat options (coming up shortly), this list automatically changes as members enter and leave the room. You can also see how many folks are engaged in the chat by looking at the status bar just below it. In the figure, it says "28 Members in Conversation." That, too, changes as members enter and exit.

The Toolbar

As with many of the windows you interact with online (and here I'm thinking of e-mail, BBS, and file library windows), there is a set of buttons you can use to facilitate your chatting. They duplicate the chat functions from the chat window's menus.

In order of appearance, they are:

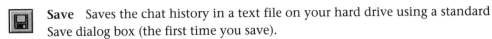 **Save** Saves the chat history in a text file on your hard drive using a standard Save dialog box (the first time you save).

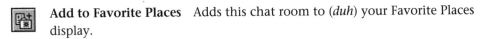 **Add to Favorite Places** Adds this chat room to (*duh*) your Favorite Places display.

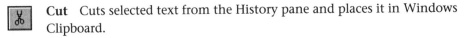 **Cut** Cuts selected text from the History pane and places it in Windows Clipboard.

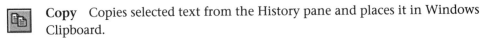 **Copy** Copies selected text from the History pane and places it in Windows Clipboard.

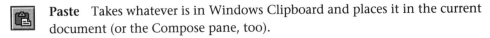 **Paste** Takes whatever is in Windows Clipboard and places it in the current document (or the Compose pane, too).

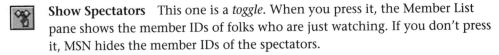 **Show Spectators** This one is a *toggle*. When you press it, the Member List pane shows the member IDs of folks who are just watching. If you don't press it, MSN hides the member IDs of the spectators.

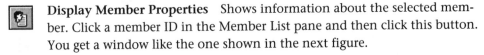 **Display Member Properties** Shows information about the selected member. Click a member ID in the Member List pane and then click this button. You get a window like the one shown in the next figure.

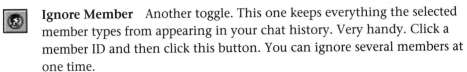 **Ignore Member** Another toggle. This one keeps everything the selected member types from appearing in your chat history. Very handy. Click a member ID and then click this button. You can ignore several members at one time.

Click these tabs for more information.

Member properties	? ✕

General | Personal | Professional

Member ID: `Completeldiot`

First name: `John`

Last name: `Pivovarnick`

City/Town: `Philadelphia`

State/Province: `PA`

Country: `United States of America`

OK | Cancel

My member properties.

Click here to close.

Create or Change Your Own Member Properties

If you missed it, I explained how to see, create, or change your own member properties back in Chapter 12. For some reason, it's done with Microsoft Exchange and MSN's Address Book. Go figure.

You can also edit your information in Member Assistance. See Chapter 23.

Spot the Room Host

When you're in a moderated chat room, there are a couple of ways to tell who's playing host(ess) with the most(est).

A host is generally the first one to say "Howdy" to you when you enter a room. A host's member ID, when she speaks, is the only one to appear in boldface type in the chat. If you look *waaayyyy* back at the figure showing the chat room, you see that Host Martha is the only member ID in bold type.

Finally, in the Member List pane, you see three kinds of icons in front of member names:

Show and No Show The Show Spectators toggle button only works in special event-type rooms where there are spectators and participants. In regular chat rooms, it does nothing, *bubkes*—less than zero.

 The dialog balloon indicates that I'm a participant in this conversation.

 The gavel indicates that this is a chat room host, or moderator.

The third is one you only see in special event-type rooms, and it's the same as the one shown on the Show Spectators button earlier (I *think* it's supposed to be a pair of opera glasses). Member IDs with that icon in front are spectators. You only see these when you press the Show Spectators button.

Getting Down to Chatting

Techno Talk

Toggle A button or command that does one thing when you select it the first time and then does the exact opposite when you select it again. Think of it like a light switch: push once, the light's on; push again, it's off.

When you first pop into a chat room, it may not look like much is happening. Give it a second—it can take a moment or two before the other members' chat appears on your screen. When it does, the other members' chat scrolls by in the History pane. It can (if the room is busy) scroll past faster than you can read.

Don't panic. When stuff starts moving up and out of sight, scroll bars appear, so you can go back at your leisure and read the chat you missed.

Take another moment to read what the members are saying to get an idea of the topic of conversation, the tone (serious, or not), before you dive in.

To enter the conversation, click in the Compose pane. This puts the cursor there. Then, type what you want to say and click **Send**. Shortly, your bit of chat appears in the History pane, in the order that MSN's computers received it.

Techno Talk

A Window Is a Window Is a Window

The chat window is just like any other window you've ever used: it has minimize, maximize, and close buttons; you can resize it by clicking the sides and corners and then dragging them. You can also resize the individual "panes," as Microsoft calls them, by click-dragging the dividers between them. Try it out.

Give folks a chance to read and respond to you, speak when spoken to, be polite and pleasant, and you'll be up to your hips in conversation (better get out your hip boots).

The Finer Points of Chat

That's really about all you need to know to get started chatting online; however, you may run into a few oddities—well, they're odd until you get used to them—and it would be uncivilized of me to let you go exploring without filling you in.

When you talk face-to-face, in addition to spoken words, you pick up a lot of information from the

Techno Talk

Scroll When too much stuff (whether that's chat, or icons, or anything) appears in a window for you to see it all at once, scroll bars appear at the right side, and sometimes across the bottom, of the window. You can use the scroll bars (indicated in the Chat World Lobby figure) to move backwards and forwards (and side to side, if appropriate) to see the hidden bits.

other person's face, the tone of their voice, and their body language. When chatting online, you don't get that, because you can't see the other people. To compensate, online chatters have come up with a series of shorthands that can help get your intent across.

Let a Smiley Be Your Umbrella

Now and then, in the course of a chat, you'll see something like this scroll across your History pane:

CompleteIdiot:

Hiya, everybody! ;)

The "CompleteIdiot" part is my member ID. The "Hiya, everybody!" is a general greeting to the room. The real mystery item here is the errant punctuation:

;)

Actually, it isn't errant. If you tilt your head to the left and look at it, you see it bears a striking resemblance to a face that's winking and smiling at the same time. That's a smiley. You can use them to show facial expressions when you're online.

Typically, smileys are made of punctuation keys, but you can use other keys. Here are some standard smileys:

:)	=	Your basic smiling face
:-)	=	Your basic smiling face, with optional nose attachment
B)	=	A face with glasses
O:)	=	I'm an angel (with a halo and everything)
}:>	=	I'm a devil
:*	=	A kiss
:(	=	A frown
:|	=	I am not amused
:P	=	A *thhppptt*, a raspberry, a Bronx cheer, a soggy salute...you get the idea
:x	=	My lips are sealed

Some folks come up with smileys that look like themselves. For example, mine looks something like:

{B{)>

It represents my receding hairline, glasses, mustache, smile, and beard.

Go nuts with smileys. You'll be amazed how many different faces you can make with the keys on your keyboard.

Special Effects

Similar to smileys, but without the faces, are another set of symbols used in chat rooms:

@—>—	=	A rose
c[]	=	A mug (as in beer or coffee)
———[}	=	A pie being thrown
{]———	=	A pie being thrown the other way

These are nice for a bit, but they get old in a hurry (for me, at least). Use with restraint, or someone will set the Too Cute Patrol on you.

Abbreviations Save Typing (IMNSHO)

Since everyone online pays for the time they spend in chat rooms, users have developed a series of standard abbreviations to save themselves some typing. For example, if someone says something excruciatingly funny online, you may see a series of LOLs scrolling across your screen. LOL means Laughing Out Loud. Other abbreviations include:

ROFL	=	Rolling On the Floor, Laughing
GMTA	=	Great Minds Think Alike
IMHO	=	In My Humble Opinion
IMNSHO	=	In My Not So Humble Opinion

Those who can't figure out how to make a decent smiley can also use:

<g>	=	Grin
<G>	=	Big grin

When in Doubt, Ask

If you're in a chat room and someone uses a smiley you don't get, or an abbreviation you can't figure out, just ask. For example, if you see me say:

CompleteIdiot:

That's what I think will fix the economy, IMNSHO.

But you don't get it, type something like this:

Complete: IMNSHO??

Naturally, when it appears on-screen, your member ID precedes it. The Complete: tells folks in the room that you're directing the question to me. The IMNSHO?? says, "What the heck does this mean??" As soon as it appears on-screen, nice folks will explain the shorthand to you—because shorthands aren't useful if nobody knows what they mean.

Room Protocols: Raise Your Hand to Speak

In some moderated rooms, including special event rooms, where there is a particular topic, or a guest speaker, everyone can't babble away at the same time. It muddies the discussion. In these situations, hosts use a *protocol* to keep things moving along without confusion. You needn't worry about the different variations, or even memorize what to do. The host explains the protocol she uses to everyone.

However, you should know that most protocols require that you "raise your hand," so to speak, before you actually speak. If you have a question, you may need to send a question mark (?) before you ask it. Before you make a comment, you may need to send an exclamation point (!).

After you send the appropriate punctuation, you can type your question or comment in the Compose pane, but don't send it. The host then keeps track of who wants to speak, and in what order. She says something like, "Now we have a comment from SO_&_SO, then a question from CompleteIdiot. Go ahead SO_&_SO."

SO_&_SO asks her question, and, at the end, types **end** so everyone knows she's done. The guest or principle speaker answers (also ending with the word **end**) and then the host asks for CompleteIdiot's comment. Only when the host asks for your comment (and only then) do you click **Send**.

Protocols keep crowds of participants from trampling all over the guest speaker so everybody gets a chance to comment or ask questions.

The Least You Need to Know

Chat can take up a serious amount of your online time each month. It's easy, it's sociable, and it's good clean fun. Keep these thoughts in mind when you sign on to chat for the first time.

➤ Chat rooms are all over MSN; you can find them in most forums and in the Chat World category.

➤ In special event-type rooms, you can either be a participant or a spectator.

➤ To chat, you need to enter a chat room.

➤ The History pane shows everything the chatters have said since you entered the room.

➤ The Member List pane shows everyone who's in the room with you.

➤ You use the Compose pane to write what you want to say in the conversation. Click the **Send** button to send it to MSN.

➤ You can use the toolbar to ignore unruly chatters (Ignore Member button), or get more information about intriguing chatters (Display Member Properties button).

➤ Chat is fun, and contains no fat, no calories, and no cholesterol. It tastes good, too.

News You Can Use

I don't know about you, but I've given up watching television news—well, except for CNN and the "Today Show" (that Katie Couric is so perky). I don't quite know when it happened, but somewhere along the line, TV news turned from an "information" medium into an "info-tainment" medium, with as much emphasis on the entertainment as on the information. It's a pet peeve of mine, and I just don't watch anymore.

Instead, if I hear about an intriguing world event (say, the outbreak of Ebola virus in Zaire, or something just as cheerful), I sign in to MSN and check out the news sources there. Even though some of these news sources are television network sources (like NBC News), I skip the stuff I'm not interested in and zero in on the stuff I want to know—that's the beauty of it. It really *is* news you can use.

There are two sorts of news available online: news about MSN, and world news hot off the wire from some heavyweight sources.

What's the Buzz Online?

To find out what's happening *online*, you need to *be* online (naturally). Sign in to MSN and, when MSN Central appears, click **MSN Today.** This opens the MSN Today screen shown in the following figure.

MSN Today: All the news that fits.

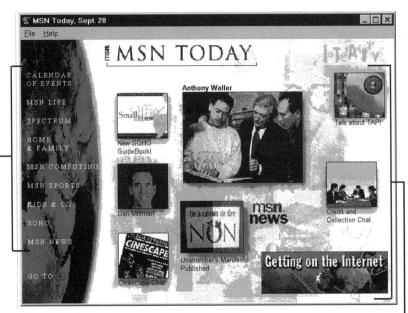

Click these titles to view more MSN news bytes.

Click these pictures for information on these events.

You looked at MSN Today back in Chapter 6 as a way of finding out what's new online today. You hopefully recall that clicking on one of the photographs opens a short description of the event with details about the time and place, and even a shortcut that takes you to the relevant forum or auditorium online. But wait, there's more!

Down the left-hand side of the MSN Today window, there's a list of nine *other* sources of news about areas and events online. If there's one that tickles your fancy, click on the title to view the display.

The titles are, in order of appearance:

Calendar of Events   Gives you a (duh) calendar of online events, featuring one event—click a date for a complete list of the day's scheduled events.

MSN Life   An online news magazine that features member interviews, advice on using MSN, and points out fun forums and other things to do.

Spectrum   Gives you news about a cross section (a spectrum, if you will) of forums and features online, with points of interest for each.

Home and Family   Tips and suggestions for making a home life for yourself and your family in the information age.

MSN Computing   News and online events for the computer addict in your life.

MSN Sports   Highlights of the sporting news and events online (more about that in a minute).

Kids & Co.   Features news, interviews, and online events of interest to the younger crowd (and the young at heart).

SOHO   Not the artsy section of New York City, but news and features of interest to folks who work in a Small Office or Home Office.

MSN News   Highlights from the world's news and related online events (more about that in a minute, too).

Using the News

When you click on a title at the left of the MSN Today screen, you open a display like the one for MSN Life shown here.

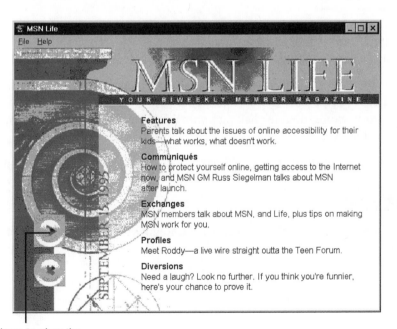

MSN Life: The biweekly member magazine.

Click here to view the
articles sequentially.

Even though each display has an individual look, they all operate much the same way. You can click on a listing to view the related article, or you can click on the right-pointing arrow to move to the next page and read everything in order.

Once you get to the second page, the controls (on the left side of the screen) change slightly. You can see what I mean in the next figure.

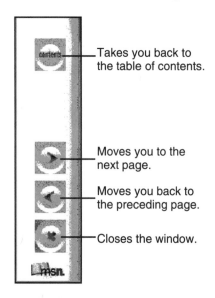

Takes you back to the table of contents.

Moves you to the next page.

Moves you back to the preceding page.

Closes the window.

The buttons look different in each of these feature areas, but all the buttons are positioned, and function, exactly the same.

Articles online are as interesting as any you've read in a paper magazine, plus there's the bonus of shortcuts that take you right to the featured area online. For example, in an article about online sports scores, double-clicking a shortcut takes you to MSN Sports in the News & Weather category.

News & Weather is where most of the real-world news is available, so let's go there now.

News of the World

To get to News & Weather (shown here), you can click **Categories** on **MSN Central**, or you can use the Go word: NEWS.

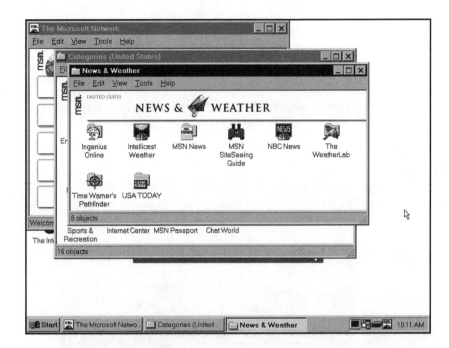

A news junkie's idea of heaven: The News & Weather Category.

News & Weather, right now, contains seven forums (and an MSN SiteSeeing Guide) that are all news or weather related. Here's a quick peek at each:

Ingenius Online

Aimed at younger folks, Ingenius Online (Go word: INGENIUS) is a joint venture of Telecommunications, Inc. and Reuters NewMedia. Reuters, you may know, is a worldwide news service that provides news to many newspapers, magazines, and television stations around the world. As a news source, they're top notch. As a name, "Reuters" is hard to pronounce: it's *Roy-ters* not *Root-ters*.

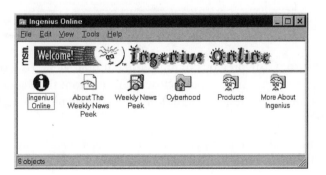

News and learning products for kids.

179

The main feature here is the Weekly News Peek, which looks at the six top international news stories of the day from a kid's point of view. It's a scaled-down version of Ingenius's What On Earth multimedia news daily for kids (which you can order in the Products folder).

You can also visit the Cyberhood (think "neighborhood," not computer criminal). Here you can join conversations about world events, educational techniques, and fun MSN and World Wide Web sites.

Intellicast Weather

Intellicast Weather (Go word: INTELLICAST), shown here, gives you access to national, regional, and (by the time you read this) even city weather maps and forecasts.

National weather information straight from NBC News.

The weather map shown in the previous figure is the national view. To look at a regional view, click on the region you want to take a closer look at. From the regional view, you'll soon be able to click on a city and get a map of the weather patterns affecting your home town (or one nearby).

In the lower-left corner, there are icons you can click to see (in addition to the forecast map) the day's satellite map, radar map, and UV (ultraviolet radiation) map.

It's more fun than the Weather Channel, and you don't have to sit around for ten minutes waiting for your local forecast (but you don't get to hear Vivaldi's *Four Seasons* either).

MSN News

MSN News (Go word: MSNNEWS), shown next, is designed to look like a daily paper. You can click a headline to read the associated story, or click one of the section headings (Business, World, and Sports) at the top of the screen to jump to the contents of those sections.

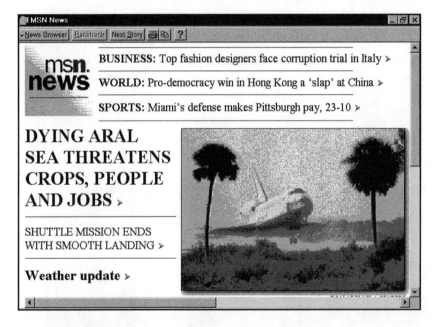

MSN News is designed like a newspaper—a newspaper you can click.

The First Time You Access MSN News...

Be prepared for a slight delay. In order to view MSN News, MSN downloads a News Browser application to your computer; this takes from two to five minutes depending on your modem and PC speeds. It's a one-time only thing.

You can also use the buttons in the toolbar to navigate through the news:

➤ The **News Browser** button enables you to select main news topics.

➤ The **Backtrack** button takes you back to stories you've seen.

➤ The **Next Story** button moves you to the next news story (aren't you glad I'm here explaining this highly technical material?).

➤ The **Print** button (the one with the printer on it) enables you to send the story you're reading to your printer, so you can read it later, on paper.

➤ The **Copy** button (the one with two sheets of paper on it) enables you to copy selected information from the article you're reading. You can then paste it into, say, a word processing document which you can store on disk for later use. That's really handy if you're a student who's writing a report on current events.

➤ The **Help** button (the one with the question mark on it) gives you help with the News Browser.

Like a daily newspaper, the stories change, well, *daily*. You can keep current with world events, and you don't have to shlepp to the recycling center when you're done.

NBC News

Like NBC Intellicast seen earlier, NBC News (Go word: NBCNEWS), shown next, gives you access to the day's top stories through its SuperNet service.

NBC News at your disposal—Hey, where's Tom Brokaw?

NBC and the Associated Press (another news service, like Reuters, with a solid reputation) brings the news in direct.

You can click highlighted (boldface or colored) text to view the related news story. You can also sneak in and see other stuff available on the SuperNet, by clicking items in the bar *above* the news page (the latest, in focus, decision '96, and so on), or by clicking the word buttons at the *bottom* of the screen (TV shows, news, sports, and hyperchannels, which, I'm guessing, are channels that can't sit still).

The WeatherLab

The WeatherLab Forum (Go word: THEWEATHERLAB), shown here, has more weather information than you can possibly use—unless you're a meteorologist, yourself.

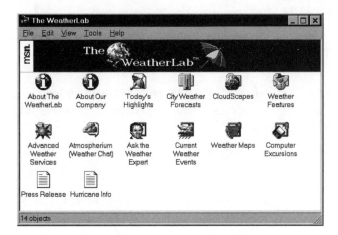

More weather information than a human being actually needs.

You can get weather forecasts for over 600 U.S. and international cities (City Weather Forecasts), weather maps (Weather Maps) for all the continents (unless it's raining, then they're incontinents), and even post your own questions for a meteorologist to answer (Ask the Weather Expert).

This one's gobs of fun, kids (of all ages), if you (like me) are nuts for weather.

Why, when I was a kid, my grandmother used to work at an airport. I used to beg her to bring home the control tower's day-old weather maps so I could study them. I won't babble too much about it, but suffice it to say, I can spot a cumulostratus cloud a mile away, and I actually know what millibars and isobars are (even if I can't quite remember how to spell them). Check it out.

Time Warner's Pathfinder

Communications giant Time Warner (publisher of *Time* and *Sports Illustrated*, among other magazine favorites—and home of Judy, the Time-Life operator), gives you access to half a dozen publications in Time Warner's Pathfinder (shown next—there's no Go word for this one yet).

The Pathfinder gives you access to Time Warner publications via the World Wide Web.

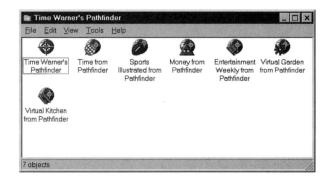

Like the NBC News areas you looked at, Time Warner's Pathfinder isn't an actual MSN forum; instead, it's a collection of access points for getting at its World Wide Web site. That means a couple of things for you:

1. You need to have Microsoft's Internet Tools or version 1.05 of the MSN software.

2. You need to read Chapter 20 to find out where to get them.

3. You also need to read Chapter 20 to find out what the World Wide Web is and how to use the Internet Explorer (that's part of the Internet Tools and MSN 1.05).

Go do that now and then come back here. I'll wait.

Back? Good.

The Websites you can access include:

Time Warner's Pathfinder (shown in the next figure) which gives you access to all of the following (or you can double-click the icon for the one you want to skip the main Pathfinder).

Time from Pathfinder takes you to the online version of *Time* magazine. Sports Illustrated from Pathfinder takes you to the online version of *Sports Illustrated*. (Are you getting the idea here?)

Money from Pathfinder takes you to the online version of *Money* magazine. Entertainment Weekly from Pathfinder takes you to the online version of *Entertainment Weekly* magazine. (Are you sure you don't get this yet?)

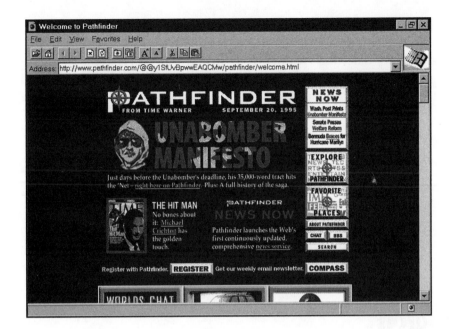

Time Warner's Pathfinder.

There's also Virtual Garden from Pathfinder and Virtual Kitchen from Pathfinder that take you to a gardening and a cooking magazine, respectively.

It's a great way to explore the World Wide Web, and there's no sales rep calling to get you to subscribe—they can't anyway: your modem's got your phone tied up.

USA Today

Like the Time Warner area in the last section, *USA Today* (shown next, also Go-word-less at this time) is available only with Microsoft's Internet Tools or MSN version 1.05 or later (see Chapter 20).

USA Today, available from the World Wide Web.

185

You can read the paper online, just as you would over coffee in your breakfast nook. Start with the USA Today Front Page, and use the Internet Explorer to view each of the usual sections: News, Sports, Money, Life, and Weather. You can also send letters to the editor with USA Today Feedback; get sports scores as they happen with USA Today Real Time Scores; look at the news photos with USA Today Snapshot; and even do the USA Today Crossword.

Software Warning for Crossword Addicts!

In order to view and do the *USA Today* Crossword Puzzle, you need to download a *puzzle browser* and configure your Internet Explorer to use it.

To download the puzzle browser, click **puzzle browser** on the Crossword Web page. That takes you to an instructional Web page that tells you what to download and how to set your Internet Explorer software so you can do the puzzles.

Other News Sources

In addition to the news sources covered here, you'll frequently find news BBSs and folders in many of the other forums online.

Forum news sources can offer access to the news services you've seen here; some forums even have news provided by the managers and members of that particular forum. The only way to tell is to check out the News folder or BBS in your favorite forums.

The Least You Need to Know

The least you need to know is that you can be an MSN freak and still keep in touch with the real world. You can often find up-to-the-minute news online, as it happens, instead of waiting for your favorite news broadcast.

The important things to remember from this chapter are:

➤ NBC News and Intellicast Weather are not part of MSN, but actually part of NBC's SuperNet service. However, you don't need any additional software to use either.

➤ Time Warner's Pathfinder and *USA Today* are both Websites located on the Internet. You need MSN version 1.05 or Microsoft's Internet Tools to use them. Chapter 20 gives you the details on acquiring and using them.

➤ No news is no longer good news.

OOOOOH...

Educational Programming

Students come in all shapes and sizes—I know, I worked on high school and college campuses for *years* (don't ask how many, I won't tell).

In spite of the variety in age, shape, and size, students all have a few things in common:

➤ A burning desire to learn

➤ They sometimes need support and guidance while making decisions about their education.

➤ A deep-seated need to avoid homework at all costs

That last one you can't really avoid, but there are resources out there to shorten the process. Likewise, there are tools available to help students make some of those tough education decisions.

In this chapter we'll look at the resources that are available for students (and educators, too) on MSN. First stop:

Education & Reference

All of MSN's educational resources are logically gathered together in the Education & Reference category (shown here). To get here, you can click **Categories** in **MSN Central**, then double-click the **Education & Reference** icon. Alternately, you can use the Go word: EDUCATION.

The Education & Reference category. Go word: EDUCATION.

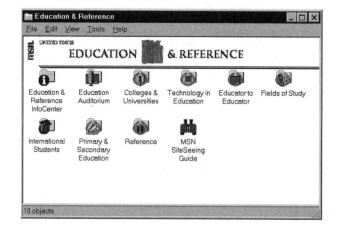

Education & Reference contains the standard category features you've come to expect: an InfoCenter (Education & Reference InfoCenter), an auditorium for online events (Education Auditorium), and the ever-popular binocular icon for the MSN SiteSeeing Guide (which, when you access it here, takes you right to a tour of the Education & Reference sites worth seeing).

MSN groups all the reference materials available online into the Reference folder (but I bet you already figured that out). We'll peek in here later in the chapter. First the educational resources.

MSN groups educational information into a number of folders: Colleges & Universities, Technology in Education, Educator to Educator, Fields of Study, International Students, and Primary & Secondary Education.

We'll look at each in turn. If you're exploring online while you're reading, double-click the appropriate folder to enter each forum.

Colleges & Universities

A major part of getting into college these days is drumming up financial aid and taking a fleet of standardized tests. The Colleges & Universities Forum (shown below) provides resources to help you cope.

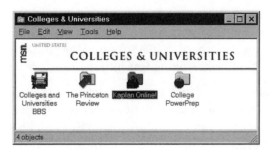

Resources for getting into college at undergraduate, and graduate, levels.

Naturally, there is a Colleges & Universities BBS where you can read and post messages, sharing your insights into the process, and getting tips from other MSN members. Chapter 10 gives you the scoop on using MSN's BBSs.

The three remaining folders each contain resources to help you round up financial aid, take those standardized tests, as well as other advice. To help you decide which resources will best meet your needs, here come the highlights:

If You're Starting A College Search... May I humbly suggest you pick up a copy of *The Complete Idiot's Guide to Getting Into College*? It walks you gently through the process, step-by-step.

The Princeton Review

Brought to you by Princeton Review Publishing, the Princeton Review Forum (Go word: PRINCETONREVIEW) contains admission and financial aid information for all levels of college. You can read the complete text of their books *Cracking the SAT* (for undergrad students) and *Cracking the GRE* (for graduate students).

The Student Message Board BBS gives you a chance to correspond with other students and ask questions of the forum's resident college admissions expert. There's a Student Chat area where you can just hang out, or attend one of the hosted discussions.

In the TPR (The Princeton Review) Software file library, you can download short practice tests to help you prepare for all of the major admissions exams.

Kaplan Online!

No, not Gabe Kaplan from "Welcome Back Kotter" (man, I *gotta* lay off the Nick at Nite), but Kaplan as in Kaplan Educational Centers, a nation-wide company that helps students prepare for standardized tests. The Go word is: KAPLAN.

They offer a similar set of services to the Princeton Review, specializing (as you may suspect) in helping students prepare to take all of the standardized admissions tests including: the LSAT for law school, NCLEX for nursing, and the MCAT for medical school. All of which have been striking fear into the hearts of students for decades.

Kaplan also offers a library of software you can download to help prepare for these tests—but look before you download, a lot of their stuff costs you money. Chapter 11 has the details on downloading software, including instructions for checking software properties for pricing information.

College PowerPrep

SSDF: Same stuff, different forum.

It's difficult to recommend one over the other, since they all offer similar sets of information and preparation. My advice is to think about what *you* need to do to get into college, review the services offered in each of the three forums, and then weigh what they offer (and cost) against what you need and can afford. In short, comparison shop before you take the plunge.

Technology in Education

I get a lot of e-mail from teachers who've read my books, wanting a little more help in dealing with the changing role of computers in education. Many are learning how to use their new hardware while they're teaching their students to use it.

If you're an educator in need of technological assistance, Technology in Education (shown in the next figure, Go word: EDTECH) may be just the ticket.

Help for folks struggling with computers in the classroom.

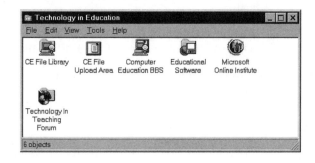

190

Technology in Education includes a library of files to help you cope (CE File Library), a BBS where you can share your own files to help other educators (CE Upload Area), and a library of educational software (called Educational Software, oddly enough) where you can download applications for yourself and your students.

Additionally, there's a Computer Education BBS where you can read and post messages on related subjects. There's also access to the Microsoft Online Institute (Go word: MOLI), a forum that's also an institute of computer learning where you can take courses in the technology you have to teach your students. Naturally, the Microsoft Online Institute covers Microsoft products, but may expand into other topics in the future.

MOLI Costs MOOLAH

Like most learning institutions, the Microsoft Online Institute costs money—some courses (aimed at businesses) cost as much as $500. Other courses leave the tuition field blank, but as much as I'd like to say "that means *free*," it really only means the field is blank.

Check the MOLI Course Catalog (in the Advising folder) before you enroll.

Finally, there's an entire forum, called Technology in Teaching, to help educators deal with the sudden influx of high-tech equipment in the classroom.

Teachers of the world, I salute you.

More for Teachers: Educator to Educator

Think of it as a faculty lounge. Educator to Educator, shown next (Go word: EDUCATOR) provides educators at all grade levels a number of ways to communicate with each other. There's a bulletin board (Educator to Educator BBS), chat room (Educator Chat), and the Educator Exchange where you can swap stories, advice, and tips for getting through to your students.

Whether you're struggling with a troubled or troublesome student, or just want to socialize with other educators, Educator to Educator is there for you. (Have I mentioned how much I admire and respect teachers? I do.)

Fields of Study

Fields of Study, shown in the following figure, (Go word: FIELDS) isn't so much a forum as much as a collection of shortcuts to other forums on MSN that may be of interest to students.

So, where you from? What's your major?

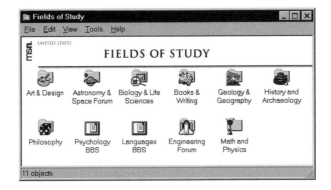

You may notice, looking at the figure, that the forum names are all related to subjects in which you might major. It's a chance for folks who think they *might* be interested in majoring in a subject to explore it a little and see if it's for them. For students already majoring in these subjects, it's an online resource for information in your field.

Check them out—they may help with your homework, if nothing else.

International Students

Did you ever think about studying abroad? (*Please,* don't make that "a broad" joke—not even quietly to yourself. Thank you.)

If you have, or if you're already studying in a foreign country, International Students (Go word: INTLSTUDENTS) has resources just for you.

Resources for world-traveling students, and folks who want to be.

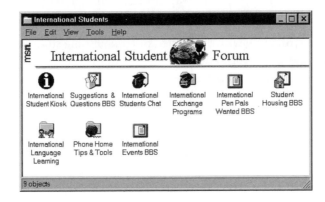

For wannabe travelers, there's a folder full of information about International Exchange Programs, a BBS full of housing information (Student Housing BBS), and a folder devoted to International Language Learning.

For students already abroad, there is a BBS where you can find an international pen pal (International Pen Pals Wanted BBS), an International Students Chat room, plus a folder to help you keep from getting too homesick (Phone Home Tips & Tools).

Studying in another country can be quite an enriching experience, but also lonely. (Hey, I miss my family, and they're only two hours away by car.) Get support and advice here.

Primary & Secondary Education

As a companion to the Colleges & Universities folder, here's one devoted to students in preschool through 12th grade: Primary & Secondary Education (Go word: PRIMARYED). In the following figure, you can see there's a BBS for Parent & Teacher communication, and another for discussions of Primary & Secondary Education.

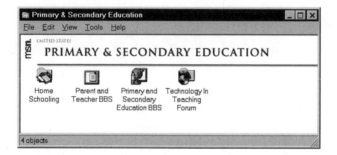

Younger students need support, too.

The area also gives access to the Technology In Teaching Forum (also seen in the Technology in Education section), and—very cool, I think—a folder devoted to teaching your kids at home (Home Schooling).

You find resources here for all of your young students, even those tikes you're just planning to send to school.

References Available upon Request

As the name implies, the Reference area (shown below, Go word: REFERENCE) provides students with information resources—some of which you've seen before.

Need a synonym for cinnamon? Look in here.

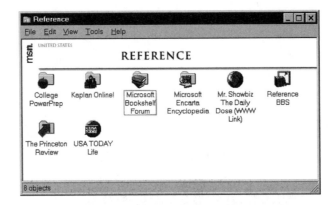

The Reference folder gives you another way to get at College PowerPrep, Kaplan Online!, and the Princeton Review (last seen in the "Colleges & Universities" section). There's also a Reference BBS where you can pass notes to other members on reference-related topics.

The actual references you find here are an eclectic mix.

Microsoft Bookshelf Forum

The Microsoft Bookshelf Forum (Go word: MSBOOKS) gives you online access to an introductory edition of the popular Microsoft Bookshelf CD-ROM—whether you've got a CD-ROM drive or not.

Bookshelf includes a dictionary, thesaurus, encyclopedia, book of quotations, almanac, atlas, and a historical timeline, all in one tidy package.

In order to use Bookshelf online, though, you have to do a little preparation work. It's easy enough, and involves three simple steps:

1. Read the **Step 1: Read me first!** file. Double-click on its icon to read it. It contains up to the minute instructions and information, including the system requirements for using Bookshelf.

2. Install the necessary software. To do that, double-click the **Step 2: Install Bookshelf Intro Edition** icon. This downloads the software to your computer (it takes about 10 minutes, depending on your modem and PC speeds) and installs it in your Microsoft Network folder. You receive an "installation complete" message when it's done. Click **OK** to continue.

3. Run the software. To start it up, double-click the **Step 3: Run Bookshelf Intro Edition** icon. You may be asked to enter your name and a company name.

When it starts up, Bookshelf looks like the next figure. It's simple enough to use: click on a book at the top of the screen, type a word or phrase to search for, then click an article title in the Articles list to read the information.

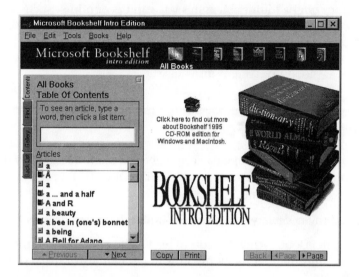

It's seven reference books in one tiny window.

Access Bookshelf Fast!

To get at the intro version of Bookshelf quickly, later, click and drag the **Step 3: Run Bookshelf Intro Edition** icon from the Bookshelf window onto your desktop. This gives you a desktop shortcut that launches MSN and takes you right to the Bookshelf Forum.

The same trick works for Microsoft Encarta in the next section.

You can also use the Find tab to search for a particular word or phrase in article titles, or in the full text of all the Bookshelf articles. Menus, buttons, and on-screen instructions are clear cut and straightforward. Should you need it, online help is available under the Help menu. The Help menu also offers advice for including footnote or endnote references for Bookshelf information you include in your papers.

When Is a CD Not a CD?

It's not a riddle. The CD-ROM versions of Microsoft Bookshelf and Encarta (in the next section) offer additional features you can't get online—such as video and audio clips, in addition to the pictures you can see online. That's why both are "intro" editions. Naturally, Microsoft wants you to buy the full versions. If you've got a CD-ROM drive, and find yourself using either online version regularly, it may be a good investment for you.

Microsoft Encarta Encyclopedia Forum

Like Bookshelf, the Microsoft Encarta Encyclopedia Forum gives you online access to the popular Encarta Encyclopedia. The forum, (Go word: ENCARTAFORUM) gives you everything you need to access Encarta online.

Again, you need to download the necessary software in a similar three-step process:

1. Read the **Readme First** file. Double-click its icon to read it. It contains up to the minute instructions and information, including how much hard drive space you need to install the software.

2. Install the necessary software. To do that, double-click the **Encarta Installer** icon. This downloads the software to your computer (it takes about 10 minutes, depending on your modem and PC speeds) and installs it in your Microsoft Network folder. You receive a "installation complete" message when it's done. Click **OK** to continue.

3. Run the software. To start it up, double-click the **Microsoft Encarta Intro Edition** icon.

When Encarta starts up, it opens to the "A" page. Each of the bars below the Microsoft Encarta title bar (Arts, Language, & Literature; Language; Find; Go Back Views; and Tools) is a drop-down menu or button you can use to navigate and customize Encarta.

As with Bookshelf, in the last section, Encarta's menus, buttons, and on-screen instructions are clear cut and straightforward.

If you need it, help is available at all times under Encarta's Help menu. Help also gives tips on including foot- and end-note references for Encarta quotations you include in your schoolwork.

Referring to the World Wide Web

The two remaining Reference resources (Mr. Showbiz The Daily Dose, and USA TODAY Life) are both shortcuts to World Wide Web Pages which means:

➤ You need to have MSN version 1.05 or Microsoft's Internet Tools installed on your computer before you can use them (see Chapter 20 for details).

➤ Also, you need to read Chapter 20 to know how to explore the Web—and what it is, too.

So, if you're dying to try the Web, why don't you jump ahead to Chapter 20 when you're finished here. USA Today's Website is covered there. Mr. Showbiz The Daily Dose (shown next) is *not* covered in Chapter 20—and I can't figure out what a Hollywood gossip page is doing in Education & Reference anyhow.

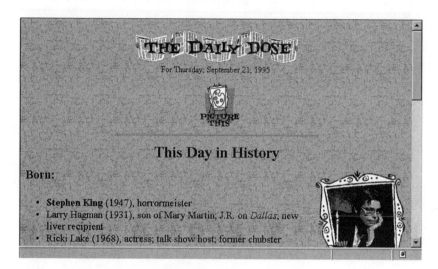

I suppose this could be a valid reference if you're taking a course in tabloid journalism...

The Least You Need to Know

There are piles of educational resources available on MSN, for teachers and students alike. Most operate like all the other forums you've seen online, so if you have difficulty, consult the appropriate chapters here.

Some, however, require a little work on your part:

➤ To use Microsoft Bookshelf Intro Edition online, you need to download and install the appropriate software.

➤ The same is true of Microsoft Encarta Encyclopedia Intro Edition: download and install the Encarta software first.

➤ To use the World Wide Web resources, you need to be using MSN version 1.05 (or later), or the Microsoft Internet Tools. Chapter 20 tells you what they are and how to get them.

Chapter 16

A Geek's Delight: Computers & Software

In This Chapter

➤ A guided tour of the Computers & Software category

➤ Points of interest for geek wannabes

➤ And stuff for geeks

Being a computer geek myself, I must say that Computers & Software is indeed a delightful category. It's the kind of place where computer geeks (did I mention that I'm one?) can wallow in geeky resources, and a place where geeks-in-training can hone their computer skills until they're actually geeks in their own right.

A Look Around Computers & Software

If you take a look at the next figure, you'll see that Computers & Software is a standard-looking category. It includes an InfoCenter, a bunch of subcategory folders, an auditorium, and some MSN guides.

The Computers & Software category— let's dive in.

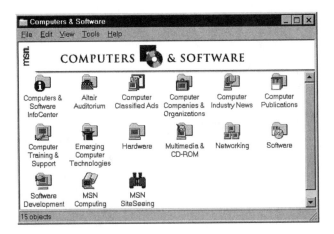

What's the Scoop?

Whenever you visit a category, or forum, for the first time, I recommend taking a look at the informational files. These files give you a better idea of what's hot and happening there. In Computers & Software, you have a couple of things to look at to help fill you in:

 Gives you the scoop on the category as a whole, including who's in charge, what's new, and what's happening.

 An online guide to all the computing resources available on MSN.

 Shows you highlights of this category (and all the others, too) that you can visit with a click of your mouse.

Take a few minutes to check them out—they'll keep you apprised of recent changes in the category not covered here.

Where Do I Find...?

After you've checked out the latest greatest category news, you can check out the rest of the folders. For now, here's a quick summary of what you'll find. A little later we'll look at some of these in more detail.

 Altair Pavilion   Computers & Software's big event room. This is where you go to meet computing celebrities and guest speakers.

 Computer Classified Ads   A BBS you can visit to buy and sell computer stuff.

Computer Companies & Organizations   Hardware and software manufacturers maintain support forums online. You can get help here with a cranky printer, hard drive, or other computer thingy.

 Computer Industry News   Get the latest press releases and news stories about the computer industry.

 Computer Publications   Read online versions of your favorite computer magazines.

 Computer Training & Support   Learn how to use your computer equipment to its full potential.

 Emerging Computer Technologies   Find out what all the fuss is about the newest computer advances.

 Hardware   Get help and support using PCs, printers, scanners, and other hardware.

 Multimedia & CD-ROM   Unearth helpful information and software to turn your PC into a multimedia monster.

 Networking   Learn what the alphabet soup of LANs, WANs, and other computer communication hookups mean.

 Software   It's my personal favorite. It's where you find forums devoted to all kinds of software that you can download.

 Software Development   Where real geeks go to get tools and resources to write their own software.

Check This Out...

Multimedia
Software that combines text, graphics, sound, animation, and video clips is referred to as multimedia, because it contains multiple media. Multimedia software takes up tons of storage space; that's why it's usually found on CD-ROM discs.

Check This Out...

CD-ROM
Acronym for Compact Disc-Read Only Memory. Cousin to the audio CDs you're probably familiar with, the computer version can hold more than 500 MB of information—compared to the 1.4 MB of a high-density floppy disk.

Techno Talk

LAN   Local Area Network. A way to connect computers that are relatively close together (in the same room, or floor of a building) so they can share files and information.

That's the category at a glance. Now let's look at some of these folders in a little more depth.

WAN

Wide Area Network. Similar to a LAN, but covers greater distances. Computers are connected and share files over several floors of a building, or even with computers in remote locations (across town, or across the country). The Internet is a WAN.

Help with Windows 95

Windows 95 got you a little cranky? Can't quite make the adjustment from Windows 3.1? There's help in the Software folder: Microsoft Windows 95 Support Desktop (shown in the next figure).

Help! Where's the Program Manager? What are these Properties?

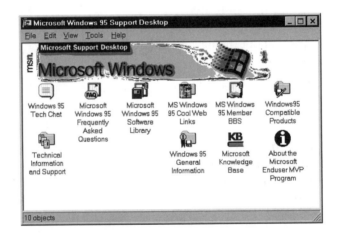

To get there from the main Computers & Software window, do this:

1. Double-click the **Software** folder.

2. Double-click the **Operating Systems** folder.

3. Double-click the **Microsoft Windows** folder.

4. Double-click the **Microsoft Windows 95** folder.

5. Double-click the **Microsoft Windows 95 Support Desktop** folder.

Of course, you can just cut to the chase and use the Go word: MSWINDOWS_SD.

Just the FAQs Ma'am...

You can find answers to the most commonly asked questions about Windows 95 in the Microsoft Windows 95 Frequently Asked Questions BBS. That's what FAQs are: Frequently Asked Questions.

Alternately, if you're not really having trouble, but just want more details, take a peek in the Windows 95 General Information folder. You find a pile of solid, basic information.

For less run-of-the-mill situations (meaning anything you can't find an answer for in the earlier suggestions), you can check out the MS Windows 95 Member BBS. Here you can peruse previously posted questions, some of which may be about your particular problem.

If your questions haven't previously been asked, you can always post them yourself—then check back regularly to see if they've been answered.

Both the Microsoft Windows 95 Frequently Asked Questions MS Windows 95 Member BBS and Questions MS Windows 95 Member BBSs are standard MSN bulletin boards. If you aren't sure how they work, check out the details in Chapter 10.

Check This Out...

Of Course, If You're Really Cranky...

If Windows 95 has you completely crazed, you may want to pick up a good book on the subject. Naturally, this is a plug for *The Complete Idiot's Guide to Windows 95*, but you figured that out, didn't you?

I Need Software!

You may have Windows 95 humming like a well-tuned engine. Good for you! Now you need some software that makes the best use of Windows 95's expanded capabilities. You've got a couple of choices here.

The Microsoft Windows 95 Software Library gives you a selection of software from Microsoft that give Windows 95 even more power (like the Power Tools).

Unlike most software sources online, the software here is not presented in BBS format. Instead, the files are available from text documents you can double-click to read—like the information files and news flashes you've read about in earlier chapters.

For details on how to download software and other files, look in Chapter 11. It's got the scoop for you.

If your need is more for commercial products designed for Windows 95, double-click the **Windows 95 Compatible Products** folder. Inside you'll find regularly updated information on all the software and hardware that works with 95. It's a great place to check before you call your favorite mail-order company, or head for your local computer store.

For the Technically Inclined

For folks who approach or surpass supreme geekdom, there's the Technical Information and Support folder.

Here you find behind-the-scenes type information about how Windows 95 does what it does. It's the sort of information programmers, system managers, and information systems professionals need and crave—but that's not to say that regular folks can't look, too.

More Information Than You Can Shake a Stick At

Though why you'd be shaking a stick at your computer, I don't know.

The MS Knowledge Base—everything you ever wanted to know about Microsoft Products but were afraid to ask.

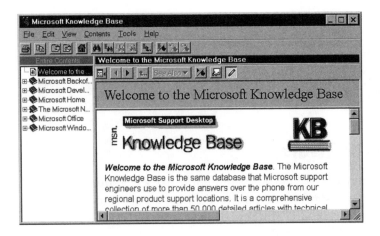

The Microsoft Knowledge Base (shown here) is an online database of just about everything there is to know about Microsoft products, including Windows 95 and MSN.

It's the same database that Microsoft's support staff uses to provide answers over the phone from their technical support locations. It contains more than *50,000* (yikes!) articles with technical information about Microsoft products, bug and fix lists, documentation errors, and answers to commonly asked technical support questions.

It works much the same as a *very large* online help file, with a powerful search capability.

You can sift through its contents manually, by clicking one of the main subject groups at the left of the screen, or you can search for all information on a particular topic by clicking the toolbar button with the big binoculars on it. This gives you a dialog box (much like the Find dialog box you've used before) where you can specify the information to search for, and it does the looking for you.

If the answer isn't here, I don't know where it is.

Software Sources

We looked at the software resources in Chapter 11, while talking about downloading files from MSN. What you didn't see then is all the categories of software. To get there, double-click the **Software** folder in the **Computers & Software** window, or use the Go word: SOFTWARE. You can see it in the next figure.

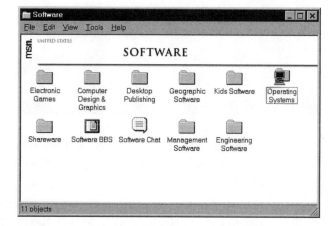

A software smorgasbord.

You can browse through software libraries devoted to Electronic Games, Computer Design & Graphics, Desktop Publishing, Geographic Software, Kids Software, Operating Systems, Shareware, Management Software, and Engineering Software.

Additionally, there's a Software BBS, where you can discuss the latest software finds (and get answers to questions about using them), and a Software Chat room where you can shmooze with other MSN members about software.

Only you know where your software needs and interests lie, so I'll let you browse at your own discretion. While you're browsing, check out the Shareware Forum, too (Go word: SHAREWARE). It's loaded with software you can try before you buy.

205

Hardware Hoopla

Computers & Software wouldn't be much of a category if you couldn't check out your hardware options, too. You can. Double-click the **Hardware** folder in the Computers & Software window, or use the Go word: HARDWARE. The Hardware Forum looks a little something like the next figure—only a little like it because pickings seem a little slim right now. Expect the area to expand as more hardware companies hop onto the MSN bandwagon.

MSN's Hardware resources.

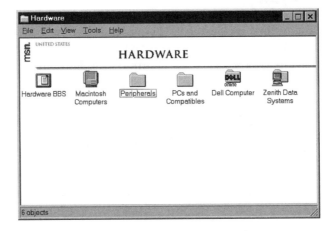

Peripheral
Supplemental computer hardware—the stuff that's nice to have, when using a computer. Basically, all the stuff that isn't the computer (monitor, printer, mouse, CD-ROM drive, and so on).

At the moment, you can check out resources for Macintosh Computers, PCs and Compatibles, Dell Computer, and Zenith Data Systems.

If it isn't your computer but one of your hardware accessories that you need help with, look in the Peripherals folder, where you find information on printers, scanners, CD-ROM drives, and other, well, *peripherals*.

I Read It in the Want Ads

When you're ready to buy (or sell) a bit of computer paraphernalia, think about buying or selling it through MSN's Computer Classified Ads (shown here). You get to them by double-clicking on the **MSN Computer Classified Ads** icon in the main Computing & Software window.

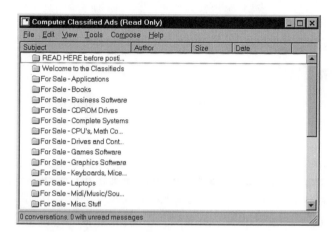

The online equivalent of the want ads—except you can't wrap fish in these.

The classifieds are set up like MSN's BBSs. You can see in the figure that there are folders that break down the ads by category (For Sale—Applications, For Sale—Complete Systems, Wanted To Buy—Games Software, etc.).

Buying Stuff Online

If you're in a buying mood, double-click the appropriate category folder and browse for subjects that meet your needs. (Chapter 10 has complete BBS information, if you need more detailed instructions.)

When you find something that interests you, the usual procedure is to e-mail the seller's member ID asking if the item is still available, plus any other questions you may have. The member responds (also by e-mail), and the negotiations begin.

Let the Buyer Beware!

The risks of buying merchandise through online classifieds are about the same as buying something through newspaper ads: you don't know who you're dealing with and, unless the seller happens to be from your hometown, you don't usually get to look at the merchandise before you buy.

Be careful. Try to get some sort of warranty from the seller, so you can return the item for a refund if it doesn't work or meet your needs. Never, never, never, just e-mail somebody your home address or credit card number. There are as many rip-off artists online as there are in the physical world.

If you're at all leery or mistrusting, this isn't the way to go. There are too many uncertainties. It's just not for the squeamish.

When you're ready to purchase, and the price has been set, you send your check or money order to the seller, who cashes it and ships you the computer doodad.

Selling Your Own Stuff

In order to sell an unused, or unwanted, bit of computer paraphernalia, you need to post an ad (in the appropriate folder) describing what you've got and how much you want for it.

You then need to check your e-mail and your posting regularly (in case someone expresses interest in a response on the BBS, rather than by e-mail). As the seller, you need to answer questions, weigh bids, and decide to whom you're going to sell the item.

You need to negotiate the price, decide who pays the shipping, and determine how payment will be made. After you settle all that, you wait for the payment and ship the item when you're paid.

I've sold stuff this way (my old Apple IIe computer, as a matter of fact). It can be fast and effective.

Let the Seller Beware, Too!

There are as many risks in selling stuff online as there are in buying. You have to be careful that the buyer isn't trying to rip you off, too. I'm not suggesting that you be *completely* paranoid, but a little healthy paranoia isn't a bad thing in this day and age. Be careful and cover your... *hindquarters.*

The Least You Need to Know

MSN's Computers & Software Category is a very rich resource for all kinds of information about computers.

Whenever something goes wrong with my computer (and it happens, believe me), I try to fix it myself. If I can't figure it out before I resort to panicking, I cruise through the relevant areas in Computers & Software looking for help and support. That often solves the problem for me.

Otherwise, when I'm bored or want a new toy to play with, I browse through all the software online. It's a constant source of entertainment for me. Maybe it will be for you, too.

Chapter 17

Outpace the Rat Race: Business & Finance

In This Chapter

➤ A quick tour of the Business & Finance category, including:

➤ Small Office/Home Office resources

➤ Finding employment online

I feel like some clichéd bubble-head whenever I admit to this, but what the heck—we're friends, right? I have no head for business, and my finances are enough to make an accountant blanch. (They actually turned my tax guy Jeff into an accountant named Blanche. It was both amazing and frightening.)

That said, let's jump into what is (for me) a strange new world of online information.

Welcome to Business & Finance

The Business & Finance category, shown below, gives you access to a world of (*duh*) business and financial information and resources.

The category is:
Business & Finance.

Giving You the Business

The Go words for the features of Business & Finance in this chapter are:

Business & Finance	BUSINESS
Business & Finance Directory	B&FDIRECTORY
Business News & Reference	BUSINESSNEWS
Business Services	BUSINESSSERVICES
Career Connection	CAREERCONNECT
International Trade	INTTRADE
Investing	INVESTING
Personal Finance	PERSONALFINANCE
Professions & Industries	PROFESSIONS
Small Office/Home Office	SOHO

Here you find a Business & Finance InfoCenter, a Business & Finance Auditorium (for online events and meetings), the MSN SiteSeeing Guide (featuring business-type highlights from MSN and the Internet), and the MSN SOHO GuideBook. All this in addition to the usual assortment of subcategories.

SOHO = Small Office Home Office

The MSN Small Office Home Office area (shown next) is chock-full of information for folks who run small businesses or work for big businesses from a home office.

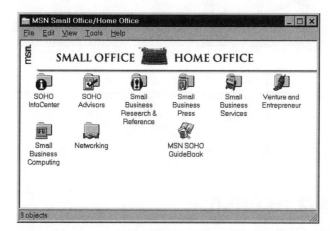

SOHO—sounds like something an indifferent Santa would say.

Of special note here is the folder SOHO Advisors, which gives you access to advice about setting up and running your own small business or home office from business professionals. There are also folders providing information tailored to small business needs in Small Business Computing, Networking (the people kind, not the computer kind), and an entire folder devoted to Small Business Research & Reference.

It's mighty scary going into business for yourself in this economic climate. You've got to marshal all the resources you can.

The Business & Finance Directory

It's not a forum, it really is a Business & Finance Directory—you can see what I mean in the following figure. The directory gives you four folders (A—E, F—J, and so on) that break down and alphabetize all of the business and finance resources scattered around MSN.

If your primary interest in MSN is its business resources, the directory gives you access to all the related areas online, and you don't have to go searching for them. Just double-click on a folder in the directory, and you're at that forum. Very convenient.

Looking for a lawyer experienced with small business matters? Check out The Law Office.

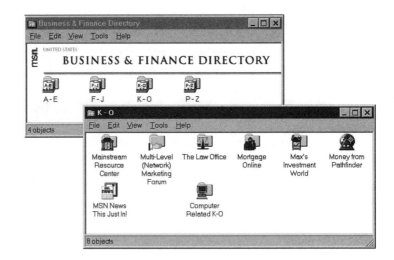

Business News & Reference

Staying on top in business means keeping apprised of current developments (at least, that's what my economics professor used to say—what do I know?). The Business News & Reference area gives you immediate business news gratification.

"What's the news across the Nation? We have got the information..." Ooh. Laugh-In reference. I'm old.

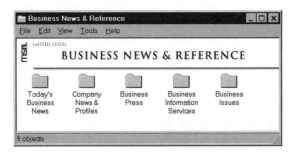

You can side-step the News & Weather category entirely and go right for the news you need to stay in touch with developments in the business world and on Wall Street.

Of interest to small businesses that cater to big businesses is the folder Company News & Profiles. Reading a profile of a company *before* you contact them can help you tailor your presentation to suit the company—and help you get them as a client.

Get a Job! (In the Career Connection)

The Career Connection (shown here) is a small area that can deliver big. If you're looking for a job (or another job) you can find job openings in the Career Opportunities folder.

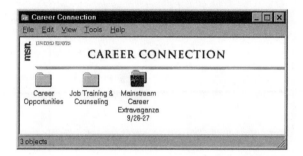

Where was this when I was looking for a job?

For those in a "transitional" stage (trying to ease yourself out of one job and into another, say) you can learn new skills and get advice from professional employment counselors and trainers in Job Training & Counseling.

The remaining folder in the figure is for Mainstream Career Extravaganza, an online job fair. It's long over, but look for MSN to host more similar events in the near future.

Investing

Something I know less than nothing about. The Investing area, shown here, gives you access to Today's Business News (so you can check stock trends, etc.). There's also a folder devoted to Market and Securities Research for information about stocks, bonds, Treasury bills, and other investment tools I don't have (I swear, I'm not bitter, I just thought an IRA was an Irish guy with a gun).

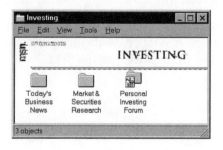

Investing in your future.

The Personal Investing Forum is an entire forum (complete with its own chat room, BBS, and library) devoted to the intricacies of investing your hard-earned money. If you do your own investing and financial planning, you may also want to check out...

Personal Finance

The Personal Finance area (shown here) gives you access to a folder full of Financial Services: service providers who can help you manage your money.

Personal Finance: everything from balancing a checkbook to buying a home.

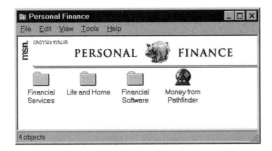

You can also get at information geared toward basic Life and Home financial issues (where stuff like mortgage rates and "points" are explained). If you're running MSN 1.05, you can also explore the World Wide Web version of *Money* magazine. See Chapter 20 for details.

The coolest thing here is the Financial Software folder because you can get free stuff. For the time being, Microsoft is *giving away* copies of its financial software package Microsoft Money. You can download a free copy here.

If you, like me, haven't done any financial planning whatsoever, Microsoft Money may be the place to start.

Professions & Industries

Like the Business & Finance Directory earlier, Professions & Industries (shown next) isn't so much a forum as a convenient gathering of other MSN forums from other areas online.

Here you find folders that cover the major professional and industrial types (such as Accounting, Civil Service, Insurance, Medicine, and so on). Each is full of information and resources of interest to employees in the field.

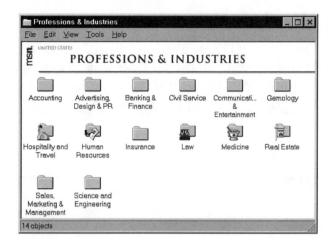

So, what do you do for a living? It's probably here.

International Trade

Jet-setting business types will love the International Trade area (seen here). It contains resources to make trading between nations a snap, including access to Federal Express and UPS shipping and tracking software. ICC Business Information supplies, you guessed it, information about foreign and domestic businesses.

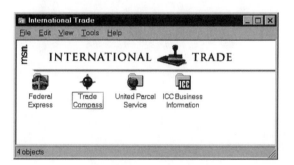

Sell your widgets in Bangkok.

Trade Compass (with MSN 1.05—see Chapter 20 for details) gets you to a World Wide Web page that can help you chart your international trading course.

The Least You Need to Know

The least you need to know is that I'm not a businessman, or a financier, nor do I play one on television. (Hey, the last part I played was a mechanic in a Pep Boys training video. You know, the *Pep Boys*: Manny, Moe, and Jack.)

Let this chapter be your guide to where things are, and you can decide on your own if they meet your needs.

Is there an accountant in the house?

Fun Stuff

Some people (I won't name names here) like to pretend that they only use an online service like MSN for practical matters: stock quotes, research, getting the latest computer software, and so on.

To them I say: *Horse hockey.*

I also say: *All work and no play makes Jack a dull boy.*

Finally, I say: *Get a life—an online life, that is.*

There's more to the online life than serious, practical matters. Sure, it helps in the tax-deduction department if you say, "I only use it for business-related research," but come on. Lighten up. Have some fun. This chapter shows you where the action is.

Special Events

"Special Events" is one of those rare phrases that does double-duty, at least on MSN. One of its duties is to act proper noun-ish because "Special Events" is the name of an MSN category (you can see it in the next figure), Go word: EVENTS.

Special Events—isn't that special...

The second job is to describe what goes on in that category: events that are special. They're "special" because they don't happen all the time. If you look closely in the preceding figure, you see that MSN has hosted events related to a pile of varied happenings in the world: America's Cup (the sailing race), the British Grand Prix (the car race—this isn't getting too racy for you, is it?), goings-on at the United Nations, the World Conference on Women that caused such a stir in China, and more.

Check This Out...

Babbage? Cabbage?

The Special Events main auditorium is called the Babbage Auditorium. It's named in honor of Charles Babbage, a pioneer in computing.

During the real-world event (whatever it may be), MSN hosts a series of related online activities. When the real-world event ends, the online event ends, too, but a record of it (called an *archive*) gets stored in the Past Events folder.

A Typical Special Event Includes...

Special Events typically include a special event chat room, where guest speakers report from the scene of the real-world event. You also find BBSs full of guest profiles, chat histories, photos from the event, and MSN members sharing their reactions to the events, both online and off.

You can see a typical assortment of event materials in the next figure, which is from the 4th World Conference on Women.

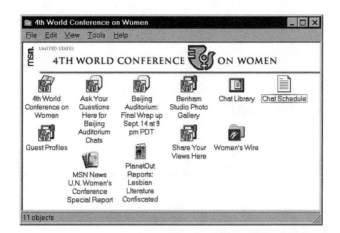

The typical parts of a Special Event.

Of special note for this event are the links to MSN News coverage (see Chapter 14) of the Conference in China and access to the Women's Wire area which features discussions of concerns and issues important to women.

Joining the Chat

One of the cooler aspects of a Special Event is the chance to chat with someone who's actually at the scene of the real-world event. It's almost as good as being there yourself.

Chapter 13 has the nitty-gritty details on entering and using MSN chat rooms. However, Special Event chats can require a little extra fiddling *if* you want to be both a spectator and a participant (to ask questions of the guest).

To do both, you need to have your MSN options set to **Browse MSN Folders By Using A Separate Window For Each Folder** (Chapter 7 tells you how). Then, in the Special Events Category:

1. Double-click the **Auditorium** icon to enter as a spectator.

2. Minimize or move the Auditorium window so you can...

3. Double-click the **Ask Your Questions Here** icon so you can enter as a participant.

4. Resize or arrange the chat windows so you can see both.

5. In both chat windows: click the **Tools** menu and click **Options**.

6. Clear the check boxes in the Notification section.

This keeps member arrival and departure news from cluttering up the event chat. You can also save a *history* of the chat in both windows (or just one—up to you). Chapter 13 has the details.

To ask a question, make sure the Ask A Question chat window is foremost (active). Type your question in the Compose pane, at the lower left corner of the window. Click **Send**, or press **Enter**.

For Longer Questions

If your question is longer than the Compose pane can hold at one time, press **CTRL+Enter** when you hit the end of the first line and then type the rest of your question. Repeat as necessary.

That's (Arts &) Entertainment

Keeping up with Hollywood happenings is a favorite pastime and passion for many. If it's one of yours, you may want to check out the Arts & Entertainment Category (shown here), Go word: ENTERTAINMENT.

If it's artistic or entertaining, it's here.

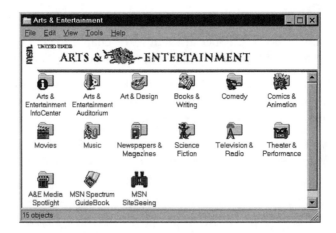

Here you'll find about a dozen satisfying areas to soothe your entertainment cravings, whether you're into art for art's sake, a voracious reader, a science fiction fan, or practically anything else.

My own personal craving, lately, has been for movies, so I checked out the Movies area (Go word: MOVIES). It includes access to the Film Forum, the Microsoft Cinemania Connection, Hollywood Online! (to satisfy that deep need for gossip), and Fangoria—which is a magazine devoted to science fiction and horror movies (another personal addiction).

Another CD-ROM Opportunity

The Cinemania Connection (Go word: CINEMANIA) gives Microsoft Cinemania '96 CD-ROM owners access to monthly updates to the information on the CD-ROM. You can download the updates and integrate them into your Cinemania database.

You can be current with movie reviews throughout the year, instead of waiting for the new Cinemania CD to be released. The updates will be available shortly after Cinemania '96 is in stores.

If the arts aren't your bag, you might want to pop into the Interests, Leisure, & Hobbies category.

The Complete Hobbyist

Interests, Leisure, & Hobbies, shown in the next figure (Go word: INTERESTS) covers the rest of the amusement spectrum. If you're interested in arts and crafts, cars, collectibles, games, indoor sports, outdoor sports, electronics, or any of a dozen broad topics, here's the place to go.

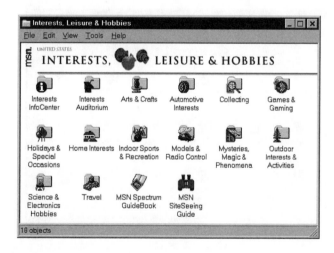

Interesting interests, from "A" to, uh, "T."

But, seriously folks, where else can you find subjects that range as widely as auto repair (in Automotive Interests) and UFOs and Alien Abductions (in Mysteries, Magic, & Phenomena)—with pottery and painting in between?

Since it's difficult to suggest, or cover, everything in such a smorgasbord of interests, I suggest you take a minute or two to cruise through and check out the areas that interest you.

If you don't feel like browsing, try using the **Find on The Microsoft Network** command on your Start button's **Find** submenu to search MSN for a topic that interests you. The Find command is covered in detail in Chapters 10 and 11 if you need help with it.

Shopping!

You. Me. A major credit card. Need I say more?

There are a number of shopping opportunities online right now: Gourmet Gift Net and American Greetings (the greeting card folks) to name two. Look for more as MSN grows.

Shopping online is a real treat (for me, anyhow) because it means I can take ten minutes out of my busy day to take care of my gift needs, without losing an hour to highway traffic and another hour to shopping mall congestion.

The figure here shows the assortment of items available from Gourmet Gift Net (Go word: GOURMETGIFT), located in the Holidays & Special Occasions folder in Interests, Leisure, & Hobbies. It's part forum, part catalog.

Shopping for gifts for the gourmand in your life.

It's part forum because there's an Information Kiosk (About Gourmet Gift Chat) and chat room (Gift Chat With Linda) where you can get gift advice from a gift professional.

The rest of the items in the Gourmet Gift Net window are like sections of a catalog—double-click an icon and you see a collection of related merchandise you can purchase, like the coffee (*yum*) related stuff in the following figure.

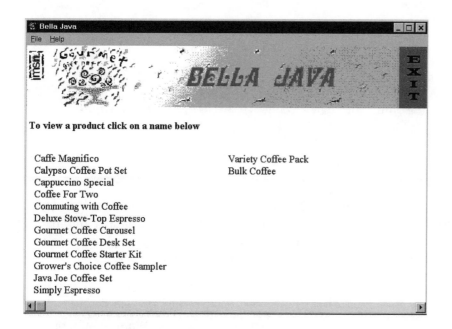

This is what heaven looks like to a coffee junkie like me.

Navigating a Catalog

Click one of the product names and you open a description of the product. Descriptions include the usual catalog-speak ("Don Francisco makes it easy to achieve beautiful results…"), with a photograph (usually) of the item. If appropriate to the product, you also get detailed information, including the dimensions and special options. All descriptions include pricing and a product number.

Write down the price, product number, and product name, if you intend to purchase the item.

At the bottom of each product screen, there are tools for navigating through the catalog. To go to the previous product description, click the **Back One** button. To see the next product, click the **Next Page** button. To jump back to the list of all products, click **Directory**.

If you want to *buy* the product, click **Order Here**.

A Price Note
The price listed in most product information does *not* include shipping charges, or any applicable sales tax.

Ordering Online

Just So You Know...

Shopping online, through a forum like this, is one of the only times when it's OK to send credit card information to someone. (The other is when you're changing your MSN payment method, covered in Chapter 23.)

When you click the Order Here button, MSN downloads an order form to your computer and opens your word processor so you can fill it out. Enter all of the requested information. Most allow you to specify a Ship To address, if you care to send your purchase as a gift to another location. You'll need to provide the product number, name, and price (which is why I told you to write them down).

You can do this online, or, if you prefer, you can save online charges:

1. Minimize your word processor (you need to be using Microsoft Word, Works, or Windows' WordPad) with the order form open.

2. Sign out from MSN.

3. Fill out the order form and save it.

4. Select **Send** from the word processor's **File** menu.

5. You're asked to specify a profile with the Choose Profile dialog box. Select **MS Exchange Settings** from the **Profile Name** drop-down menu, and click **OK**.

Your PC churns while it gets your e-mail together, then it presents you with a Microsoft Exchange window like the one below.

1. Enter the e-mail address in the To box (the order form tells you what member ID to use).

2. Enter a subject in the Subject box (I used the product name).

3. Click the **Send** button (the one with the speeding envelope on it).

If you're online, MSN sends your mail immediately. If you're signed out, as a money-saving tactic, your MSN software launches. Click **Connect**. You sign in, send your mail, and sign out again. You receive an e-mail confirmation of your order, and it tells you about how long it will take for your order to be shipped.

Click here to send. ——
Enter e-mail address here. ——
Enter a subject. ——
Your completed order form. ——

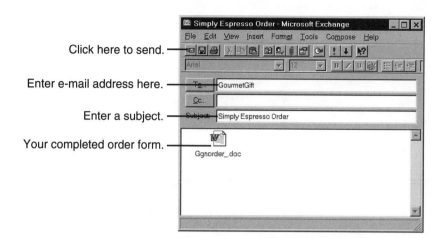

Your order, ready to go.

If E-mail Is a Muddle

Chapter 12 has in-depth e-mail information for you, if the process is at all confusing.

The Least You Need to Know

All work is no fun (trust me on this one, kids). There are a lot of diverting forums and features online, no matter where your interests lie. This chapter gives you just a taste. Explore, enjoy, have fun.

Chapter 19

Centering on the Internet

In This Chapter

➤ The Internet explained

➤ The Internet Center explored

➤ The newsgroup experience

➤ Babbling about Bitnet

The Internet. *Oooh. Ahhh.*

If you've paid any attention at all to the media hoopla that's been buzzing around for the last couple of years about the Internet, you probably have one of two ideas about it:

1. The Internet is the cure for all the ills of the world. It's the gateway to a future so promising and so much like "Star Trek," we'll all have to pay the Roddenberry estate a royalty just to exist.

2. It's the hiding place for international and domestic terrorists, pornographers, perverts, and other scum buckets like that.

Both kind of miss the mark.

The Internet: What's That?

Internet is an abbreviated form of International Network. It started out as a way for related computer systems (say, military computers, or systems on college campuses) to easily pass messages and information back and forth over great distances.

Once the similar computers could talk to each other, connections were established that enabled the military-type computers to communicate with the educational-type computers, which in turn could talk to corporate-type computers, creating a world-wide network of communications. It was strictly the domain of scientists, academics, and military types.

Since nobody "designed" it, the Internet is more of a crazy quilt of different computer systems that cooperate in passing stuff around. It grew organically, which is to say, with no real plan, so it can seem fairly complex and intimidating to the uninitiated.

In the past couple of years, regular folks, like you and I, have swarmed onto the Net (as some call it) and have pretty much commandeered it from its original use. Its popularity is due in part to the wide variety of material available on it, plus the "all's fair" attitude that pervades it.

Unlike commercial online services (like MSN) where someone is "in charge," the Internet is, on the whole, unsupervised (though some individual pockets of it are tightly controlled). You can find such disparate information as:

➤ The latest medical research

➤ Scientific information and data

➤ Recreational and social topics

➤ Pure silliness, like collections of knock-knock jokes

Parental Advisory

Because the Internet is so vast, and mostly unsupervised, you can find adult and controversial information, files, and discussions out there. You should check out the Internet yourself before you turn your child loose on it (see Chapter 22 for more about this).

Once you've seen it with your own eyes, you can decide if you want your child to have access.

Some adult material—the stuff that's actually retrieved from the Internet and stored on MSN's computers (newsgroups, mostly)—is automatically screened from MSN members who have not filed for full adult access. Chapter 22 has the details on how to file for access for yourself, or how to officially deny adult access to younger members of your household.

That takes care of *some* of the adult material. However, once you leave MSN's computers and start looking at information stored on other systems (with the World Wide Web, say, covered in the next chapter) there's no such screening device. You either have access to every bit of it, or you don't have access at all.

Newsgroup
The Internet's version of a BBS, where users can read and post messages on a dizzying array of topics.

Start at the Internet Center

The Internet Center, shown here, is one of MSN's categories. To get there, click **Categories** in MSN Central, then double-click the **Internet Center** icon. You can also use the Go word: INTERNET.

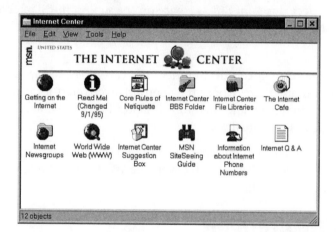

Welcome to the Net. So where's Sandra Bullock?

The Internet Center Go Words

These are the Go words that take you to the main Internet folders in the Internet Center:

The Internet Center	INTERNET
Core Rules of Netiquette	CORERULES
Getting on the Internet	GETONINTERNET
Internet Newsgroups	NEWSGROUPS
World Wide Web	WWW

There's a handy list of Go words on the tear card at the front of the book. Go nuts.

Like the other categories, the Internet Center has information files available (such as Read Me!, Information about Internet Phone Numbers, and Internet Q & A all shown in the preceding figure). You just double-click on one to read it. There's also a chat room (the Internet Café), BBS (in the Internet Center BBS Folder), and file libraries (in the Internet Center File Libraries Folder). The BBS and file libraries work the same as those discussed in Chapters 10 and 11.

Be Thoughtful and Courteous

One of the information files you see in the Internet Center is called the Core Rules of Netiquette, which is a set of guidelines for how to behave on the Internet. You should read it before you begin. It also doesn't hurt if you check out Aunt Effie's advice on the subject in Chapter 8. Please and thank you.

These all work the same as their cousins in other MSN categories, so I won't bore you with a rehash on how to use them. Check the appropriate chapters for details, if you need a refresher: Chapter 10 for forum and BBS stuff; Chapter 11 for file library information; and Chapter 12 for details on e-mail.

The real meat of the Internet Center is contained in two little items: Internet Newsgroups and World Wide Web (WWW). Chapter 20 covers the World Wide Web, so I guess we'll have to look at the newsgroups here.

Exploring the Newsgroups

As I mentioned earlier, a newsgroup is like a BBS on the Microsoft Network, except it may originate from nearly anywhere in the world.

To get at the newsgroups, double-click on the **Internet Newsgroups** folder in the Internet Center window. Inside, there are five folders full of all the newsgroups available in the Internet Center. These are arbitrary divisions to help sort the groups by topic and type. They are: NetNews, Usenet Newsgroups, Other Popular Newsgroups, Regional and International Newsgroups, and The Most Popular Newsgroups. Let's look at each in turn. Double-click on the **NetNews** icon.

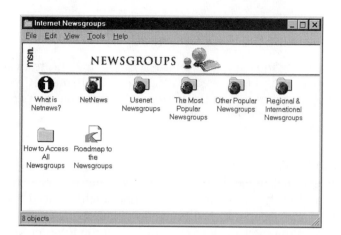

Newsgroups, newsgroups every-where...

NetNews

NetNews contains all of the newsgroups available through MSN. They're sorted alphabetically, by name, into folders (shown in the following figure). If you're looking for a newsgroup about aardvarks, you start with the "a" folder, double click on it to open it, and then sort through the contents to see if there's an aardvark newsgroup.

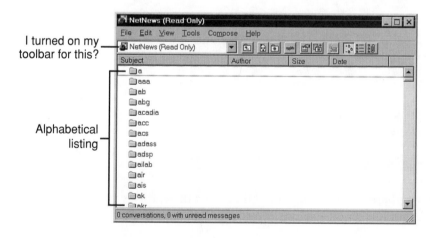

I turned on my toolbar for this?

Alphabetical listing

All the newsgroups available. These folders may contain newsgroups or another set of folders.

Save Time with the Find Command

You can use the Find command on the Start Menu to locate an appropriate newsgroup, too. Find is covered in detail in both Chapters 10 and 11. When entering your search information, select **Internet newsgroups** from the Of type drop-down menu.

There are something like 10,000 newsgroups on the Internet (with more added every day), so manually searching through NetNews may not be the speediest way to find what you're looking for (it is awfully fun to browse through, though). Instead, you may want to try one of the other newsgroup folders, first. In the NetNews dialog box, click on the **Up One Level** button on the toolbar. When you're back in the Internet Newsgroups window, double-click on the **Usenet Newsgroups** folder.

Using Usenet Newsgroups

Usenet (for User's Network) is the name of a moderated set of newsgroups—there are actually people who monitor these newsgroups and keep them from getting too chaotic. In order to add a newsgroup to Usenet, the new group actually has to be approved by a committee.

The Usenet news-groups.

Since the Usenet newsgroups are more organized than the others, this is a good place for beginners to start exploring.

Usenet maintains six broad subject categories, each containing a variety of newsgroups on that subject. They are:

Comp   Computer related newsgroups

Misc   A hodgepodge of groups that don't fit in the other categories

Rec   Recreational subjects: leisure, hobbies, sports, humor, and so on

Sci   Science and technology stuff

Soc   Social and society-related topics

Talk   Discussions on assorted hotly debated topics

To get to the topic that interests you, simply double-click the topic icon.

Newsgroup Navigation Tips

I find it helpful to use MSN's navigation toolbar to get through the newsgroups without getting lost—or *too* lost. I also prefer MSN to display new windows for each folder I open (Chapter 7 tells you how to set your display options).

To show the toolbar, select **Toolbar** from the Tools menu. The tools are similar to those in the Windows Explorer, so you shouldn't have a problem using them.

Other Popular Newsgroups

The newsgroups contained in this folder aren't from Usenet. These aren't supervised or moderated, and they tend to be a little bit, shall we say, disorganized—but they can be gobs of fun.

Alt   For alternative. Alternative lifestyles, medicine,…if you can name it, it probably has a group here. There's lots of outrageous and bizarre material here.

Bionet   Biology related topics, mainly.

Bit   Mailing lists from Bitnet, posted for public consumption. More about Bitnet in, well, a bit.

Biz   Business topics, not that laundry detergent.

One from Column A and One from Column B

The remaining two newsgroup folders are selections from the preceding three.

Regional & International Newsgroups are newsgroups pulled from NetNews that are area specific. If you're looking, say, to buy a used car in your area, you can probably find one or two posted here. I did—the posting is shown in the next figure.

Would you buy a used car from this newsgroup?

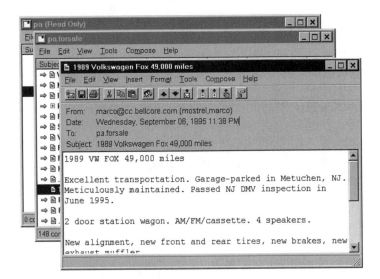

In the regional newsgroup grouping, I found the listing for Pennsylvania, found the For Sale group, and then found the '89 Volkswagen listed in the figure. Unfortunately the "PA" newsgroup also covers New Jersey and Delaware, and I don't think I want to shlep to Metuchen to see this car.

The last grouping is called The Most Popular Newsgroups. Here you find nine or ten of the most active groups that have been pulled from the other groupings.

Because these are very popular (and limited to a handful) this is an excellent place to get a feel for the variety, and uneven quality, of the stuff that gets posted on the Net.

Finding What You Want in Newsgroups

I mentioned earlier that, on MSN, newsgroups work much the same as the BBSs you find in other forums online. Some of the newsgroups are read-only, which means (*duh*) that you can only read them; you can't post your own response (these are mainly in the moderated, Usenet newsgroups). In other newgroups, you can respond to postings as you would to any BBS online. If you're not sure how that works, Chapter 10 explains it for you.

Because of the disorganized nature of many of the newsgroups (except Usenet), it can take some digging and reading to find what you want. In the next figure, I was desperately in need of a new joke—I haven't heard one in *weeks*.

To get at that lowly little snippet of humor, I did the following (all the windows in the background in the figure back me up on this):

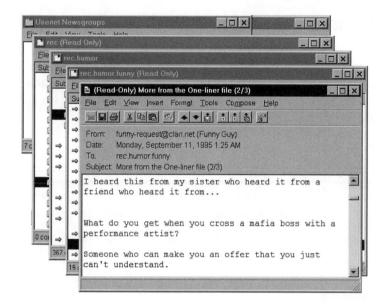

The joke's on me.

1. I went to the **Internet Center** (Go word: INTERNET).

2. Double-clicked on the **Internet Newsgroups** folder.

3. Double-clicked on the **Usenet Newsgroups** folder.

4. Double-clicked the **Rec** icon.

5. Double-clicked the **Humor** folder.

6. Double-clicked the **Funny** folder.

7. Scanned the listing of subjects there until I found one that appealed to me.

8. Double-clicked the posting named **More from the One-liner file**. I'm a sucker for a good one-liner.

That gave me the message shown in the figure. In truth, I went through about a half-dozen postings before I found one that was: (a) actually funny, and (b) clean enough for a general audience-type book (I printed the dirty ones out for my own personal enjoyment later though, *tee-hee*).

That's the sort of digging you need to do. It can be time-consuming (therefore expensive) and frustrating (if you can't find what you need), but it can also be as entertaining as all get-out. Don't say I didn't warn you.

A Word About Newsgroup Names: Yikes!

Often, when cruising through the newsgroups, I find myself thinking, "What the heck does *that* stand for?" Newsgroup names are often abbreviated within an inch of their lives. Newsgroups are named so that an experienced Net Surfer (one who cruises the Net regularly) can tell at a glance where to find the original newsgroup. For example, in the last section, the name of the newsgroup where I found that joke is...

    rec.humor.funny

That's not as bad as some, but still not really helpful to a *newbie* (a new user). If you know that "rec" is a Usenet newsgroup, you can tell from the above that the joke is from the Usenet, in the **rec** newsgroup, in the **humor** section, in the **funny** group.

Don't panic. With a little practice and experience using the newsgroups, you'll be able to figure out these names without even thinking about it.

A Bit About Bitnet

Bitnet (short for Because It's Time Network), as I mentioned earlier, is normally a network used for mailing lists. On MSN, the mailing list messages are posted as a newsgroup for the convenience of browsers who don't want to subscribe to a mailing list.

In many ways a mailing list is like a cross between a newsgroup and a magazine: You get a variety of messages and responses from the mailing list members, much as you do in a newsgroup or BBS, but, you don't have to go looking for them. When you subscribe to a mailing list, as when you subscribe to a newspaper or magazine, the messages are delivered to right to your mailbox—in this case, they arrive at your PC via e-mail.

Subscribing to Mailing Lists

If you browse the Bit newsgroup (in the Other Popular Newsgroups folder) you may find something of interest to you. You can subscribe to that mailing list, if you care to. Generally you find subscribing and unsubscribing information in one or more of the Bit postings in each category.

Mailbox Overflow Warning!

If you *do* decide to subscribe to a mailing list, you better be prepared to have your mailbox *flooded* with e-mail. You can get tons of it. Make it a point to sign in to MSN at *least* two or three times a week to retrieve your mail or you'll get buried in unread e-mail. Consider yourself warned.

Subscribing to a mailing list involves sending e-mail to a particular Internet address (Chapter 12 explains those) to request a subscription (these are free—it's not *that* kind of subscription. There's no standard subscription form, so you have to check the postings for specific instruction for each mailing list you're interested in joining.

Save That Message!

When you find a message that includes information on how to subscribe and unsubscribe to a mailing list to which you think you want to sub- scribe, save that message to your hard drive!

Click the **Save** button on the toolbar (the one with the floppy disk on it). Print it out, file it, keep it handy. If for some reason you change your mind and want to unsubscribe, you need the information in the message again, and you don't want to have to go looking for it online. If you don't keep it, and can't find the unsubscribe instructions online, you'll never be free of that mailing list—never, never, never (insert maniacal laugh here).

After your mail is sent, wait a few days (some poor soul somewhere has to retrieve and read your mail before he can add your e-mail address to the mailing list), and then check-in on MSN. You should start receiving mail from the list soon. Read it, delete it, or respond to it, as you wish.

Cancel My Subscription, Please

Sometimes a mailing list goes astray: it's not what you thought it would be, it's not fun, it's impossible to keep up with, whatever. To unsubscribe to a mailing list, you need to send *another* piece of e-mail requesting that someone remove your name from the list. Again, it takes a few days to kick in, so be patient.

Cutting to the Mailing List Chase

If you're really taken by the idea of mailing lists and want to find more of them than are represented on MSN, you can cut MSN out of the loop, here's how:

Compose e-mail (Chapter 12 covers e-mail in depth) addressed to:

> **listserv@bitnic.educom.edu**

(Type the address carefully, or it will bounce back to you.)

In the body of the message (not in the subject, or anywhere else) type: **list global**. By return e-mail, you'll receive a list of all the current, active mailing list discussion groups. You can then pick-and-choose from the list, instead of the postings on MSN.

I do, however, suggest you try to find representative postings in the Bit area before you subscribe to a mailing list for two reasons:

1. You can't tell an awful lot about the mailing list from the description; it may not be what you're looking for (or even what you think it is).

2. It's *very* rude to subscribe to and then cancel a mailing list subscription in short order. If you subscribe, give it a chance. Wait a couple of weeks before you unsubscribe.

The Least You Need to Know

The Internet is a big, wide, wonderful...uh...doohickey. It literally brings the world to your doorstep. There's no way this chapter (and the next, where we look at WWW) can cover all there is to know about the Internet. If you're interested, you may want to check out *The Complete Idiot's Guide to The Internet,* and *The Complete Idiot's Guide to Protecting Yourself on the Internet* at your local bookstore. Just a thought. In the meantime, check out these bits of tid:

➤ There's adult material on the Internet, so check it out yourself before you let your kids go exploring. See Chapter 22 if you want to restrict your child's access to the Internet.

➤ Newsgroups behave much the same as the BBSs you find in all MSN forums. You can read and respond to messages from people all over the world. Chapter 10 explains how.

➤ Some newsgroups (mostly in the Usenet Newsgroups folder) are read-only, which means you can only read them; you can't post a response.

➤ Mailing list discussions (posted to the Bit BBS in the Other Popular Newsgroups folder) are normally conducted via e-mail. You can subscribe to mailing lists and have all their postings delivered to your PC—but that can be a lot of e-mail. Be prepared.

➤ It's very easy to get addicted to the Internet (just ask my friend Juliet Cooke, Info-diva and Goddess-babe). If you don't believe me, wait until you get a look at the way-cool World Wide Web stuff covered in the next chapter. Dig it.

Browsing the WWW—World Wide Web, Not Wild, Wild West

In This Chapter

➤ What you need to get started

➤ The World Wide Web

➤ What's a URL and why should you care?

In the last chapter, we looked at part of the Internet Center, specifically newsgroups and features which are similar to other MSN forums.

This time out, we're going to look at the World Wide Web (WWW) which is way too cool, and lots of fun. Before we get started, though, we need to make sure you've got the right stuff to cruise the Web.

What in the World Is the World Wide Web?

Before I actually show you what the World Wide Web looks like, and how to zip around through it, here's a little background information for you.

The World Wide Web is a *hypertext* based system. If you've ever seen or used HyperPad on a PC, or played with HyperCard on a Macintosh computer, you know that individual cards in either sort of hyperdocument are linked together. If you click on a word or phrase that's highlighted (colored blue, say), you're zapped at hyperspeed to a card that contains information related to that highlighted word or phrase. That's how the Web works, too.

Instead of cards, though, the basic Web component is a page, often called (oddly enough) a *Web page*. It can contain text, photographs, buttons, or other graphic elements. Some of these elements are just there for you to see, others are clickable links to other Web pages.

Each Web page is assigned an address, called a *URL*, which stands for Uniform Resource Locator, which is just a three dollar phrase for address, so there you are.

The computer system where a mass of Web pages are stored is called a Website.

All this sounds rather dull and academic compared to the reality of Web pages. Let's cut to the chase and get you set to cruise the Web.

Web Junkies Take Note

Literally, take notes. A lot of companies, and practically everyone else on the planet, are using the Web as a marketing tool. None of them are shy about sharing their Web page addresses (URLs); the Sci-Fi Channel, for one, shows its URL at the bottom of the screen during many of its "Coming Up Next" spots. Write 'em down. Then you can check out those pages next time you're online.

What You Need to Get Started on the Web

I'm sorry to say that you probably aren't prepared for World Wide Web access—the MSN software you got with Windows 95 isn't Web-capable. But don't panic, it's easy to pick up the odds and ends you need.

Those odds and ends are included in Microsoft's Internet tools, and there's two ways you can get your hands on them: download them from MSN (probably the easiest option), or you can purchase Microsoft Plus! for Windows 95.

Microsoft Plus! Companion for Windows 95

Plus! is a package of Windows 95 enhancements that expand its capabilities in a number of ways: it automates the fine-tuning of your PC; gives you better DriveSpace hard drive compression; and gives you a pile of look-and-feel customizing options. You can find it in your favorite computer store or mail-order catalog for $40–50.

The Plus! features we're interested in, though, are the Internet-related tools, including the Internet Explorer, a Web browsing application you need to access the World Wide Web through MSN.

Plus! is easy to install—the installer starts up automatically on the CD-ROM version; or you can use the Add/Remove Programs Control Panel for floppy disks.

Downloading MSN Version 1.05

You can accomplish the same goal by downloading the latest version of the MSN software from MSN. Here's how (you can start whether you're signed in to MSN or not):

1. Click your **Start** button.

2. Point at the **Find** command.

3. Click on **The Microsoft Network**. This opens the Find dialog box you've used in Chapters 10 and 11.

4. In the Containing text box, type **MSN 1.05**.

5. Click **Find Now**.

   If you aren't signed in to MSN, the software launches and the Sign In screen appears. Click **Connect**, and MSN connects you. If you are already signed in to MSN, the search begins immediately.

   When the search results appear (you can see what I turned up in the preceding figure):

6. Double-click the entry named **UP**. It stands for upgrade. This gives you to the screen shown in the next figure.

7. Sit back, relax, and read the instructions on the screen—it's all pretty much automatic from this point onward. You just need to keep an eye on things in case something wonky happens.

It takes about ten minutes or so (depending on your modem and computer) while MSN downloads the file to your PC (there's no charge for the download, beyond the usual online fees). When it's done, MSN automatically disconnects you.

> **Check This Out...**
>
> **DriveSpace** An application that comes with Windows 95. It compresses your hard drive so you have more room to store files. See your Windows 95 manual or online Help for details.

> **Check This Out...**
>
> **Higher Is Good, Too** At the moment, the latest version of the MSN software is version 1.05. If, when you read this, you turn up a higher version number (1.06, 1.1, or even 2.0), go for it.
>
> Once MSN gets really going, there's no way to tell how fast the upgrades will come pouring out of Microsoft. Go for the latest, greatest version online.

*My find results in
the Find dialog box.*

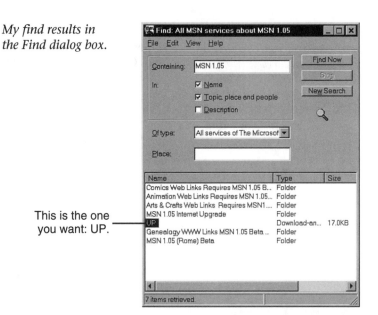

This is the one
you want: UP.

*MSN is delivering
MSN 1.05 to
your PC.*

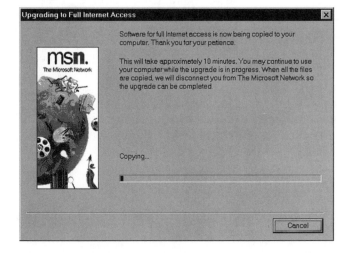

The automation continues: once you're signed off, MSN updates your previous version of MSN. The software restarts your PC and Windows 95 to enable the changes to kick in.

You may need to fiddle with MSN's settings a little before you can sign in and browse the Web. Start MSN by double-clicking its icon on your desktop, or selecting it from the Start menu.

When the Sign In screen appears, click **Settings**. This opens the Connection Settings screen shown in the following figure. If the information next to the Access Numbers button says:

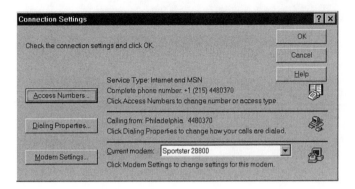

This is what your Connection Settings looks like when you're ready to ride the Web.

Service Type: Internet and MSN

Complete phone number: +1 (area code) 7 digit phone number.

Then you're set to go. If not, click **Access Numbers**. This calls up the dialog box shown in the next figure. From the **Service type** drop-down menu, select **Internet and The Microsoft Network**.

Next, click the first **Change** button, beside the first phone number and select an access number (Chapter 5 describes this procedure in detail). Repeat the process with the second **Change** button, for your backup phone number.

Click **OK** when you're done, and, well, *you're done.*

You can now sign in to MSN and access all of the Internet, not just the newsgroups we saw in the last chapter.

Check This Out...

Local Access Numbers May Not Be Available
The phone numbers you use to access the Internet through MSN are completely different from the regular MSN access numbers. You may not be able to find one that's actually a *local* call for you.

Be patient. MSN is adding more domestic, and foreign, access numbers all the time. Current access number lists are available online in Member Assistance—see Chapter 23 for details.

By Jove, I think we've set these settings before...in Chapter 5.

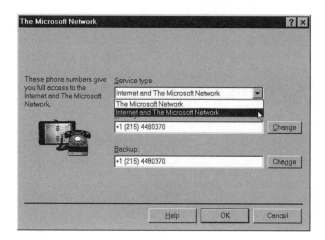

Spinning onto the Web

There are two ways to begin your exploration of the Web, one is for when you're already connected to MSN (online, even), the other is for when you're offline (not connected to MSN). The obvious choice is shown in the following figure: go to the Internet Center and double-click on the **WWW** icon.

The World Wide Web icon in the Internet Center window.

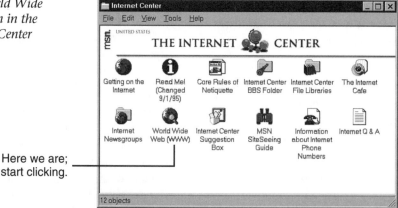

Here we are; start clicking.

Starting on MSN

Alternatively, if you're cruising around another forum online, check and see. In most forums in the Resource Center, there's often a folder called Related Areas (like the one in the following figure). In it, you sometimes find a folder called Related Internet Resources, and that, in turn, may contain access to WWW pages that are related to the forum's topic.

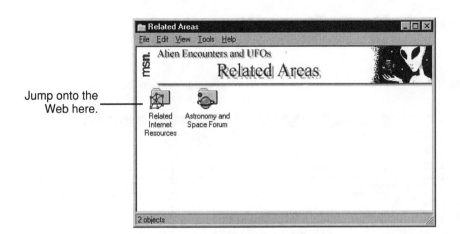

A sneaky way to get at WWW resources.

Jump onto the Web here.

To use them, double-click on the **Related Internet Resources** folder and then double-click on the icon for the resource you want to use. You go right to the designated Web page (or other Internet resource).

Starting Offline

If you're not signed in to MSN, but you're Jonesing (that means craving, for the slang impaired) for WWW access, you can also begin offline.

WWW I'm not going to type World Wide Web anymore... I mean, after this time...it's too much to type. WWW, the Web, the World Wide Web—it's all the same thing (okay, after *this* time).

The Internet

When you installed MSN 1.05, or added Plus! to your PC, you gained a new desktop icon called The Internet (it's shown next). Double-click **The Internet** icon; this does a few things automatically:

➤ It launches the Microsoft Internet Explorer (more about that in a moment or two).

➤ It signs you in to MSN (by giving you the Sign In screen—just click **Connect** when it appears).

➤ And it takes you immediately to the Microsoft WWW home page.

The next few sections show you what a Web page looks like, how to get around, and how to use the Internet Explorer.

I Got Them Cosmic Home Page Blues Again, Momma!

The Microsoft home page.

Toolbar

The arrow cursor changes when you point at something clickable.

URL

Things to click

The status bar shows a description of what you point at.

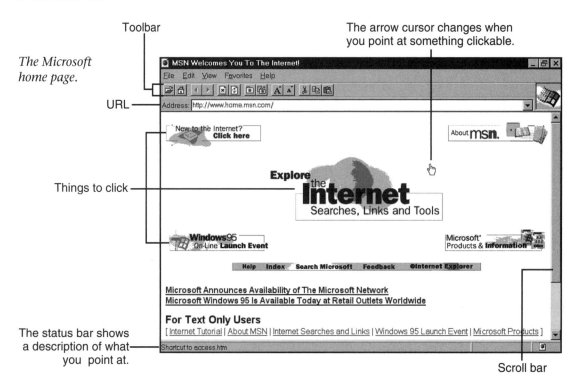

Scroll bar

Starting Elsewhere Don't want to start with Microsoft's home page? You can change your start page to any page on the WWW. I'll show you how shortly.

The first thing you see is the Microsoft home page (a home page is the *first* page of a series of Web pages), shown in the last figure. Microsoft's home page is your *start page*, meaning this is where you start your adventures on the Web.

You don't get the full effect of this (or any) Web page because they're normally presented in color, and this is a black-and-white image. Bear with me. Moreover, the words and phrases you click to go to another Web page are indicated by color—you can't see this in the pictures here.

After you click the colored word or phrase, jump to the associated Web page, and then return to the original page, the word or phrase you clicked is now in a different color (the default is purple), so you know you've "been there, done that."

There are also buttons on Web pages (like the Explore the Internet one at the center of the preceding figure). You know you can click something because the regular arrow cursor changes to a pointing hand when you point at something you can click.

All of these clickable items on the page, because they're connected to other Web pages, are called *links*. When you click a link, you're taken to the associated Web page, no matter where it is on the Internet—on the same computer, or one halfway around the world.

"Paging Dr. Page" Web page, home page, start page, whatever. They're all different kinds of Web pages and function pretty much the same.

Links are a great way to explore randomly, but you may need some help getting to a specific place, or getting back to where you started. That's where the toolbar helps.

Tools You Can Use: The Toolbar

The toolbar gives you instant access to the most-used commands in the Explorer's menus. I'll briefly introduce them here, and we'll use them in the next section to float around the Web.

Open   Enables you to enter a specific URL to visit.

Home   Takes you back to your start page. Do not pass Go, do not collect $200.

Back   Takes you back to the last Web page you visited.

Forward   Takes you to the next Web page in the series you've visited (you need to have used the Back button already).

Stop   Cancels whatever the current Web page is doing (moving you to a link, say).

Refresh   Reloads the current Web page.

Favorite Places   Opens your Favorite Places display—not the MSN Favorite Places, though. The Explorer has its own Favorite Places list.

Add To Favorite Places   Adds the current Web page to the Explorer's list of your Favorite Places.

Use Large Fonts   Substitutes larger fonts on Web pages—easier on the eyes.

Use Small Fonts   Substitutes smaller fonts on Web pages—reduces the amount of scrolling you may have to do to see the whole page.

Cut, Copy, & Paste   The Good 'Ol Boys of the toolbar—they work the same as ever.

Now that you know what these tools are, let's put them to work.

Getting Where You Want To Go and Getting Back Again

Microsoft's home page is nice enough, but it isn't the most interesting thing on the Net (not to me, anyhow). There are much cooler and weirder pages out there.

Going There

If you have the URL for a page you want to visit (and I'm going to give you one, here, so don't panic), get online and open Internet Explorer. Now click the **Open** button on the toolbar. This gives you the Open Internet Address dialog box shown in the next figure.

Stand back! I'm gonna URL!

Type the URL here.

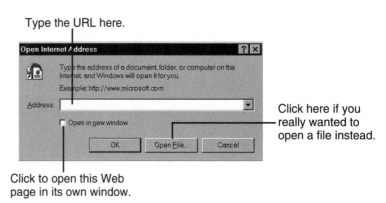

Click here if you really wanted to open a file instead.

Click to open this Web page in its own window.

Then, in the Address text box, type the URL for the Web page you want to visit. For this example, carefully type:

http://gnn.com/gnn/wic/best.toc.html

This takes you to a Website called Best of the Net where you can explore some of the cooler and stranger Web pages and sites available. I'm intentionally not showing you what it looks like, for two reasons. First, I want you to be surprised, and, second, it changes frequently—so even if I showed you, it wouldn't look the same when you got there.

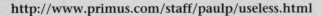

'Cause I'm the Duke of URL

Here are URLs for some other fun Websites you may (or may not) want to check out:

> **http://www.primus.com/staff/paulp/useless.html**

Takes you to a Web page that highlights the most useless pages on the WWW. They're funny, sometimes, but *boy* are they useless.

> **http://www.scifi.com/**

Takes you to the Sci-Fi Channel's Website, called the Dominion. Very bizarre, very science fiction-y.

> **http://home.mcom.com/fishcam/**

Takes you to a Web page that features (sort of) live pictures of a salt-water aquarium. The picture gets updated every five minutes. Can you say, "Too much free time?" I thought so.

Have fun. Explore. Come back here when you're done playing, and I'll tell you how to get home again. I won't wait up.

Home Again, Home Again

When you're done exploring this particular series of Web pages, you have two choices for getting back to your start page. You can select it, or any other Web page you've visited, from your File menu. The Internet Explorer keeps track of 300 (*yikes!*) of your recently visited Web pages, so you can return to them easily. Select the one you want from the menu.

If the one you want isn't listed, select **More History** at the bottom of the menu. It opens a window. Double-click the icon for the Web page you want to visit, and, before you know it, you are there.

You can also simply click on the **Home** button on the toolbar, and this returns you to your start page.

> *Techno Talk*
>
> **http://gnn.com/gnn/ wic/best.toc.html— What the * ! # Does That Mean?** You don't really need to know. For the terminally curious (hey, curiosity *has* done in a few felines, you know) here's a breakdown:
>
> The **http** is a command telling the Explorer to use the *HyperText Transfer Protocol.* The slashes (/) are dividers like the backslashes (\) used in PC path statements. The **gnn.com/gnn/ wic** is the part of the address that identifies the Internet address where the Web page you want is located. The **/best.toc.html** is the actual filename of the Web page you want to open.
>
> Aren't you glad you asked?

249

The Internet Explorer's File menu: it proves you can go home again.

```
File
  Open...                              Ctrl+O
  Open Start Page
  Save As...                           Ctrl+S

  Page Setup...
  Print                                Ctrl+P

  Create Shortcut

  Exit

  1 Our Favorite Websites
  2 Explore the Internet
✓ 3 MSN Welcomes You To The Internet!
  4 Windows 95 - News and Events
  5 Microsoft Windows 95 Home Page
  6 Microsoft Corporation Products
  7 Microsoft Corporation
  8 MSN Welcomes You To The Internet!
  More History...
```

The MSN home page ——

Other sites I visited ——

Opens a list of more sites I visited.

Leaving the Web Altogether

To completely leave the Web, select **Exit** from the **File** menu, or click the Internet Explorer's **Close** button.

If you originally connected to the Web from a forum on MSN, you are still connected to MSN, and you can explore other areas online if you care to.

If you originally connected to the Web, starting offline with the Internet Explorer, MSN disconnects you when you exit the Explorer application.

So, What Are My Options?

You can customize a number of features of the Explorer to your liking. To change them, of course, the Explorer needs to be running. Launch it by your favorite method and then select **Options** from the **View** menu.

Your options appear on a typical, tabbed Windows dialog box. To look at a different set of options, click the appropriate tab.

Appearance

The Appearance tab gives you three sets of options: Page, Shortcuts, and Addresses.

The Page options enable you to hide or show pictures in the Web pages you view. Hiding them speeds things up online, but cuts down on the coolness, too. The default setting is for pictures to be shown. To hide them, click the **Show pictures** check box.

You can also select custom text and background colors for Web pages (click the **Use custom colors** check box and then click each of the buttons below to select the colors). However, I don't recommend it. You should see them the way their creators designed them.

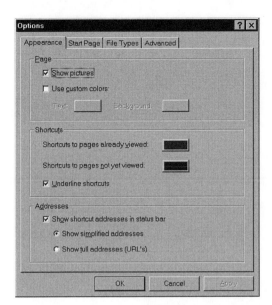

Appearances cannot only be deceiving, they can also be changed.

The Shortcuts options enable you to select the colors for link text. You can change both **Shortcuts to pages already viewed** and **Shortcuts to pages not yet viewed**. Click the appropriate button to select your new colors. You can also have the Explorer stop underlining shortcut text, click in the **Underline shortcuts** check box, and it stops.

The Addresses options enable you to set how (and *if*) the Explorer displays the addresses in the status bar across the bottom of the Explorer window. To stop it displaying them (they're turned on as the default), click in the **Show shortcut addresses in the status bar** check box.

If you keep addresses set to appear, you can choose to **Show simplified addresses** (which eliminates some of the address information, or **Show full addresses (URLs)**. Show full addresses if you share your URLs with your friends.

Start Page

Your default Start Page is the MSN home page, shown earlier in the chapter. If you want to change it:

1. Go to the URL you want as your start page.

2. Select **Options** from the **View** menu.

3. Click the **Options** tab.

4. Click **Use Current**.

This is where you (duh) change your start page.

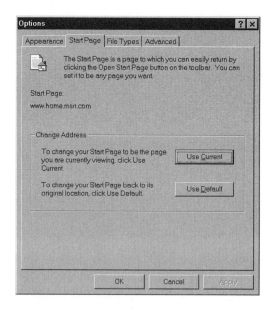

The Web page you're looking at is the first Web page you go to whenever you access the Web with the Explorer.

Your File type options

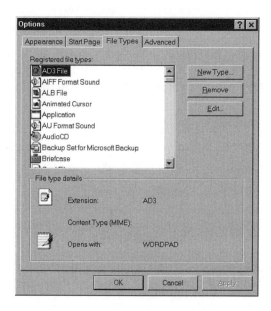

To change it back to the MSN Home Page, click **Use Default**.

File Types

This is where you tell Windows 95 what documents to open with which applications. I have *yet* to run into a file type that hasn't been listed in the Registered file types list, so I wouldn't lose any sleep over this one.

Advanced

The Advanced tab gives you two sets of options you can fiddle with, History and Cache.

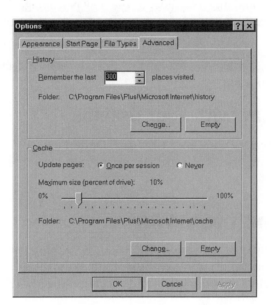

My, aren't these settings advanced!

The History options tell the Explorer how many URLs to remember after you visit them, and where to store them. The default number is 300—and that's a lot of URLs. To change the number, double-click on the number to select it and then type the number you want in its place.

> **Check This Out...**
>
> **Cache** The amount of disk space set aside to store information from, and about, the Web pages you've visited.

Explorer stores your history at C:\Program Files\Plus!\ Microsoft Internet\history. If you want it saved elsewhere, click **Change**. If disk space is low and you want to delete your WWW history, click **Empty**. That deletes it.

The Cache options take a little experimentation. If you've got a slower computer, you may want to change the **Update pages** option from **Once per session** (the default setting) to **Never**.

253

On slower computers, updating can slow down the browsing process. Clicking the **Never** button keeps the Explorer from looking to see if the page has changed and speeds things up a little.

I suggest you try browsing the Web with the update option set to **Once per session**. If it slows things down too much, then change it to **Never**.

The **Maximum size (percent of drive)** option tells the Explorer how much of your hard drive it can use for this cache of Web pages. The default is 10 percent. To change the Maximum size, click and drag the slider to the new percentage. You can delete all of the saved files in your cache (freeing up some hard drive space) by clicking the **Empty** button.

If you want to change where the Explorer saves your cache file, click the **Change** button and enter the new location.

When You're Done with Your Options

You can click **Apply** after you finish with each Option tab, or you can make all the changes you want, and then click **OK**. This applies your changes and closes the Options display.

Things to Do on the WWW

The Web is more than just Web pages that take you to other pages, and so on until goofiness sets in. You can do stuff like: listen to (and download) audio clips; look at (and download) pictures like the one below; and watch (all together now: and download) video clips.

A cast shot from the 60s show "UFO," from the Sci-Fi Channel's archives.

Whatever the file, or kind of file you're dealing with online, the process remains the same:

254

You click on the name and description of the file on the Web page. The file gets downloaded to your computer's memory and an appropriate application gets launched (if necessary) on your PC to display the file.

Make Sure You've Got the Right App for the Job

When viewing some files online, the Explorer launches an application from your PC to display the file. Sound files, for example, launch Windows 95's Sound Recorder.

You need to have an appropriate application for the file you want to see. If you don't have an application that can handle the file, don't waste your time trying to see it online—it won't happen, my friend.

You can stop, look, listen to the file and then get on with your life. If you decide you want to keep it, you have to save it first—because, at the moment, it's just hanging out in RAM. Click **Save** on the **File** menu. You receive a standard Save As dialog box. Use it to name the file and specify where to save it and then click **Save**.

Virus Reminder

We talked briefly about computer viruses back in Chapter 11.

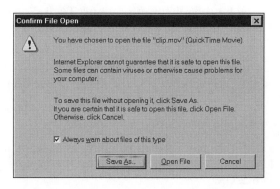

Danger, Will Robinson! (Sorry, too much Sci-Fi Channel, I guess.)

When you tell the Explorer to open a file, it reminds you of the virus danger (with the dialog box shown in the previous figure). If you insist on seeing the file now, click **Open File**, and the Explorer does just that. If you'd rather play it safe, click **Save As**, and the Explorer saves the file to disk so you can take a whack at it with an anti-virus utility before you open it.

If you completely chicken out, click **Cancel**, and the Explorer acts like you never asked it to do a thing.

Late-Breaking News

As I write this, Microsoft has just started testing version 2.0 of its Internet Tools. The main differences between the new version and the version discussed here are:

➤ The addition of a Search button on the toolbar, which takes you to a Web page with tools for searching WWW for particular information.

➤ New Security options, so you'll know if there's a chance someone is watching what you're doing on the Internet (it can happen).

➤ Some fun stuff: animated titles and integrated sound and video.

The new version may be available by the time you read this—if so, you can acquire it by the methods described in the "What You Need to Get Started on the Web" section.

The Least You Need to Know

Oh, what a strange new world that has such Web pages in it! I think that the very least you need to know about cruising the Web is that it's so much fun it can become an addiction. Consider yourself warned: The Betty Ford Clinic is opening a WWW wing. Otherwise keep these thoughts in mind:

➤ To access WWW, you need Microsoft's Internet Tools. You can download them with MSN version 1.05 (or higher), or purchase them in Microsoft Plus! Companion for Windows 95.

➤ Links that take you to other Web pages appear in one color before you use them, and in another after, so you always know where you've been.

➤ Pictures and other graphics can also be links. You know you can click something when your arrow cursor turns into a pointing hand.

➤ You can go to any Website for which you have an URL, by using the **Open** command in the **File** menu, or the **Open** button on the Explorer's toolbar. Type in the URL and then click **OK**.

➤ You can return to your start page at any time: just click the **Home** button on the toolbar.

Part 3
Tips, Tricks, and How-To Stuff

Up to now we've been looking at your basic, everyday operation of the Microsoft Network, with an eye toward just finding our way around and getting things done. Now we're going to get a little fancier.

The tips and tricks in this section include ideas for getting around online so fast it'll make your head spin, and tips on how to fix problems with MSN and how to get help when you need it.

In the how-to department, I'll show you how to set up MSN on a portable computer, so you can take it on the road with you, and show you how to prevent your child from getting an eyeful of some of the adult information available online.

Chapter 21

On the Road with MSN

In This Chapter

➤ Create a new Dialing Properties location

➤ Finding local access numbers

➤ Travel tips

Sometimes, in the course of human events, it becomes necessary to hit the road, Jack. You're finally taking a vacation, or you need to attend a conference, convention, or other work-related event. Maybe you're even moving to another city. You just need to be somewhere *else* for a bit.

When it happens, you'll want to be able to keep up with your e-mail, friends, and other online adventures. You can.

First Things First

If you're moving, or your everyday computer is portable, you can skip ahead to the next section.

If you're traveling with a laptop that you don't use regularly—one that you borrowed or rented for the occasion—you may need to read this section.

Before you can access the Microsoft Network from the road, you need to be sure the computer you're going to be using is up to the job. That means:

1. It has the MSN software (and Microsoft Exchange) installed on its hard drive.

2. It's equipped with a working modem that is connected properly (internal or external).

3. Wherever you go, you need to be sure there's a phone line handy that you can plug your modem into.

If your traveling computer doesn't have the MSN software installed, install it from your original Windows 95 disks or CD-ROM disc. The process is exactly the same as way the heck back in Chapter 3.

When you install the software, make sure the modem works by connecting it to a working phone line. You set up the software just like you did in Chapter 4, but with one *big* difference.

The first MSN registration screen.

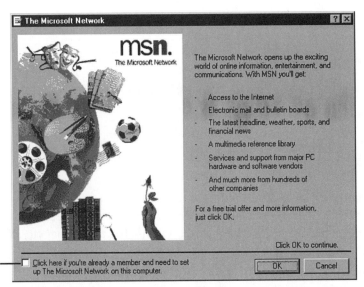

Click here to set up MSN on a portable.

Since you're already a member of MSN, when you start the registration process (see Chapter 5), instead of re-entering all that personal information again, just click the **Click here if you're already a member and need to set up The Microsoft Network on this computer** check box.

MSN sends you directly to the Sign In screen—do not pass go, do not collect $200. Type your member ID and password as usual, and click **Connect**.

When you do that, your laptop's modem calls MSN, and MSN's computers update the software on your traveling PC so it has all of your account information.

Change Your Dialing Properties

Before you hit the road, you can save yourself some time if you set up a new Location file for your destination in your Modems Properties dialog box.

Chapter 4 describes this process in detail, but, essentially you're just providing Windows 95 with information about where you'll be, and what sort of phone line you'll be using to connect with the outside world.

If you're setting up in advance, you may need to ask the reservations person at the hotel you're staying at (or the friend with whom you're staying) for information about the kind of phone line (pulse dial or touch tone) and what special numbers, if any, you need to dial to get to an outside line or make a long-distance call. Also, check to see if the phone line has call waiting.

If You're Moving, Not Visiting

After you create a new location file for your new home town, you can delete your old location file. In the Dialing Properties dialog box, simply select the old location file from the I am dialing from pop-up list and click **Remove**.

Don't delete your old location file until you're feeling comfortable in your new location. If you do so too soon, you may bring on a bout of homesickness—trust me.

You may want to have a location file for your home, your office, and any place you visit regularly. I have one set up for my home (which *is* my office), one for when I visit my family, and one for when I go to New York City—which isn't as often as I'd like.

I also keep a miscellaneous location file for places I don't go to very often—that way I'm not cluttering up my hard drive with location files for every place I've ever been with my laptop. All I need to do is enter the new local access numbers and fiddle with the dialing prefixes.

If you *do* wind up with a pile of extraneous location files, select the unnecessary location from the **I am dialing from** menu and click **Remove**. This deletes the location files from your system.

Calling All Calling Cards

As long as you're getting ready for your big travel adventure, now is a good time to set up your Dialing Properties so you can use your long distance calling card. (Chapter 4 covers this also.) You won't be using your calling card to call your home MSN access number. That's way too expensive. Instead, you will be using your calling card to charge the cost of the call from your hotel to MSN's local number wherever you're visiting (see the next section) to your home phone bill.

Hotels charge *outrageous* sums for calls (even local calls), but only minor change for the 1-800 numbers you use with most calling cards.

Use a calling card, too, if you're staying with a friend. Even if they say it's okay, it's still kind of rude to run up the phone bill of someone nice enough to put you up for a few days in their home. I think Aunt Effie will back me up on this.

Finding Local Access Numbers

When you travel to another city, you *don't* want to access MSN through your home town local access number. If you're out of your local calling area, you will run up a long distance call of the highest order. Instead, you can find a local access number for the city you're visiting. Fortunately, MSN enables you to choose from all of the available access numbers whenever you want. Here's how to do it.

1. If it isn't running already, launch the MSN software on your laptop.

2. On the Sign In screen, click the **Settings** button. This opens the Settings dialog box.

3. Click the **Access Number** button. This opens the screen that shows your two access numbers (Chapter 5 shows you all of this).

4. Click the **Change** button beside the first access number. This opens the next screen, shown in the next figure.

5. Select a new **Country**, **State/Region**, and **Access number** as appropriate from the pop-up lists.

6. Click **OK**.

7. Repeat steps 4 through 6 for the second access number. This time, select a *different* local number (if there's one available) for your destination, in case your first choice is busy.

You're good to go.

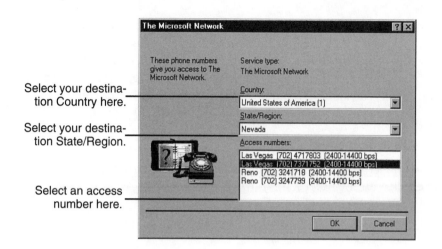

Select your destination Country here.

Select your destination State/Region.

Select an access number here.

Choosing a new access number for the road. I only wish I was heading for Vegas.

Pick Up the Phone

If you have any trouble locating a local access number for your destination city, you can give MSN's Member Support line a call.

To get a Member Support number, you need to run MSN Help. Click on the **Start** button. Click **Run**. In the Run dialog, type **C:\WINDOWS\HELP\Msn.hlp** and click **OK**. Help starts right up, as shown in the following figure.

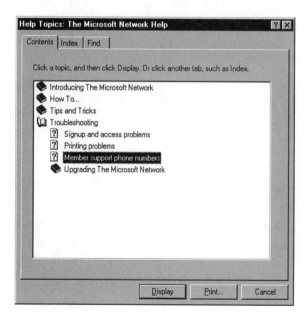

MSN's Help files.

Now, click the **Contents** tab and click the **Troubleshooting** entry from the list that appears. The list (as shown in the figure) of troubleshooting help titles drops down. Double-click the **Member support help numbers** (it's the one that's highlighted in the figure), and a list of member support numbers opens. Find the one appropriate for you (there are support numbers for spots all around the world) and give them a call.

When you call, be sure to have the following handy:

➤ Paper and a pencil to write things down.

➤ The telephone number from which you will be calling the Microsoft Network. You may want to check with the hotel staff, or wherever, to find out what this number is before you call—just so you know.

➤ The speed of the modem you will be using, from 2400 to 28,800 baud.

Travel Tips

Whether it's for business, pleasure, or out of necessity, traveling is traumatic enough without computer glitches to give you grief, too. Here are some tips to make traveling with your computer a little less stressful.

Call Ahead

If you're staying at a hotel, call and make sure that you can use the phone line in your room to connect your modem. You need to check two things in particular:

➤ Make sure there's a phone jack you can plug into (either a spare jack, or the phone's jack). If you use the phone's jack, you have to unplug the phone.

➤ Make sure that the hotel doesn't use a PBX phone system. Most modems, especially fax modems, don't work with PBX phone systems.

If you simply cannot get a room with a phone jack you can plug into, you either need to go into MSN withdrawal, or you can buy a modem adapter—called an acoustic coupler, if you must know—the kind you put the telephone's handset on. With the modem adapter, everything goes through the phone's ear and mouth pieces, instead of directly into the phone line. You can call your modem's manufacturer for details.

PBX phone systems are digital and much more powerful than standard phone lines. You can damage your modem. Ask before you plug into it. (You'd *think* modems and digital phone systems would get along great, but *noooo*. Go figure.)

You can sidestep the PBX problem with an adapter like the one mentioned above. Check with your modem's manufacturer, a PC mail-order company, or your favorite computer store.

When You Make Your Plane Reservations...

Airlines have gotten weird about passengers who use electronic equipment on flights. The airlines claim the electronics interfere with their navigational systems. Unfortunately, none of the airlines seems to agree on the type of electronics that cause this problem.

If you need or want to use your computer during your flight, ask if it's allowed when you make your reservations. Better still, call the airline before you make your reservations.

Other Stuff

Naturally, if you've traveled with a computer before, you know enough to do the following:

➤ Bring a spare battery or two, especially if the flight will last longer than one battery is likely to last (only you know how long your batteries last with normal use).

➤ Bring your power cord and/or battery charger, so you can plug in and recharge whenever possible.

➤ Carry your equipment in a padded bag. Take it on the plane with you. Even if you don't want to work, *never* check your delicate electronics unless you have indestructible stainless steel luggage.

➤ At airport security, you *can* have your laptop and accessories X-rayed. Contrary to popular wisdom, it does *not* damage your disks or hard drive. I've done it, and my laptop lives to tell the tale.

➤ If you're too chicken to have your laptop X-rayed, be prepared to turn it on to prove to security that it *is* a computer and not an instrument of international terrorism.

➤ Never leave your computer in the trunk of a car for more than a few minutes. Car trunks get too hot, or too cold. Plastic (like that in your laptop's case and floppy disks) melts, or freezes and cracks—bad, and expensive, news.

➤ If your computer does get too hot or cold, don't use it until it's back to room temperature. It may take an hour or two. Read a magazine, freshen up, or take a nap.

➤ Make sure you have a game or two loaded on your laptop—you can't work all of the time.

➤ Have fun and send me a post card.

The Least You Need to Know

Taking your MSN friends with you when you travel can be enjoyable and keep you from getting too homesick while on the road. It's very easy, and only takes a little planning.

➤ Location files, created with your Modem's Control Panel and the Dialing Properties button (see Chapter 4), spare you a lot a hassle on the road—and who needs the pressure? The most you need to do is tinker with the pre-dial stuff for outside lines and disable call waiting.

➤ You can get local access numbers by clicking the **Settings** button on the MSN Sign In screen and clicking **Access numbers**. Finally, click **Change** for each of your existing access numbers and select new ones for your destination.

➤ Before you leave, make sure that the place where you'll be staying is equipped to deal with your computer. This means you need a phone jack you can plug into and a non-PBX phone system or at least an adapter.

Kids and MSN

A couple weeks ago, I had some friends come to visit for four days—six of them. Four of them boys, aged 4–12.

You don't really get an appreciation for what parents go through until you find yourself looking at the stuff in your apartment thinking, "What here is okay for kids to mess around with?" In a single man's apartment, there isn't much. I had to put so many personal possessions out of reach, my place looked empty. It gave me a whole new outlook on the "adult/child appropriateness" thing.

(Though, to be fair, it was almost as frightening to realize how much of my stuff *is* appropriate for a 5-year-old to play with. A lot of it—toys, games, stuffed animals. Think about *that*.)

Adult Material

Our society is such that, whenever you use the words "adult material" in a sentence, everyone automatically thinks about pornography and obscenity. That isn't always the case.

Sure, much of the material rated "Adults Only" online is sexual in nature, and inappropriate for kids. It's an easy out to slap an "Adults Only" label on anything sexual. No one argues with the label, and no one gets offended.

However, other material (in areas that are rated "General Audience") are, in my opinion, just as inappropriate for young folks.

For example, in the Alien Encounters & UFOs Forum in the Mysteries, Magic, & Phenomena Category, there's a document that contains photos from a controversial film that allegedly shows aliens from the Roswell, NM UFO crash being autopsied. Real or not, I don't think scenes from an autopsy are appropriate for children—and my stomach wasn't too happy with them, either.

When I saw those pictures, I thought (well, *first* I thought *eeeeewwwwwww*) if I wasn't such a mature, sophisticated, '90s sort of guy, this would give me nightmares.

So, the point is, even if you do follow the advice given here and restrict your kids from areas rated "AO," it doesn't mean your job is done. You still need to supervise kids' online activities.

Check This Out...

Disclaimer: Your Kids, Your Decision

I'm skating on thin ice here (I also talk about politics and religion at parties, so be warned). I'm trying to make a point about online access in terms of what I think and believe. If you disagree with me, that's fine. Adults reading this need to think about what material is online and make up their own minds about letting their kids at it.

In no way am I trying to tell you what's good or bad for your kids, or what you should do. That's a parent's job and always will be.

The Full Access Issue

When you share your life with kids (your own, or loaners, the way I do it), you often find yourself saying things like, "I would really like to have this (whatever it is), but I don't want the kids to see it/use it/break it." Then you decide, based on how much you want the thing versus how little you want to explain it, or hide it, from the kids in your life, whether to get it.

The same is true of the Microsoft Network or any online service.

In terms of MSN, you've got three options:

1. Forget about the kids. Keep MSN and its adults-only content all to yourself. That stiffs the kids out of some fun.

2. Let the kids use *your* account, but don't get full adult access. That will make the kids happy, but you'll be cheating yourself.

3. Get the best of both worlds: your own, full access account and a limited access account just for the kids.

You need to decide, if you're going to use it, whether you're also going to let your kids use it, too. If you do decide to let your kids use it, you need to figure out how much access you're going to let the children in question have, because there *are* adult areas online.

Your Call

I'll explain how to set up a separate account for the kids in your life and how to restrict that account's access in two ways: by limiting access to areas rated "Adults Only" and to other areas on an as-needed basis.

Setting up an account for the child or children in your life is not a complicated affair.

On a Separate Computer

Apparently, it's not as unusual as I thought; there are a lot of people who have more than one computer in their homes. Parents upgrade their own PC, and give the older one to their kids. It eliminates a lot of arguments.

If the kids have their own modem-equipped PC, running Windows 95, simply follow the instructions in Chapters 3 through 5 to install the necessary software and create an MSN account with a different member ID and password than your own.

On the Same Computer

Money Warning! Money Warning! Unlike some online services, MSN's software doesn't allow for the creation of different member IDs under one master account, so there's only one bill.

With MSN, you have to create individual accounts, and MSN bills each account separately. You should know that before you set up an account for your kid(s).

If you're all one big happy family, sharing one big happy computer, you can still set up an MSN account for your kids. Here's how.

1. Click the **Start** button.

2. Click **Run**.

3. In the Run dialog box, carefully type (yes, including the double quotes (")): "**C:\Program Files\ The Microsoft Network\Signup.exe** in the text box.

4. Click **OK**.

5. This launches the registration routine you used to create *your* account back in Chapter 5. Simply repeat the registration process, entering a new member ID and password (different than your own) for your kids' account.

Limited Access

All new accounts are restricted from Full Adult Access. You don't have to take the steps outlined in this section, unless you want there to be absolutely *no question* about Adult Access for your kids.

To officially limit the new account's access to areas rated "Adults Only," *before* you turn the account over to your kids, sign on using their member ID and password. Then go to an "Adults Only" forum:

1. Click the **Edit** menu.

2. Point to **Go To** and click **Other Location**.

3. Type the Go word for the Adults Only forum you want to open (the Go word for the Sexuality Forum is **sexy**, though I don't want to seem like I'm picking on that forum) and press **Enter**.

4. Double-click on the adult forum's **BBS** icon.

5. Every adult forum BBS has a message explaining how to get full adult access. In the Sexuality Forum, it's called **Full Access for 18+** (other forums use similar, if not identical, names). Find the message thread and double-click on it to open it. (If you're reading ahead, the use of BBSs is covered in Chapter 10.)

6. Find the message called **How to Sign Up** and double-click on it to read it. It explains Full Adult Access, and how to get it (or not). At the end of the message, there is a shortcut to the Access EForm, like the one shown below.

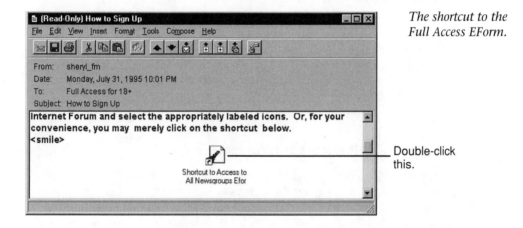

The shortcut to the Full Access EForm.

Double-click this.

7. Click on the shortcut. MSN thinks about it for a moment or two, then presents you with the Full Access EForm, as shown in the next figure. The **Request Access** tab is foremost.

Gimme access.

Don't gimme access.

Click here.

Then click here.

8. Click on the **Remove Access** tab.

9. Click in the **I agree with the following** check box.

10. Click **Send**.

You have officially removed Full Adult Access from your children's account. You'll receive a piece of e-mail confirming the change in a day or so.

To Get Adult Access for Yourself...

If you want to get Full Adult Access for yourself, repeat the process described here while signed on with your own member ID and password (if you don't use your own ID and password, you'll just give your kids account Full Adult Access, which kind of defeats the purpose of this chapter).

When you get to step 8, skip it. Leave the **Request Access** tab in the front. Click in the **I agree with the following** check box and click **Send**. You'll receive e-mail in a day or so confirming your Full Adult Access status.

Restricting Access to Other Forums

As I mentioned earlier, you may find material inappropriate for children in forums that are otherwise rated GA (for General Audiences).

To limit your child's access to a forum, you need to send e-mail to the forum manager requesting that he exclude the child's account from the forum.

First, go to the category that contains the forum in question. Click on the forum's icon to select it and then select **Properties** from the **File** menu.

More Kids & Computers Stuff By the way, *The Home Computer Companion* (Alpha Books, 1994) has an excellent section on kids and computers. It also includes scheduling tips, and lots of ideas for other stuff you can do with your computer. Check it out.

When the Properties window opens, click on the **Context** tab. This gives you information about the forum, including the member ID(s) for the forum manager(s), like those shown in the following figure.

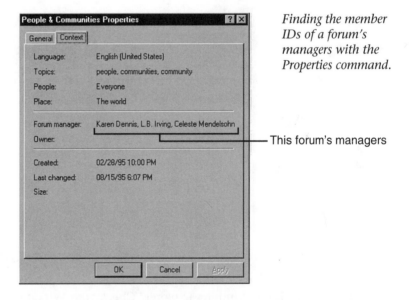

Finding the member IDs of a forum's managers with the Properties command.

— This forum's managers

Jot down the names and compose e-mail (explained in Chapter 12) addressed to one/all of the forum managers asking them to exclude your child's member ID from this forum.

Make sure you include your *child's* member ID, or you could wind up restricting yourself, not your child, from the forum.

You can repeat the process for any and all areas that you want to keep your child from using.

Restricting Access to the Internet

Unlike other areas on MSN, the Internet is not rated or moderated, and there is some *very* adult content out there, indeed. (I'd give you some examples, but I'm blushing at just the *thought* of some of it.)

If you want to prevent your child getting in over his or her head in the adult material available on the Net, you have to do two things:

1. Eliminate the Internet Tools

You can keep kids with MSN installed on their own, kids-only PC, from accessing much of the Internet by *not* installing Microsoft's Internet Tools. Without the tools installed, they cannot access Web pages.

If Microsoft's Internet Tools are already installed on your child's computer, you can delete them, using the Windows Explorer.

Deleting the Internet Tools with the Windows Explorer.

Delete this. ——

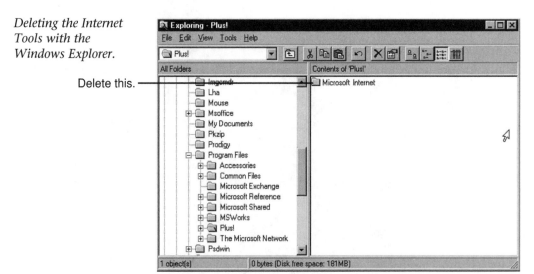

Unfamiliar with the Windows Explorer? Check your Windows 95 manual, or online Help files, for details.

You find the folder **Microsoft Internet** at the end of the path **C:\Program Files\Plus!\ Microsoft Internet**.

Click on the **Microsoft Internet** folder to select it and click the **Delete** button (it's the one with the X on it). Windows asks if you really want to delete the folder. Click **OK**. You also get a warning that you're about to delete an application file; when you get this warning, click **Yes to All**. The Internet is now out of your hair.

If your children use the MSN software installed on your computer, and you want to retain Internet access for yourself, *don't* delete the Microsoft Internet folder, as described above. Instead, you need to do the following before you let your kid(s) sign in:

1. Launch **MSN**.

2. Click the **Settings** button on the Sign In screen. This opens the screen shown in the figure here.

Click here. ——

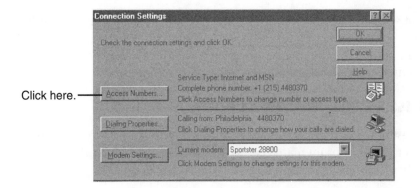

Changing your service type, temporarily.

3. Click the **Access Numbers** button. This opens the following screen.

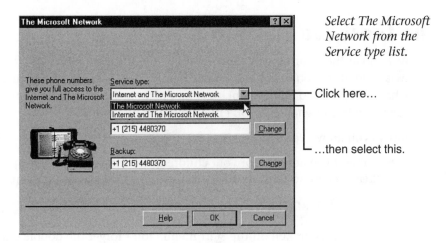

Select The Microsoft Network from the Service type list.

Click here...

...then select this.

275

4. Click the **Service Type** drop-down menu.

5. Select **The Microsoft Network** from the menu.

6. Click **OK**.

When You Want to Access the Internet...

Repeat the process described here before you sign in to MSN; however, when you reach step 5, select **Internet and The Microsoft Network**. This returns your Internet access.

MSN tells you that you need to restart the MSN software before the change takes effect. Click **OK**, and MSN shuts down. Then restart the software again. MSN is now incapable of accessing certain portions of the Internet. However, your kids can still enter and use MSN's Internet Center, which is why you need to do one more thing.

2. Restrict Access to the Internet Center

To eliminate the rest of your child's access to the Internet, you need to drop an e-mail note to the Internet Center's forum managers, as described earlier, asking them to restrict your child's member ID from the forum.

Once you receive confirmation that your child's member ID is restricted, you don't have anything to worry about.

The Least You Need to Know

As I said at the beginning of this chapter: your kids, your call. I won't presume to tell you what's good for you or your children (if more people would stop telling everybody else what to do, this would be a much happier planet). If you care to do any of the things suggested in this chapter, cool. I'm honored. If not, still cool.

Just so you know, your options are:

➤ To set up an account for your children, just run the Setup.exe application again and create a new account for the kids only. It's at the path statement:

C:\Program Files\The Microsoft Network\Signup.exe

If you're using Run on the Start menu, don't forget the double quotation mark (") in front, or you just get a cranky error message.

➤ A second, kids-only account, means a second MSN bill.

➤ All new accounts are restricted from Full Adult Access. You don't have to file the Full Access EForm unless you want there to be no question about Adult Access for your kids.

➤ You can further restrict your child's access to forums online by dropping an e-mail note to the forum manager(s).

Chapter 23

Member Assistance, or Help, Help! Oh, Help!

In This Chapter

➤ Touring the Member Lobby

➤ Checking your MSN bill

➤ Changing your method of payment

➤ Helpful resources

I don't care how big a computer geek you are—sooner or later you run into a situation you just don't know how to handle. It happens to me, it happens to Bill Gates (of course Bill has a fleet of technicians he can call), and it will happen to you.

If it so happens that the unknown whatever has something to do with MSN, there's an area online that's just dripping with helpful information: Member Assistance.

Getting to Member Assistance

Techno Talk

blah blah blah blah blah blah

Get Help Offline First Don't forget—you can run MSN's online Help files offline. Select **Run** from the **Start** menu. Type this: **C:\WINDOWS\HELP\Msn.hlp** in the text box. Then click **OK**. Why pay online fees if you don't have to?

To get to Member Assistance, click the **Member Assistance** bar on MSN Central. You can also use the Go word: LOBBY. The Go word is "LOBBY" because the main window of Member Assistance (shown in the next figure) is called the Member Lobby, and the theme, if you will, is that of an office building's lobby.

Like an office building lobby, there's a place to get information (About the Lobby), a Reception Desk, a map of the joint (Maps & Information), and other information.

A very cool Member Lobby feature is the MSN Suggestion Box. It's a BBS that enables you to post your comments and ideas on MSN, like a new forum you'd like to see, or a feature you'd like added to the software.

Let's start at the Reception Desk.

The Member Lobby is where you begin your quest for information.

Check This Out...

Flash!

The icon shown in the Member Lobby, the one with the lightning bolt on it, is an MSN System Flash. These documents contain important information about the MSN computers, such as scheduled times when the computer will be offline (inaccessible to you) for repairs, maintenance, or upgrades. Each news flash is dated so you can tell when it was released. You should read new flashes when you see them (just double-click its icon) so you don't get cranky trying to get online when the system is offline.

Welcome to the Reception Desk

The Reception Desk, shown next, is a great place for newbies to check out (in?). It contains a lot of basic, introductory material to help them get a handle on MSN quickly. The Go word is: RECEPTION.

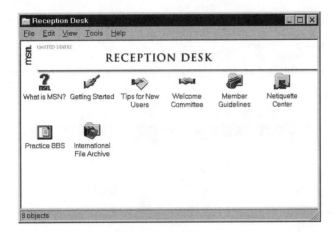

Basic information is available, all day, every day, at the Reception Desk.

Here you find several information displays that work like the MSN Today page (just click a topic to see the related details). Topics include:

➤ What is MSN?

➤ Getting Started

➤ Tips for New Users

➤ Welcome Committee

You can also access the Member Guidelines which you *should* have read when you joined MSN. They're available in the Member Guidelines folder if you didn't, or if you need to brush up.

The Netiquette Center folder gives access to tips and techniques for being a polite resident of MSN and the Internet. See Chapters 19 and 20 for more details.

Best for really new users is the Practice BBS which gives you a bulletin board where you can practice reading and posting messages. That way, you won't be completely surprised by the process when you try a regular forum BBS.

Finally, there's the International File Archive folder. This contains greetings in all the languages that are used on MSN. You can see a "Howdy-do" note from Bill Gates in German, Spanish, and other languages I don't speak.

Maps & Information: Online Tour Guides

Can you guess what you find in the folder named Maps & Information? I thought you could. Maps & Information (Go word: MSNMAPS), shown here, contains more information displays like those in the Reception Desk, just double-click to view them. Topics here include:

➤ How MSN is Organized

➤ Finding Things Fast

➤ Tips for International Travelers

➤ Getting on the Internet

The Maps & Information Window— and these maps you don't have to refold.

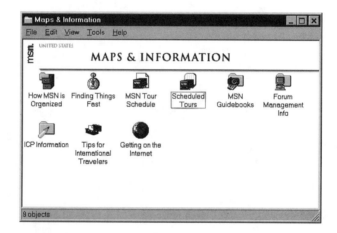

Additionally, Maps & Information contains a chat room where you can take part in a guided tour of the service given by MSN personnel. It's called Scheduled Tours, and the tours occur daily at 3:00 p.m. and 6:00 p.m. Pacific Time (that's 6:00 p.m. and 9:00 p.m. on the East coast).

The MSN Guidebooks folder contains copies of the titles you can also access from the MSN Today screen—MSN Life, MSN Kids & Co., and so on. They're all covered back in Chapter 14.

The remaining two folders contain information of interest to only a few folks. The Forum Management Info folder gives you the details on becoming an MSN Forum Manager. The ICP Information folder gives you the scoop on becoming an Information Content Provider, which is a fancy way of saying you want to buy and run your own forum online.

The Scoop on the Member Directory

Now, you probably think that the Member Directory folder (shown next, Go word: MSNDIRECTORY) explains, and enables you to play with, MSN's Member directory, but it only does half that. This area offers three information displays:

➤ Member Information

➤ Member Guidelines

➤ Welcome Committee

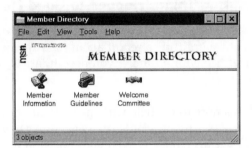

It's like the telephone book, but for MSN members only.

We saw both the Member Guidelines and Welcome Committee back at the Reception Desk. The Member Information display shows you how to use the MSN Member directory to find MSN members by information provided in their member profiles. It also shows you how to turn the information you find into a personal Address Book.

You can't actually do any of that here. It's done through the Microsoft Exchange (since the Address Book is e-mail related). E-mail, Microsoft Exchange, the Member Directory, and personal address books are covered in Chapter 12.

Getting Some Member Support

Member Support (Go word: USSUPPORT), shown next, is where you find answers to the most commonly asked (and uncommonly asked) questions about MSN.

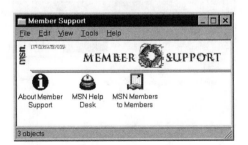

MSN's Member Support area.

The MSN Help Desk icon opens another informational display where you can read answers to the most common questions about MSN's BBSs, chat rooms, e-mail, the Internet, and more. Click on the appropriate title to scan for the information you need. If you can't find the answer you need here, the For More Information page gives you a number of options for getting help, including dropping a note to a live MSN support person.

When Bad Things Happen to Good Members

The MSN Help Desk's For More Information page also gives you the option of submitting a report about harassment, junk mail, or disruptive member behavior online. If you need it, use it.

Before you drop MSN a note to get help with an MSN question, check out the MSN Members to Members BBS. Any difficulties you encounter have probably already happened to someone else. Check here to see if your question has been asked and answered already. If it hasn't, you can post it yourself and wait for a reply.

The Members to Members BBS is broken down into the same categories as the Help Desk (in alphabetical order): Bulletin Boards, Chat, Connecting to MSN, E-mail, Internet, MSN General Discussions, and Navigation. There's also a folder for Windows 95 questions. Make sure you're reading —and posting—in the area most suited to your question.

Accounts & Billing

The Accounts & Billing area (Go word: MSNACCOUNTS), shown next, has two principal information displays: Accounts and Billing Information and Membership Plans. (The third icon in the window below is Tips for International Travelers again. Been there, done that.)

Learn all there is to know about MSN's accounting and billing here.

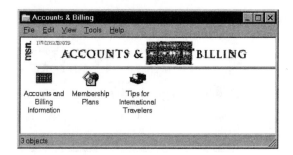

Accounts and Billing Information tells you how to check your current bill and previous months' bills and how to change your membership plan and method of payment. It also tells you how and why you should change your MSN password.

I do the same thing, later in this chapter.

Membership Plans explains the different subscription rates for MSN. You should check here from time to time. One thing that fluctuates regularly with a new-ish (funny, you don't look new-ish) online service is pricing. You may find a better deal here.

What's Hot and Happening Online: Activities & Promotions

If you're online and you don't know what to do, check in here. Activities & Promotions (shown in the following figure) may give you some ideas. If nothing else, it gives you direct access to the MSN Calendar of Events and MSN Life (both covered in Chapter 14) which contain scads of "Things to Do."

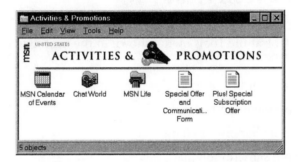

The Activities & Promotions area. Go word: MSNACTIVITIES.

If nothing strikes your fancy, you can double-click the **Chat World** icon and be hip-deep in chat rooms in nothing flat.

Before you run off to chat, though, look for document icons like the two shown in the preceding figure. These give details of any MSN promotional offers—maybe ten free hours when you buy a particular Microsoft product. Or, it may be a great deal on a product you planned to buy anyway. It never hurts to look for a bargain.

The MSN Newsstand

What would a lobby be without a newsstand? MSN's Newsstand (following, Go word: NEWSSTAND) offers easy access to MSN Today, all of the MSN Guidebooks, MSN Life, MSN Calendar of Events, and the whole News & Weather category (all covered in Chapter 14).

All the news you can stand, I guess.

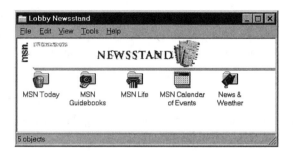

Practical Matters: Passwords & Billing

While Member Assistance is *rich* in practical information about your personal MSN account and bill, there isn't much you can actually *do* about them here. Actually, you can look at and change your billing information from MSN Central. This section shows you how.

You Start with the Tools Menu

You can fulfill all of your billing and password needs, while online, with a few clicks of your mouse. If you look at the Tools menu, shown in the next figure, you see that you can...

➤ Change your password,

➤ Change your payment method,

➤ See a summary of your online charges,

➤ And change your subscription plan.

All that with one little menu.

MSN's Tools menu, with the Billing submenu showing.

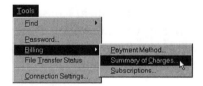

Password Paranoia

I admit it. I'm password paranoid. I'm convinced that someone is going to figure out my password and run up my MSN charges until I land in debtor's prison. Hey, stranger things have happened. Didn't you see *The Net* and *Hackers*?

To keep my (somewhat tenuous) grip on reality, I change my password regularly—every two to three weeks. Here's how to do it. Start from MSN Central, then:

1. Click on the **Tools** menu.

2. Click on **Password**. This opens the Change Your Password dialog box.

3. Type your current password in the text box labeled First type your current password.

4. Then type your new password in the Next type your new password text box—you can just use the Tab key to get to it.

5. Finally, type your new password again in the text box labeled Type the new password again.

6. Click **OK**.

You type your password *twice* as a way to make sure you typed it correctly, because, as you're typing, you don't see the letters and numbers you type on-screen. Instead you see just a string of asterisks (***). Type carefully.

MSN's Password Rules

Your password can be anything you like (and can remember) as long as it meets a few simple rules. It has to be at least eight characters long and no more than 16. It must be different from your member ID, and it cannot contain blank spaces. It can, however, include any character on a standard keyboard.

Changing Your Method of Payment

If you go on a shopping spree and max out the credit card to which you bill your MSN charges, you may want to change your payment method. You may also want to change it if you close the credit card account in favor of one with lower rates, or if your card gets lost or stolen.

Safety Alert!

If something ever does go wrong with your credit card, as described here, MSN may send you a note telling you there's a billing problem and ask you to change your method of payment following the steps outlined here.

No MSN employee will ever ask you to e-mail them your name, address, or credit card number. If someone does, it's probably a scam. Don't do it. Report the perpetrator to MSN as described in the "When Bad Things Happen To Good Members" sidebar earlier in this chapter.

You can also change your name and address information at the same time.

To start, click on the **Tools** menu in MSN Central. Point your cursor at the word **Billing** and click **Payment Method**. The dialog box shown next pops up.

Click either button to change your name, address, or payment method.

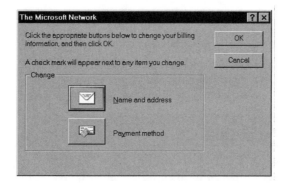

To change your name and address, click the **Name and address** button. To change your payment method, click the **Payment method** button. In each case, MSN presents you with simple dialog boxes in which you provide the new information. In fact, they're exactly the same as the ones you used to provide this information when you registered with MSN originally, back in Chapter 5. You can check there if you've forgotten what they look like.

Getting a Look at Your MSN Bill

To see how much money you've spent so far this month, or what your total was for any previous month, select **Summary of Charges** from the **Billing** submenu on the **Tools** menu.

When you do, a blank Online Statement window opens. It shows your current balance, the remaining free connect time you have left, and when the billing period ends. If you need more information, click the **Details** button.

Click on the billing period you want to check in the Period list box and click **OK**. MSN thinks about it for a moment and then displays the details in the Online Statement window (shown next).

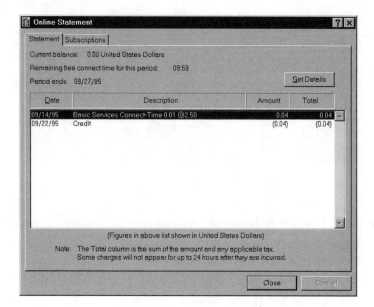

Details on my current bill—I don't owe them a cent.

When you're done, click **Close**, and the display goes away. Or, if you want to check which Subscription plan you have, you can click the **Subscriptions** tab.

Changing Subscription Plans

If you use more or less time online than you anticipated when you first chose a subscription plan, you can change plans easily enough.

Normally, you discover changes in usage while looking at your bill (as described in the last section). If your Online Statement is still open, you can simply click the **Subscriptions** tab. Otherwise, from anywhere else online, select **Subscriptions** from the **Billing** submenu on the **Tools** menu. A window like the one shown here opens.

If the Trial Plan was still valid when you joined (it's supposed to be a limited time thing, but who knows?) you may have *two* subscription plans as I do here. The Trial Plan followed by the plan that kicks in when the trial period ends.

The Subscriptions display.

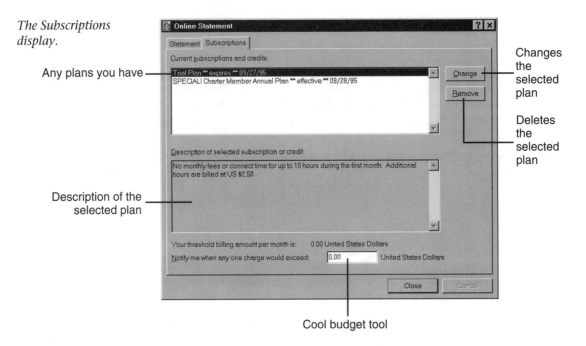

Any plans you have

Description of the selected plan

Changes the selected plan

Deletes the selected plan

Cool budget tool

To view the details of the plan, click the plan's name in the Current Subscriptions and credits display. A description appears in the box labeled Description of selected subscription or credit.

To change the selected plan, click **Change**. You receive a dialog box of your subscription options. Click the plan you want and click **OK**.

To remove the selected plan, click **Remove**. It's gone.

Stay Within Your Budget

Money's tight. You've only allowed yourself to spend X amount of dollars each month on MSN. To help you stay within your budget, enter the maximum amount of money you want to spend *per session* in the text box labeled Notify me when any one charge would exceed. MSN warns you if you're about to go over your budget for an online session. Cool. Cheap. I like it.

Changes Take Time

Any changes you make online to your billing or personal information take a day or so to kick in. The changes don't affect your current online session, and they may not be in place when you sign in the next day (depending on how busy they are in Member Services). Just so you know.

Canceling Your MSN Account

It can happen. If you decide MSN isn't for you and you want to cancel your MSN account, call MSN's nearest Member Support number. In the North America, that's 1-800-386-5550. Tell the service representative you want to cancel, and he will walk you through the process.

The Least You Need to Know

Member Assistance is a wonderful source of information, and a sneaky way to get at some of the more popular areas online. The absolute least you need to know is that you get there by clicking **Member Assistance** in MSN Central.

Billing, membership information, and subscriptions are all changed by way of the Tools menu. You don't have to go to Member Assistance; you can make any changes you like right from MSN Central.

Chapter 24

Troubleshooting the Microsoft Network

In This Chapter

➤ Easy solutions to common problems

➤ Sources of help when you aren't connected to MSN

➤ Sources of help when you *are* connected

In my experience, once you get your Microsoft Network software installed and configured, and you use it correctly, things rarely go wrong—at least, not anything that *you* can do anything about. But that's *my* experience. Your experiences may vary.

To help you over the rough spots, here's a bunch of advice culled from other places in the book, plus some additional information on how to figure out what's wrong, why it's wrong, and how to fix it.

Generally Speaking

Generally speaking, there's nothing that can go *so* wrong with the Microsoft Network that your computer explodes or anything, so don't panic.

Also generally speaking, there are only four places where things can go wrong when you're trying to do something with MSN: your hardware, your software, the local connection (*node*), or with MSN's computers in the jolly state of Washington.

When things go wrong, and *what* goes wrong, can give you an indication of *where* something is boogered up (*boogered up*—a highly technical term; use it to impress your friends).

For example: if you're trying to get MSN started up and connected, but *nothing* is happening, the problem is with your hardware or software. It has to be because you haven't called out and attempted to connect.

On the other hand, if MSN starts up fine, and dials out fine, but you run into trouble trying to connect to your local access number, then the troublemaker is probably your software or your local node. It isn't likely to be your hardware because you wouldn't have gotten as far as you did if your modem was broken—that's not to say it *can't* be your hardware, just that it's low on the list of things that could be wrong.

On the other hand (which would give you three hands, and make you a heck of a touch-typist), if the problem occurred once you were connected to the Microsoft Network, then it's probably being caused by its computers. Depending on what happened, it could also be your local node, or your computer.

Get the idea? It's kind of like the food chain. In the food chain, the smaller and weaker you are the more things can eat you. With the connection chain, the further along you go, the more things there are to mess with your computer.

MSN Software Won't Launch

If you're having trouble getting your Microsoft Network software up and running, you may have installed the software incorrectly, incompletely, or even damaged it by some unknown mishap. It happens.

Reinstall and reconfigure your software following the instructions in Chapters 3, 4, and 5—but make sure to click the **Click here if you're already a member and need to set up The Microsoft Network on this computer** check box when MSN asks you to re-register. This simplifies the process greatly.

Modem Woes

Your software starts fine, but when you try to get it to use your modem, all sorts of craziness happens. You get an error message saying "MSN can't initialize your modem," and the modem won't accept commands. Your first step: check the obvious:

➤ Is your *external modem* connected properly? Cables tight? Correct port?

➤ Plugged in?

➤ Turned on?

➤ Is your *internal modem* seated properly in its expansion slot?

➤ Is the phone line working and connected to the modem properly? Double-check, carefully. Looks can be deceiving.

If that all seems to be fine, try this: turn off your external modem. Wait about 30 seconds, or so. Turn it back on and try again.

For an internal modem, save any open documents and exit all open applications. Next select the **Shutdown** command from your Start menu. When the dialog box appears, click **Restart the computer**. This puts your PC, Windows 95, and your modem through a *soft boot*.

If that doesn't fix it, repeat the process, but this time when the dialog box appears, select **Shut down the computer**. When your screen tells you it's safe to turn off your computer, do so. Wait about a minute, then turn it back on and try again.

You may also want to try using your modem with the plain communications software that came with it (either on a floppy disk, or installed on your hard drive), or with another online service (maybe CompuServe, Prodigy, or America Online if you're a member).

Soft Boot
Term for restarting your computer *without* turning it off or cutting the power to it. It's much easier on your PC—it spares it that jolt of electricity inherent in turning it off and on again.

If you've got Microsoft Works for Windows 95, or a similar package, you probably have a communications module. You may want to test with that. Check the software's manual or online Help for details.

If your modem works with the *other* software, your MSN software is probably the culprit. Try removing it with the Windows Setup tab of the Add/Remove Programs Properties display (in the Control Panel window). Then reinstall it and set it up again as described in Chapters 3, 4, and 5.

If your modem is connected properly and doesn't respond to *any* communications software, there's something wrong with the modem. Check out the modem trouble-shooting guidance that follows, which includes how to access Windows 95's Modem Troubleshooter.

Modem Peculiarities

Since there are so many makes and models of modems (and so many Ms in this sentence), it's difficult to say what to try if your modem is giving you grief. You do have some options, though.

Try the Modem Troubleshooter

If your modem isn't working properly with MSN, or it just isn't working at all, you can try using Windows 95's Modem Troubleshooter to help you sort out the problem.

Select **Help** from the Start menu and double-click **Troubleshooting** in the Contents list. Finally, double-click the entry **If you have trouble using your modem**. It asks you a series of questions about the problem you're having in order to help you resolve it.

Try the Manufacturer's Technical Support Line

Most manufacturers of computer hardware and software maintain technical support lines that you can call and ask questions about their products.

They'll know their products the best (at least you'd think so). If you're having a modem problem you can't sort out, give them a call. This number is usually listed in the troubleshooting or technical support section of most owner's manuals.

You need to have a pencil, paper, and relevant information about your system: the CPU (386, 486, Pentium), RAM, operating system (Windows 95), make and model of the modem, and a brief description of the problem, including any error messages you may have gotten, when you call.

High Speed Hassles

If you're using a high speed modem (say 14,400 BPS and higher) and you want to use that extra speed with the Microsoft Network, check your modem's manual for configuration tips.

What About 28.8 BPS Access?

You *can* access MSN at 28.8 BPS, if your modem can handle it, but you must have Microsoft's Internet Tools installed on your PC. The Internet Tools are included with the upgrade to MSN 1.05, which is being tested at this writing. Check in Member Assistance for more information. At the moment, 28.8 access is through a very limited set of local access numbers, but there should be way more by the time you read this.

Some modems require that you configure the Modems Control Panel's Advanced setting for hardware handshaking. Others require different settings for X-On/X-Off or flow control.

You don't really need to know what all that means (they're just buzzwords applied to how modems connect to each other and regulate the flow of junk back and forth). You *do* need to know how you set those options in your Modems Control Panel. They're covered in Chapter 4.

If your modem's manual doesn't explain it clearly, you may want to call the modem manufacturer's technical support line, or call one of MSN's Member Support numbers (they're coming up soon).

Can't Connect to Local Access Number

You launched MSN fine, it initialized your modem, and dialed the local access number, but, for some reason, it doesn't connect to your local node. There are a couple of things that may cause this to happen.

No Dial Tone

If your modem doesn't hear a dial tone when you try to dial your local access number, you get a message that says (*duh*) No Dial Tone.

Chances are one of the following is happening:

➤ Your modem isn't connected to your phone line (check to make sure).

➤ Your modem isn't connected *correctly* (many modems have two jacks: one for the phone line and one for a telephone—make sure you plugged each into the proper jack).

➤ Your phone line isn't working.

If you have a phone connected to the same line, try picking up the receiver and listening. If you don't hear a dial tone, press the cutoff button a few times. ("Flash" is the modern, cordless, cellular sort of term, I guess, but hey, we used to have a *party line* when I was a kid. I'm not used to this newfangled stuff.) This may get you a dial tone again. If not, you may want to have a friend or neighbor call your number and then report the line trouble to your phone company if there's no answer. Of course, you can do this yourself if you have a second phone line that's working.

When you do hear a dial tone, hang up the phone and try your modem again. If it still doesn't work, chances are that the modem is set up wrong, or defective. Check the modem manual for installation, setup, and configuring information.

Access Number Is Busy

It happens. That's why you have *two* local access numbers. If both are busy, try the numbers several times, waiting five to ten minutes between attempts. If the numbers are *still* busy, try selecting another set of access numbers, as described in Chapters 5 and 21.

Don't Just Change Stuff: Keep Track

Before you go changing anything, write down your settings the way they are *now*. If you go into an ecstasy of info-swapping, you may forget what your settings looked like before you started—and you may want or need to change them back the way they were.

It also doesn't hurt to make sure you've got the correct telephone information entered in your Modems Control Panel. Check to see if you entered the phone number correctly, selected touch-tone vs. Pulse dial, entered the number (like 9) that you have to use to get an outside line, and disabled call waiting (if you have call waiting). Chapter 4 has the details.

Can You Say "Duh?" I Thought You Could.

It may seem like a *really* obvious point to make, but I'm going to make it anyway. If you don't have call waiting, *don't* click in the Disable call waiting check box. It confuses the heck out of your phone line, and you won't be able to connect to MSN.

If you *do* have call waiting, disable it as described in Chapter 4.

No Answer at Local Access Number

Same deal as in "Access Number Is Busy." Try a few times, waiting a few minutes in between tries. While you're waiting, double-check to see if you set the phone number(s) and other phone information correctly in the Set Up screen. If you make any changes, be sure to save the new settings (just click **Save**), then try again. Chapters 4 and 6 have the details on how to set up.

If you *still* don't get an answer from the access number, try an alternate access number, as described in Chapters 5 and 21.

No Carrier Signal

Your modem dials the number, the number answers, but you don't get that digital "Hi, how you doin'?" squeal from the modem at your local access number.

Same solutions as "busy" and "no answer," above: try again or change access numbers.

Final Connection to MSN Didn't Happen

Sometimes you call up your local access number, connect fine, and then something goes wonky (another technical term) when the local node tries to connect you to the Microsoft Network.

What happens to *me* is that I sit there while the Sign In screen says Verifying Account or Verifying Internet Access and then I get a polite error message saying I am no longer connected to the Microsoft Network. I didn't know I was connected in the first place.

Remember the old saying: If at first you don't succeed, try, try, again.

Before you fool around with any of your hardware or software, try a few more times, waiting a few minutes between attempts. The problem, most likely, is with your local node, or MSN itself. Don't panic.

If it takes too long, and you're too impatient, or it happens too often, check out Chapters 5 and 21 for advice on picking new local access numbers.

Problems After You've Connected to MSN

Sometimes apparent poop starts to happen after you've signed on to the Microsoft Network, and you have no idea why. The following are typical.

Everything Is Sooooo Sloooowwwww

If you're in a chat room, or downloading a file, and it seems to be taking forever to get anything done, the problem is that there's a lot of traffic on MSN or on your local access node.

There are *thousands* of people using the service, and they're all trying to do the same stuff. It slows things down and, because it takes longer to do stuff, runs up your phone bill and online charges. Here are a few things you can try.

➤ Sign off and connect again. That often solves the problem if the source is your local node.

➤ Try another local access number—one that's less active. Unfortunately, the only way to tell if it's really less active is to try it.

➤ Stop downloading files and use the Transfer Status window (see Chapter 11) to retrieve or send your files when you're done exploring MSN. It automatically disconnects you from the service when the transfer is done.

➤ Sign off, wait a while, and try again later.

MSN Disconnects You

Suddenly being knocked offline is known as being *punted* to those in the know. For no apparent reason, you're treated like a football and drop-kicked off the service. It happens from time to time, and for a number of reasons you don't really need to know.

The only thing to do about it is pick yourself up, dust yourself off, and start all over again.

If it happens regularly, make sure that you disabled call waiting (if you have it) in your Modems Control Panel. Chapter 4 tells you how. The clicking sound an incoming call makes can disrupt the flow of information to your computer, making MSN's computer think you've hung up.

If call waiting isn't the problem, you can also try another set of local access numbers.

Trouble Downloading Files

When you download files, whether one at a time, or in a bunch with the Transfer Status window (covered in Chapter 11), you can't seem to get MSN to finish the job. You get disconnected, or otherwise interrupted.

The first thing to do is try again. The problem may be a slow down, or "punt" situation like those described above. There may just be too many people trying to download files at the same time.

If the problem happens *all the time*, there may be another difficulty. Check the following:

➤ If you have call waiting, make sure you've checked the Disable Call Waiting check box in your Set Up screen. See Chapter 6 for instructions.

➤ If you use a screen saver (the one that comes with Windows 95, After Dark, or any other one) turn it off before you sign in to MSN.

Most screen savers kick in if there isn't any keyboard or mouse activity for a few minutes. During a download, there isn't any activity like that, but your computer is still busy. If the screen saver starts up in the middle of a download it can booger up the process, or even damage the files as you download them. Check your screen saver manual for instructions on how to temporarily turn it off.

Sources of Help

There are a number of ways you can get Help to resolve problems with the Microsoft Network, both offline and on. If you're having trouble connecting to MSN, naturally you need to use the offline resources first. If you can connect to MSN, but run into trouble online, you can try both online *and* offline help.

Offline Help

You can use the information from the Microsoft Network's Help menu—even though you can't *see* the Help menu when you're not connected to MSN.

Click the **Start** button and click **Run**. When the Run dialog box opens, type: **C:\WINDOWS\HELP\Msn.hlp** in the text box. Click **OK.** The Microsoft Network's Help fires right up.

MSN's Help works like any other Windows 95 Help files you've ever used. You can select topics from the Contents list or Index, or find Help by searching for a pertinent word or phrase.

Member Support

The Microsoft Network also maintains Member Support lines all around the world, so you can call and find answers to your questions. Worldwide Member Support phone numbers are listed in MSN's Help files (as discussed above) in the Troubleshooting section.

Member Support Numbers

At the moment these are the telephone numbers for reaching Member Support in North and South America.

English	800-386-5550
Spanish	95-800-2156987
French Canadian	800-952-1110
Other Countries in South America (Spanish)	813-577-9916

The numbers listed are subject to change, however. You can download the latest numbers from Member Assistance online (see Chapter 24).

Member Support offers two sorts of assistance: live and automated. When you call up, an automated system (you know, "Press 1 for Automated Help, *now*.") answers your call and directs it (if you're using a touch-tone phone).

With automated help, you're given a series of choices, and you need to select the one that sounds like the problem you're having (connection problems, membership or account questions, and so on). Some of the automated help choices even offer you the option of receiving the information by fax (if you're fax-capable).

At the moment, automated support is available the same hours as live Help, below. That may change as MSN picks up steam—or it may not. The only way to find out is to give a call.

With live support, real live people take your questions from 7 a.m. until 2 a.m., Monday through Friday, and from 12:00 p.m. to 10 p.m. on weekends (that's Eastern Standard time, by the way).

Whether you're calling to talk to a live person or to listen to the automated stuff, you should have a pencil and paper handy to write down the information you get. When talking to a real flesh-and-blood person you should also have some additional information at your fingertips: your computer's processor (386, 486, Pentium), amount of RAM installed, the make and model of your modem, and a brief description of the problem, including any error messages you may have gotten.

Online Help

There are almost as many ways of getting help with a problem online as there is offline.

Forum Foibles

It's easy for beginners to get lost and confused online. Don't panic. Most forums online have an Information Kiosk and Visitor's Center where you can find all manner of useful information to help you find your way around the forum and MSN.

Ask in a Chat Room

If you're having trouble, you can always pop into a chat room and ask a host or another member for help. Hosts are a great resource—if they don't know the answer to your question, they can at least point you in the right direction. You can usually find a host in all moderated chat rooms—that's what makes them moderated, after all.

Other users are also good for help. A lot of folks online have been using the service for months (even before it was opened to the general public) and know the ins and outs pretty well.

Chapter 13 has the scoop on hosts, chat rooms, and chatting.

Check Out Customer Service in Member Assistance

Member Assistance is *completely* devoted to helping you figure out what the heck is going on, online. There are dozens of helpful resources, from chat rooms to guidebooks, and even guided tours you can take.

Member Assistance is so chock-full of information that it's got a chapter all its own: Chapter 23. Check it out.

The Least You Need to Know

With all of these helpful resources around, you should never encounter a problem so bizarre that no one can help you out of it. *Life* should be so fully explained.

➤ When trouble happens, *don't panic*.

➤ Problems tend to crop up in one of four places: your hardware; your software; the local access node; and on MSN itself. Knowing *when* the problem happened, and *what* happened, can help you figure out *where* or *why* it happened.

➤ You can get help offline with your Start menu, and through MSN's worldwide Member Support numbers.

➤ You can get help online from Help files and Information Kiosks, hosts, other MSN members, and Member Assistance.

I LOVE THIS PLACE.

Chapter 25

Go Words, Short-cuts, and Favorite Places

In This Chapter

➤ The art of getting where you're going, fast

➤ Finding and using Go words

➤ Creating and using shortcuts

➤ Adding a favorite place to Favorite Places

I hope you think (as I do) that saving money is a good thing (because it is), and that speed (online, at least) is of the essence.

Getting Around Quickly

I live in a pretty big city. After you live somewhere for a while (in my case, five years), you get to know the sneaky and roundabout—but *fast*—ways to get where you're going. Getting around on MSN (which is like a big digital city) has the same sort of learning curve—but, thankfully, not five years' worth.

There are three main ways to get from point A to point B, quick like a bunny, online. They are: using Go words, using shortcuts, and adding to (and using) MSN's Favorite Places screen. Each method takes you on an online trip that normally (if you were plotting it like a mall "You Are Here" map) looks like this:

> **MSN Central/Categories/Interests, Leisure, & Hobbies/Alien Encounters,** ➡**& UFOs**

and turns it into this:

> **MSN Central/Favorite Places/Alien Encounters, & UFOs**

or even:

> **Your Desktop/Alien Encounters, & UFOs**

Of these three (for me, anyhow), shortcuts are the fastest because they can take you from being *offline* to being online and then to the MSN area of your choice. Go words come next because they can take you from point A to point Z without all that double-clicking of Category and Forum folders in between.

Finally, Favorite Places is not *as* fast, but it can save you considerable online time—especially if you visit a set of forums every time you're online.

Each method takes a little preparation before you use it, and we'll look at each in turn: how to set them up, and then how to use them.

Shortcuts

If you've forgotten, a shortcut is an icon that you create. It's like a trail of bread crumbs leading from your PC's desktop to a particular location on MSN. When you double-click a shortcut, you go to the area the icon represents—even if you weren't connected to MSN when you double-clicked.

Creating Shortcuts

To create some shortcuts of your very own, you need to first connect to MSN. Next, go to the category of your choice and locate the folder for the forum for which you'd like to have a shortcut. Then...

1. Click the forum's folder with your *right* mouse button to select it. This calls up the menu shown in the following figure.

The old right mouse button click trick...

2. Click **Create Shortcut** on the menu. MSN creates the shortcut and then shows you a confirmation message (like the one shown in the next figure).

Click here to skip this confirmation forever after.

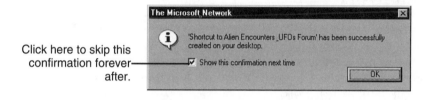

Shortcut confirmation— just click OK.

3. Click **OK**. The message goes away, and you're left with a lovely little shortcut on your Windows desktop.

Shortcut to Alien Encounters & UFOs Forum.mcc

A shortcut to Alien Encounters.

If You're Using Your Right Mouse Button for Something Else...

Some mice are programmable so the right mouse button does something funky, such as double-click with one click or some similar funkiness. If you've got such a mouse and you've programmed the right mouse button to do something other than call up this sneaky menu, you can *still* create a shortcut. All you have to do is click the **Forum** icon to select it and then click **Create Shortcut** in the File menu.

However, you should really think about reprogramming your mouse buttons so you can access this *very* convenient pop-up menu. It's too cool for school. Check your mouse manual, or its online Help files for details, if you're interested.

307

Using Shortcuts

Using a shortcut is simple enough: just double-click the shortcut for the forum you want to visit. If you're online, you go to the forum. If you aren't connected to MSN, your MSN software fires up and presents you with the Sign In screen. Enter your member ID and password and then click **Connect**.

You connect to MSN and go directly to the shortcut's forum. Very simple and very cool.

Managing Your Shortcuts

The Windows 95 desktop is already a pretty cluttered affair. Depending on the installation choices you made, you probably have a string of icons running down the side of the desktop already. Mine has: My Computer, the Inbox for Microsoft Exchange, my Recycle Bin, the MSN shortcut, a briefcase for Microsoft Office, *and* the shortcut I just created. It's getting crowded—all right, crowded for someone as anal-retentive as me.

If you don't want to clutter up your desktop with still *more* icons, do this:

1. Click your desktop with your right mouse button. This calls up the shortcut menu shown in the following figure.

Son of the right mouse button click trick...

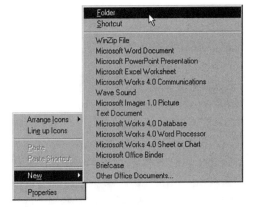

2. Point at the **New** command. That calls up the submenu (also shown in the figure).

3. Click **Folder**. Windows thinks about it for a moment, and then a new folder appears on your desktop. The folder's name is selected and ready for editing (like the one shown in the next figure).

4. Type a name for the folder. I called mine **MSN Shortcuts**.

5. Press **Enter**.

6. Click-drag your **MSN Shortcuts** icon and drop it on your new desktop folder.

My Computer   New Folder

A new folder: call it "MSN Shortcuts."

Poof—your shortcut is out of the way, but nicely organized in a folder of its own. To get at it, double-click the folder to open it and then double-click the shortcut of your choice.

Deleting Shortcuts

If you should ever tire of an area, why clog up your desktop (or new, way-cool MSN Shortcuts folder) with useless junk? Get rid of unwanted shortcuts. Here's how:

Click the unwanted shortcut with your *right* mouse button. When the clever little menu pops up, click **Delete**. As always, Windows asks if you're really, really, really sure you want to send the shortcut to the Recycle Bin. Click **OK** and that puppy's gone to shortcut heaven (well—*after* you empty the Recycle Bin).

Share Your Shortcuts!

This Works for BBS Postings, Too!

If you want to share an online discovery with everybody online, you can post a shortcut to a BBS message. Just follow the instructions here, but instead of using Microsoft Exchange, you use your favorite word processor (to compose the posting offline), or the message editing dialog box online.

Message board postings are covered in Chapter 10 if you need more details.

If you have a friend online and you want to share one (or more) of your shortcuts with her, it's easy. Mail 'em to her!

Write an e-mail note addressed to your friend using Microsoft Exchange (as described in Chapter 12). It is nice if you include a description of the shortcut and where it takes her when she uses it.

Before you send the note, minimize Microsoft Exchange. Then, open your MSN Shortcuts folder and do a *right* mouse button click on the shortcut you want to send. Select **Copy** from the pop-up menu.

Next, maximize Microsoft Exchange. In the body of the e-mail click once to place the cursor—where you want the shortcut to go. Then select **Paste** from the Edit menu. Your shortcut appears there shortly. Next time you're online, send the e-mail to your friend.

When she gets your note, your friend can use your shortcut too—she can copy and paste it to her desktop, or just double-click it in the e-mail window to access the forum.

Go, Go, Go Words

Go words, like shortcuts, take you quickly to a designated area on the Microsoft Network. Unlike shortcuts, you can only use them while connected to MSN.

Before you can *use* Go words, you have to find them—but that's easy enough.

Finding Go Words

Most forums have Go words, and they're not secret. To find them, all you have to do is check the forum's properties (so you need to be connected to MSN to do this). Here's how: first, go to the category of your choice and locate the folder for the forum for which you want a Go word. Then click the **Forum** icon with your right mouse button.

Checking a Forum's properties.

When the shortcut menu pops up (as shown in the last figure), click **Properties**. This opens a standard Windows 95 Properties display for the forum (much like the one shown in the next figure). The Go word appears in the second line of the General tab, the one labeled (get ready for a shock) *Go word*.

You can jot the Go word down on a pad of paper you keep near your PC, or you can type it into a text file of Go words that you keep open when you're online.

Techno Talk

Save Steps

If you decide to keep a text file of Go words on your hard drive, use the same word processor to create it that MSN uses to display its online text files (Chapter 25 explained how to find out which word processor to use). I mean, it's going to be open when you're online anyway, so why not save some steps?

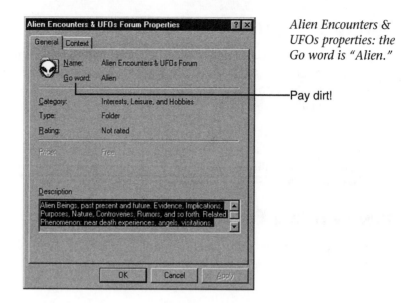

Alien Encounters & UFOs properties: the Go word is "Alien."

Using Go Words

Once you acquire some Go words for your favorite areas online, here's how to use them. (Do I need to remind you that these only work while you're signed on to MSN? I didn't think so.)

1. From any location online, click the **Edit** menu.

2. Point at **Go to**, which is at the bottom of the menu. A submenu pops up.

3. Click **Other Location**. The Go To Service dialog box (shown in the following figure) appears.

Sorry, gotta Go…

4. Type the Go word in the text box.

5. Click **OK**.

Bang—you're there.

Favorite Places

In my opinion, Go words are good for forums that you *like* and that you visit from time to time, but not for those forums you visit every time you sign in to MSN. For the handful of things you do every time you're online, I think you'd do better to add them to your Favorite Places.

Favorite Places, if you've forgotten, is your online storage area for shortcuts to, well, your favorite places. It's accessible from MSN Central and the Edit menu's Go to submenu all the time you're online, so you're never more than a click or two away from the things you want to do.

How To Add a Favorite Place

When you first join MSN, Favorite Places is completely empty—how would the folks at MSN know what you're going to visit often online? You have to add stuff to it, and then you can use it.

First, go to the category of your choice, and locate the folder for the forum you'd like to add to Favorite Places. Click the forum's icon with your *right* mouse button.

When the menu pops up, click **Add To Favorite Place**. The selected forum now has a shortcut all its own in your Favorite Places window. Repeat the process for all the forums you visit whenever you're on MSN.

There's Always the File Menu, Too You can also add any forum to Favorite Places with the File menu. Click the forum's icon to select it and then click **Add to Favorite Places** in the **File** menu.

Using Favorite Places

There are two ways you can use Favorite Places: the MSN way, and *my* way.

The MSN way is simple, and it's shown here. From anywhere online, click the **Edit** menu. Point your mouse cursor at the **Go to** option and then select **Favorite Places** from the submenu. You magically open the Favorite Places window, with all of your recent icon additions waiting for you.

Look through the shortcuts that appear in the Favorite Places window (like the one in the following figure) until you find the one you want. Double-click the icon for the place you want to visit, and there you are.

Now, *my* way is a little different. *I* open Favorite Places as soon as I sign in to MSN, and I leave it open (or minimized) so I can always get at it—of course, I have my MSN options set so that everything I open online opens its own window. This trick doesn't work otherwise. (Chapter 7 shows you how to change your display options, if you want to try it out.)

Going to Favorite Places the MSN way.

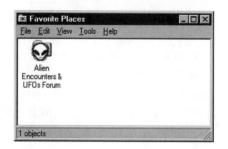

One lonely little favorite place... poor thing.

Deleting Your Favorite Places

If you're fickle and get disenchanted with one of your Favorite Places, you can delete it. Here's how:

1. Go to **Favorite Places**.

2. Click with your *right* mouse button on the icon you want to delete.

3. Select **Delete** from the menu, and that sucker is *gone*.

Alternatively, you can:

1. Go to **Favorite Places**.

2. Click the icon you want to delete, to select it.

3. Select **Delete** from the **File** menu, and that sucker is gone.

313

Check This Out...

Organizing Your Favorite Places Unlike the shortcuts on your desktop, you can't create a folder in Favorite Places to help you organize. Maybe you're not as anal-retentive as I am, and this doesn't bother you. Maybe they'll add it as an option for later versions of MSN. Maybe I should get out more.

The Least You Need to Know

Shortcuts, Go words, and MSN's Favorite Places are three really zippy ways of navigating your behind around the online world. Just remember:

➤ Shortcuts are created by selecting the forum's icon and then selecting **Create Shortcut** from the **File** menu (or by using the handy right mouse button click trick).

➤ To use a shortcut, simply double-click its icon.

➤ You find Go words by looking at a forum's properties and use Go words by selecting **Other Location** from the **Edit** menu's **Go to** submenu.

➤ You add a forum to your Favorite Places display by selecting the forum's icon and then selecting **Add to Favorite Places** from the **File** menu (or, again, by using the handy right mouse button click trick).

➤ You can open Favorite Places by clicking the **Favorite Places** bar of MSN Central, or by selecting **Favorite Places** from the **Edit** menu's **Go to** submenu. Then just double-click the icon for the place you want to visit.

Speak Like a Geek: The Complete Archive

.arc   Short for archive. File extension you find on some PC files that are *compressed*. For example: DOCUMENT.arc. See also *compression*.

.bmp   Short for bitmap. It's one of the more common PC graphics formats, and the one Windows uses for desktop wallpaper.

.lhz   File extension that indicates the file is compressed with the LHZ compression method devised by Lempel, Ziv, and Haruyasa. See also *compression*.

.zip   Short for PKZip, a compression utility, .zip is a file extension you find on some PC file names (*i.e.,* DOCUMENT.zip) that are *compressed* with PKZip, or a zip utility like WinZip. See also *compression*.

anti-virus software   Software designed to detect and destroy computer *viruses* before they can affect your PC. You should always use anti-virus software on files retrieved from the Internet, as it's the source of most computer viruses you hear about. See also *virus*.

AO   The ratings acronym that stands for "Adults Only." It indicates that the selected forum contains material that is inappropriate for folks under 18 years of age.

AT commands   The standard set of modem commands (referred to as the AT command set); these commands are called AT commands because each command begins with the letters "AT" (for "attention") to tell your modem that an instruction is coming.

baud rate   A measure of how fast a modem transfers data: a higher baud rate means you've got a faster modem.

BBS   Acronym for bulletin board system. See also *bulletin board*.

Bitnet Acronym of Because It's Time Network. On MSN, Bitnet is a posted newsgroup in the Internet Center. Normally, on the Internet, it's a *mailing list*. See also *mailing list*.

boogered A highly technical term that means "it's broke." It's a much more acceptable word for use in polite company ("It's all boogered up!") than some others you may be tempted to use. See also *wonky*.

bps Acronym for *bits per second*. It's a measure of how fast a modem transfers data: a higher BPS rating means you've got a faster modem.

buffer A section of memory (RAM) set aside to hold information you send/receive through a modem. Because computers and modems often cannot handle the same amount of information at the same speed, buffers store surplus information until the slower piece of hardware is ready to deal with it.

bulletin board Like its cork cousin, a bulletin board is a place online where you can read and post messages to and from other people.

cache A storage area, or hiding hole. In this instance, the amount of hard drive space set aside to store information from, and about, the Web pages you visit.

CC An old business term that stands for Carbon Copy. The term is still used with e-mail, to show who is getting a copy of the letter, even though carbon paper isn't involved.

CD-ROM Acronym for Compact Disc-Read Only Memory. Cousin to the audio CDs you're probably familiar with, the computer version can hold more than 500 MB of information—compared to the 1.4 MB of a high-density floppy disk.

chat Chatting online is the same as chatting face-to-face or by phone, just with a couple of computers and a few more miles between the chatters.

compatible When computer equipment is *compatible* to another, similar piece of equipment, it means they both work pretty much the same (accept the same commands, and so on). An IBM-compatible computer works pretty much the same as a computer actually made by IBM, a Hayes-compatible modem by one manufacturer is much the same as one made by another.

compress See *compression*.

compression A method of making computer files smaller so they take less time to upload and download. Compressed files also take up less space on your hard drive. It's accomplished with compression software that replaces repetitive data (like all of the E's in a text file) with little placeholders. See also *decompression*.

Crtl Abbreviation used to represent a computer's Control key. You find this abbreviation in many IBM-compatible keyboard shortcuts.

conversation   A group of BBS messages on a related topic. Like a verbal conversation, you can follow the series of messages back and forth between the participants.

conversation archive   See *message archive.*

cyan   A really chi-chi way of saying "light blue." Cyan colored text on MSN (as in the Calendar of Events) takes you to the area indicated when you click on it.

decompress   See *decompression.*

decompression   Before you can use a file that is compressed, you must decompress it with software that swaps the original data for the placeholders in the file, returning the file(s) to their original size.

demo   A trial version of software that has some vital element disabled (like the ability to save or print a file). It gives you a chance to try the product before you shell out the bucks for it.

dialog box   When you ask MSN (or any software) to do something, a dialog box appears if MSN or the software needs more information to do what you've asked. It's called a dialog box because it asks a question, and you answer it (that's "dialog"), and it's box-shaped (that's "box"). Go figure.

download time   How long it will take to transfer a file from the MSN computer to yours.

downloading   Retrieving a file from a remote computer for use on your own. See also *uploading.*

driver   A bit of software that tells Windows 95 how to deal with a particular piece of hardware. Printers require printer drivers. Modems require modem drivers.

DriveSpace   An application that comes with Windows 95. It compresses your hard drive so you have more room to store files. See your Windows 95 manual or online help for details.

e-mail   Electronic mail, there's no paper involved unless you decide to print it out. E-mail gets where it's going almost immediately, which is why I use it more than regular mail.

emoticons   Contraction for *emotion icons.* See also *smiley.*

export   The ability of an application to save a file in the format of another application (or one that another application can *import,* at least). For example, Microsoft Word can save files in a number of formats (like WordPerfect) for both Macintosh and IBM-compatible computers. Exporting is usually done with the Save As command, but check your manual.

FAQs   Frequently Asked Questions. Before you post a "Help Me" question, you should always scout around to see if there's a topic (in a message area) or file (in a file library) of FAQs. Your answer may already be there, and folks can get a little cranky answering the same question over and over.

317

FIFO   A term borrowed from retail accounting that stands for "First In, First Out." With Windows 95, it's also a buffering option for information you send out and receive through your modem.

file library   As with book libraries, a file library is a storage place—only instead of books, you find application, text, and graphics files. You can browse through them, download them, and even upload files of your own to share with other MSN users.

flame   When someone's post to a BBS is more about name-calling and anger-venting than actually discussing something, the message is called a *flame*. Writing such a message is called *flaming*. If someone posts a message like that about something you posted, you've been *flamed*. Flaming can be fun, but it's not something you'd call productive.

font   Another name for the typefaces you use in computer documents. Much of the terminology of computerized type is borrowed and adapted from the language of typesetting.

forum   MSN has 16 basic categories. Within each category there are dozens of individual areas geared to a specific aspect of the general category. Each individual area provides an assembly place for the discussion of the subject at hand. Members can speak out, learn from each other, and generally kibitz about their mutual interest—which is why they're called *forums*.

freeware   As the name implies, freeware is *free software. Yippee!* You can download it, use it, give copies to your friends, and never spend anything more for it other than the cost of the phone call and online charges incurred while downloading it. Freeware is great.

GA   The ratings acronym that stands for "General Audiences." It indicates that the forum's contents are generally suitable for all members of the family.

geek   *Not* an offensive or insulting term (or at least, not meant to be). When I use "geek," I mean a person who is heavily into computers and the related technology—I call myself a geek. It has nothing to do with biting the heads off chickens, or other old, mean-spirited connotations.

GIF   Graphics Interchange Format. A picture file format that is supposed to work on all computer platforms. It was developed for use on CompuServe, the granddaddy of all online services.

Hayes-compatible   A term that identifies a modem that conforms to the standard set of modem commands developed by the Hayes Corporation. Hayes-compatibility is fairly standard among modems. I wouldn't mess with one that isn't—it will complicate your life unnecessarily.

HTML   The format people use to create World Wide Web Pages. It stands for *Hypertext Markup Language.*

http The first part of every *URL*; it tells the Internet Explorer to use the *HyperText Transfer Protocol* to retrieve this particular Web page at this particular address.

home page The starting place for a series of Web pages by one person or company. Think of a home page like home plate; it's where you start and where you can easily return.

hypertext The World Wide Web is based on hypertext. Information on one Web Page is dynamically linked to information on other pages. A click on highlighted text takes you to the related Web page, no matter where it is on the Internet.

Hypertext Markup Language See *HTML*.

import The ability of an application to open a file created in another application with a minimum of fuss. In the process, the application translates the file into its own format so you never have to bother with it again.

Internet An international network of computers that let people exchange information, files, e-mail, and bad, bad jokes with each other.

JPEG A graphic file format that enables images to contain millions of colors while still taking up minimal space on a disk. The files are automatically compressed to save that space; however the more the files are compressed, the worse they look: they lose detail and get splotchy looking.

keyboard shortcut A combination of two or more keys that have the same effect as selecting a command from a menu.

kiosk A fancy word for "booth." MSN's information areas are sometimes referred to as kiosks.

LAN Local Area Network. A way to connect computers that are relatively close together (in the same room, or floor of a building) so they can share files and information.

launch A fancy-shmancy way of saying "start." You launch an application (like MSN).

link A clickable item on a Web page. They're connected (linked) to other Web pages. Clicking on a link takes you to the connected Web page.

local access number MSN's central computers are located in Seattle, Washington. Calling in is a long distance call for most people. Instead of socking you with long distance charges, you access MSN by calling (usually) a local phone number, and the computer at that location (called a *node*, if you care) connects you to MSN.

MA-13 The rating that stands for "Mature Audiences." It indicates that the selected forum has content that is inappropriate for folks under 13 years of age.

mailing list A mailing list functions like an Internet newsgroup, except that instead of posting messages through in a central location, all mailing list exchanges go through e-mail, hence the name.

member support   The part of MSN devoted to answering questions about the service. Member support phone numbers are available in MSN's online help files, under the heading Troubleshooting.

message archive   In order to save space on the message boards, MSN turns old or inactive conversations into text files for storage; you can download these files from the forum's library. These are also called *conversation archives*.

modem   A contraction of *modulating* and *demodulating*. It's a communications device that turns commands and other computer information into sounds (that's the modulating part) that can be sent over telephone lines to another computer. At the other end, the receiving modem turns the sounds back into commands and other information (that's the demodulating part) that the receiving computer can use.

newbies   A term used for new users of MSN. It's descriptive, not judgmental, so don't take offense.

newsgroup   The Internet's version of a BBS, where users can read and post messages on a dizzying array of topics.

node   A term borrowed from the language of networking. When you dial your local access number, you're actually calling an intermediary computer, the local node, that in turn connects you to MSN.

Not rated   Some areas on MSN, when you check their properties, have not been given a rating based on content. The Rating area says Not Rated. You should examine the content for yourself, before you allow your children to visit unrated areas online.

offline   You are not connected to MSN (or any other online service).

online   You *are* connected to MSN (or any other online service).

online chat   See *chat*.

page   See *Web page*.

PBX   A type of telephone system used in some hotels and business locations. They're high-powered and digital and may damage your modem. Ask before you plug into a strange phone system.

peripheral   Supplemental computer hardware—the stuff that's nice to have when using a computer. Basically, all the stuff that isn't the computer (e.g., monitor, printer, mouse, CD-ROM drive, and so on).

pixel   A contraction of *picture element*. It's geek-speak for the dots that make up the images you see on your computer monitor and your television set.

PKZip   The file compression utility that is the standard for IBM-compatible computers. See also *compression.*

post   A message added to a BBS is sometimes called a post. Message and post may be used interchangeably. The act of adding a message to a board is also known as *posting*, and shouldn't be confused with that little bouncy move you're supposed to do on horseback.

public domain   Legal term for software (or anything, really) where the copyright has lapsed and so no one owns it. Authors can also release software into the public domain, surrendering their rights to it.

punt   Slang term for suddenly being disconnected from MSN. MSN is treating you like a football and drop-kicks you from the service.

RE   Abbreviated form of "regarding," borrowed from business memos. All responses to BBS messages are automatically named "RE:" followed by the name and subject of the first message in the conversation.

read-only   A BBS or newsgroup where you can only read what's been posted; you can't post your own messages.

real time   Chat is one of the few things that happen in "real time" online. That means you're seeing it *as it happens*, as opposed to the time-delay involved in sending e-mail or posting a message to a BBS.

RTF   Rich Text Format. It's the file format of choice for many of MSN's online text files because it enables the documents to retain their original formatting (fonts, margins, colors, etc.) regardless of what application you use to view them.

scroll—When too much stuff (whether that's chat, or icons, or anything) appears in a window for you to see it all at once, scroll bars appear at the right side, and sometimes across the bottom, of the window. You can use the scroll bars to move backwards and forwards in the display to see the hidden bits.

shareware   Software that the author has chosen to distribute on a "try before you buy basis." You download it, try it out for a week or so, and, if you decide to keep it, send the author a registration fee.

shortcut   a tiny icon that appears on your desktop. When you click on it, it takes you to a particular area on MSN. Chapter 25 covers shortcuts.

sign in   The process of connecting to MSN.

sign off   Disconnecting from MSN.

site   See *Website.*

smiley   A facial expression you can use in chat rooms; you create smileys with your computer's punctuation keys. ;-)

soft boot   Term for restarting your computer *without* turning it off or cutting the power to it. It's much easier on your PC.

system requirements   The least amount of computer stuff you need to have before you can use a product (whether it's hardware or software) with your computer. Generally it includes a specific kind of computer (386 or better, for instance), with a certain amount of random-access memory (8 MB of RAM), other hardware (like a SVGA monitor, hard drive, and/or modem), and a version of your computer's operating system (Windows 95). Matching your system to the system requirements is the easiest way of telling if you can use a particular product.

SVGA   Super Video Graphics Array. A type of monitor and video controller popular for PCs. SVGA is the next step up from a regular VGA monitor.

toggle   A button or command that does one thing when you select it, then does the exact opposite when you select it again. Think of it like a light switch: push once, the light's on; push again, it's off.

troubleshooting   What you wish you could when things go wrong with your computer: shoot it. Actually, it's the process of making something that doesn't work, work.

UART chip   You don't really need to know what it is, just if your internal modem has one. For the truly curious, though, it stands for Universal Asynchronous Receiver/Transmitter. It's a chip on an internal modem that makes an internal modem behave like a COM port.

unmoderated   Chat rooms where there is no host present are called unmoderated, which means folks can pretty much say whatever they want to whomever they want. Conversation in unmoderated chat rooms can get pretty adult in nature, which is why these rooms are rated MA (for Mature Audiences).

uploading   Sending a file to a remote computer for storage or distribution.

URL   A fancy-shmancy acronym for the address of a World Wide Web page. It stands for Uniform Resource Locator. It tells your Web browser where to find the Web page you want to see.

Usenet   Abbreviated form of User's Network. It's the name of a moderated set of Internet newsgroups. Unlike most newsgroups, there are actually people in charge of Usenet who monitor and keep the newsgroups from getting too chaotic.

uudecode   A utility that turns an encoded file back into a real, usable file. See *uuencode*.

uuencode   In order for Internet users to attach applications and other files to e-mail being sent to an MSN user, the file must first be turned into coded text that can be put in an e-mail message. UUENCODE is the name of an application that does just that.

version number   This is the system that software manufacturers use to identify the latest greatest versions of their product. Version 2.0 is newer than version 1.0. Version 2.5.1 is newer than version 2.5.

VGA   Abbreviation for Video Graphics Array, a type of monitor and video controller popular for PCs.

virus   A bit of computer code hidden inside another file. Like the viruses that cause colds and AIDS, when you use an infected file, it infects your computer. The virus may be harmless, flashing an amusing message on your screen, or it may be harmful—destroying all of the data on your hard drive. Practice safe computing. Use anti-virus software.

WAN   Wide Area Network. Similar to a LAN, but covers greater distances. Computers are connected and share files over several floors of a building, or even with computers in remote locations (across town, or across the country).

Web page   The basic component of the World Wide Web; it's a single *hypertext* document.

Website   The computer system where a mass of Web Pages is stored is called a Website.

wonky   Another highly technical term meaning "Not quite broken, but not quite right." See also *boogered*.

World Wide Web   Part of the Internet, World Wide Web is a hypertext-based system where information appears graphically on *pages*. Clicking on a highlighted icon, word, or phrase, takes you automatically to another Web page that contains related information.

WWW   See *World Wide Web*.

Index

C

336

T

U-V

Up One Level command
(File menu), 60, 72
uploading files
    defined, 322
    file libraries, 140-141
URLs (Web addresses), 240
    defined, 322
    http, 319
    saving history of, 253
    typing, 248-249
USA Today online, 185
Usenet newsgroups,
    232-233, 322
utilities
    anti-virus, 139, 315
    compression software,
    142
    PKZip utility, 321
uudecode/uuencode,
    defined, 322

version numbers, defined,
323
VGA (Video Graphics
    Array), 323
    checking properties,
    10-11
    Windows 95 require-
    ments, 8
View menu commands,
73-74, 77
viruses
    defined, 323
    protection against, 139
    World Wide Web files,
    protecting, 255-256
volume, speaker (modems),
31

W-X-Y-Z

WANs (Wide Area Net-
    works), 202, 323
Water Sports area, 104
weather, *see* News &
    Weather category
WeatherLab forum, 183
Window Control Menu
    commands, 70
Windows 95
    DriveSpace program,
    317

help for, 202-203
installing, 20-21
Microsoft Knowledge
    Base, 204-205
modem configuration,
    14-15
Modem Troubleshooter,
    296
removing features, 24
software for, 203-204
system requirements, 8
Windows 95 Compatible
    Products folder, 204
WinZip 6.0, 142
wizards
    Add New Hardware
    Wizard, 15, 28
    Add New Modem
    Wizard, 30
    New Modem Wizard, 28
    Setup Wizard, 20-21
word processors
    composing BBS messages
    offline, 123
    launching before signing
    on to MSN, 113
    online catalog orders,
    224
    reading online text with,
    66, 112
    RTF file compatibility,
    113
World Wide Web, 239-240
    accessing
        from Internet
        Explorer, 245
        from MSN, 244-245
        Internet Center, 244
    defined, 323
    downloading files,
    254-255
        anti-virus protection,
        255-256
    exiting, 250
    home pages, 319
    HTML, 318
    hypertext, 239-240, 319
    Microsoft WWW home
    page, 246-247
    navigating, 247-248
    restricting childrens'
    access, 274-277

software requirements
    Microsoft Plus!,
    240-241
    MSN Version 1.05,
    downloading,
    241-243
URLs, 240, 248-249
    defined, 322
    saving history of, 253
Web pages, 240, 323
    entering URL,
    248-249
    magazines online,
    184-186
    Mr. Showbiz The
    Daily Dose, 196
    navigating, 246-247
    returning to starting
    page, 249
    Time Warner's
    Pathfinder, 184-185
    USA Today, 185-186
Websites, 240, 323

341

We live in a world of constant change. New technologies, new releases—it's almost impossible to keep on top of all the changes. Not so anymore! Check out Macmillan's home page—you'll find monthly Microsoft Network updates—a great way to keep abreast of the changes going on around you. You'll find more in-depth information in Chapters 20 and 29—but, for now, remember this address:

http://www.mcp.com/que/new_users

Don't get left behind!
Get connected to MCP and
stay ahead of the pack!

Complete and Return this Card
for a *FREE* Computer Book Catalog

Thank you for purchasing this book! You have purchased a superior computer book written expressly for your needs. To continue to provide the kind of up-to-date, pertinent coverage you've come to expect from us, we need to hear from you. Please take a minute to complete and return this self-addressed, postage-paid form. In return, we'll send you a free catalog of all our computer books on topics ranging from word processing to programming and the internet.

Mr. ☐   Mrs. ☐   Ms. ☐   Dr. ☐

Name (first) [_____]   (M.I.) ☐   (last) [_____]

Address [_____]

[_____]

City [_____]   State ☐☐   Zip [_____]

Phone [___][___][___]   Fax [___][___][___]

Company Name [_____]

E-mail address [_____]

1. Please check at least (3) influencing factors for purchasing this book.

Front or back cover information on book .... ☐
Special approach to the content .... ☐
Completeness of content .... ☐
Author's reputation .... ☐
Publisher's reputation .... ☐
Book cover design or layout .... ☐
Index or table of contents of book .... ☐
Price of book .... ☐
Special effects, graphics, illustrations .... ☐
Other (Please specify): _____ ☐

2. How did you first learn about this book?

Saw in Macmillan Computer Publishing catalog .... ☐
Recommended by store personnel .... ☐
Saw the book on bookshelf at store .... ☐
Recommended by a friend .... ☐
Received advertisement in the mail .... ☐
Saw an advertisement in: _____ ☐
Read book review in: _____ ☐
Other (Please specify): _____ ☐

3. How many computer books have you purchased in the last six months?

This book only .... ☐   3 to 5 books .... ☐
2 books .... ☐   More than 5 .... ☐

4. Where did you purchase this book?

Bookstore .... ☐
Computer Store .... ☐
Consumer Electronics Store .... ☐
Department Store .... ☐
Office Club .... ☐
Warehouse Club .... ☐
Mail Order .... ☐
Direct from Publisher .... ☐
Internet site .... ☐
Other (Please specify): _____ ☐

5. How long have you been using a computer?

☐ Less than 6 months   ☐ 6 months to a year
☐ 1 to 3 years   ☐ More than 3 years

6. What is your level of experience with personal computers and with the subject of this book?

	With PCs	With subject of book
New	☐	☐
Casual	☐	☐
Accomplished	☐	☐
Expert	☐	☐

Source Code ISBN: 0-7897-0603-2

7. Which of the following best describes your job title?

Administrative Assistant .... ☐
Coordinator .... ☐
Manager/Supervisor .... ☐
Director .... ☐
Vice President .... ☐
President/CEO/COO .... ☐
Lawyer/Doctor/Medical Professional .... ☐
Teacher/Educator/Trainer .... ☐
Engineer/Technician .... ☐
Consultant .... ☐
Not employed/Student/Retired .... ☐
Other (Please specify): _____ ☐

8. Which of the following best describes the area of the company your job title falls under?

Accounting .... ☐
Engineering .... ☐
Manufacturing .... ☐
Operations .... ☐
Marketing .... ☐
Sales .... ☐
Other (Please specify): _____ ☐

9. What is your age?

Under 20 .... ☐
21-29 .... ☐
30-39 .... ☐
40-49 .... ☐
50-59 .... ☐
60-over .... ☐

10. Are you:

Male .... ☐
Female .... ☐

11. Which computer publications do you read regularly? (Please list)

_____
_____
_____
_____
_____
_____
_____
_____
_____
_____

Comments: _____
_____
_____

Fold here and scotch-tape to mail.